Oxford Pocket Basic English Usage

Michael Swan

Oxford University Press

Oxford University Press,
Great Clarendon Street, Oxford OX2 6DP

Oxford   New York
Auckland   Bangkok   Buenos Aires   Cape Town   Chennai
Dar es Salaam   Delhi   Hong Kong   Istanbul   Karachi
Kolkata   Kuala Lumpur   Madrid   Melbourne   Mexico City
Mumbai   Nairobi   São Paulo   Shanghai   Taipei   Tokyo   Toronto

OXFORD and OXFORD ENGLISH are
trade marks of Oxford University Press

ISBN: 978 0 19 431416 9
© Oxford University Press 1984, 1992

Oxford Pocket Basic English Usage is
a reprint in a smaller format of
Basic English Usage.

Basic English Usage first published 1984
Oxford Pocket Basic English Usage first published 1992
2011   2010   2009   2008   2007

10   9

Illustrations by Maric-Hélène Jeeves

The flowchart in section 84 is reproduced from *The
Cambridge English Course*, Book 2, by Michael Swan
and Catherine Walter (Cambridge University Press
1984), by kind permission of the publishers.

Typeset in Postscript Concorde and Univers by
Tradespools Ltd., Frome, Somerset
Printed in China

Contents

Introduction

The purpose of this book

This is a practical guide to common problems in English grammar and usage. It is written for foreign students who would like to know more about English, and who want to avoid mistakes.

Level

The book is written especially for intermediate students, but more advanced learners may also find it useful. The explanations are made as simple as possible. Students who want more detailed and complete information should read my more advanced book *Practical English Usage*, also published by Oxford University Press.

Language

Explanations are mostly in ordinary everyday English. It has been necessary to use some grammatical terminology (for example, *adverb*, *subject*, *clause*, *modify*). These words are explained on pages 10–12.

The kind of English described

The book describes standard modern British English, and gives realistic examples of spoken and written language (both formal and informal). Incorrect forms are shown like this: '(NOT ~~I have seen him yesterday~~.)' There is some information about American usage, but the book is not a systematic guide to American English.

Organization

This is a dictionary of problems, not a grammar. Points are explained in short separate entries, so that you can find just the information you need about a particular problem—no more and no less. Entries are arranged alphabetically and numbered. A complete index at the back of the book shows where each point can be found. (There is also a list of all the entries on pages 5–9.)

How to use the book

If you want an explanation of a particular point, look in the index.
Problems are indexed under several different names, so it is usually easy
to find what you want. For example, if you need information about the
use of *I* and *me*, you can find this in the index under '**I**', '**me**', 'subject and
object forms', 'personal pronouns' or 'pronouns'.

Exercises

Basic English Usage: Exercises, by Jennifer Seidl and Michael Swan,
gives practice in the various points that are explained in *Oxford Pocket
Basic English Usage*.

Thanks

I should like to thank the many people whose suggestions and criticisms
have helped me with this book, especially Norman Coe, Stewart Melluish,
Jennifer Seidl and Catherine Walter. I am also most grateful to all
those—too many to name—who have sent me comments on my book
Practical English Usage. Their suggestions have helped me to improve
many of the explanations in this book.

Comments

I should be very glad to hear from students or teachers using this book
who find mistakes or omissions, or who have comments or suggestions of
any kind. Please write to me c/o ELT Department, Oxford University
Press, Walton Street, Oxford OX2 6DP.

5

List of entries

Words used in the explanations

active In *I paid the bill*, the verb *paid* is **active**. In *The bill was paid*, the verb *was paid* is **passive**, not **active**.

adjective a word like *green*, *hungry*, *impossible*, used to describe.

adverb a word like *tomorrow*, *here*, *badly*, *also*, which is used to say, for example, when, where or how something happens.

adverb(ial) particle a word like *up*, *out*, *off*, used as part of a verb like *get up*, *look out*, *put off*.

adverb(ial) phrase a group of words used like an adverb. Examples: *in this place*, *on Tuesday*.

affirmative *I was* is **affirmative**; *I was not* is **negative**.

auxiliary (verb) a verb like *be*, *have*, *do*, which is used with another verb to make tenses, questions etc. See also **modal auxiliary verbs.**

clause a structure with a subject and verb, and perhaps an object and adverbs. Examples: *I know that man*. *I came home last night*.
A **sentence** is made of one or more **clauses**. See also **main clause**.

comparative a form like *older*, *faster*, *more intelligent*.

conditional *I should/would* + infinitive, etc. See 88.

conjunction a word that joins clauses. Examples: *and, so, if, when*.

consonant *b, c, d, f* and *g* are **consonants**; *a, e, i, o* and *u* are **vowels**.

contraction two words made into one. Examples: *don't*, *I'll*.

determiner a word like *the, my, this, every, more*, which can come at the beginning of a noun phrase. See 96.

direct object In *I gave my mother some money*, the **direct object** is *some money*; *my mother* is the **indirect object**.

direct speech reporting somebody's words without changing the grammar. In *She said 'I'm tired'*, the clause *I'm tired* is **direct speech**. In *She said that she was tired*, the structure is **indirect speech** or **reported speech**.

emphasize You **emphasize** something if you make it 'stronger'—for example, by saying it louder.

expression a group of words used together, like *in the morning*.

first person *I, me, we, us, our, am* are **first person** forms.

formal We use **formal** language when we wish to be polite or to show respect; we use more **informal** language when we talk to friends, for example. *Good morning* is more **formal** than *Hello*; *Hi* is very **informal**.

gerund an *-ing* form used like a noun. Example: *Smoking is dangerous*.

hyphen a line (-) that separates words. Example: *milk-bottle*.

imperative a form (like the infinitive) that is used to give orders, make suggestions, etc. Examples: *Come on*; *Wait a minute*. See 170.

indirect object see **direct object**.

indirect speech see **direct speech**.

infinitive In *I need to sleep* and *I must go*, the forms *to sleep* and *go* are **infinitives**. See 175.

informal see **formal**.

irregular see **regular**.

main clause Some sentences have a **main clause** and one or more
  subordinate clauses. Example: *When I got home I asked Mary what
  she thought*. The **main clause** is *I asked Mary*; the other two clauses
  are like parts of the main clause (the first is like an adverb, the other is
  like an object): they are **subordinate clauses**.

modal auxiliary verbs *can, could, may, might, must, will, shall, would,
  should, ought* and *need*.

noun a word like *oil, memory, thing*, which can be used with an article.
  Nouns are usually the names of people or things.

object see **direct object** and **subject**.

omission, omit leaving out words. In the sentence *I know (that) you
  don't like her*, we can **omit** *that*.

participle When we use the *-ing* form like an adjective or verb, we call it
  a **present participle**. Examples: *a **crying** child*; *I was **working***. Forms
  like *broken, gone, heard, stopped* are **past participles**. See 234.

passive see **active**.

past participle see **participle**.

perfect a verb form made with *have*. Examples: *I have seen*; *They had
  forgotten*; *She will have arrived*.

phrasal verb verb + adverb particle. Examples: *stand up, write down*.

phrase a group of words that are used together. *Our old house* is a **noun
  phrase**; *has been sold* is a **verb phrase**.

plural a form used for more than one. *Books, they, many* are **plural**;
  book, she, much are **singular**.

preposition a word like *on, through, over, in, by, for*.

present participle see **participle**.

possessive a form like *my, mine, John's*, used to show possession.

progressive *I am going, I was going* are **progressive** verb forms; *I go,
  I went* are **simple** verb forms.

pronoun We use a **pronoun** instead of a more precise noun phrase.
  Examples: *I, it, yourself, their, one*.

proper noun, proper name a noun that is the name of a person, place
  etc. Examples: *Peter, Einstein, Birmingham*.

question tag a small question at the end of a sentence. Examples: *don't
  you? wasn't it?*

regular a **regular** form follows the same rules as most others. An
  irregular form does not. *Stopped* is a **regular** past tense; *went* is
  irregular. *Books* is a **regular** plural; *women* is **irregular**.

relative pronouns, relative clauses see 277–280.

reported speech see **direct speech**.

second person *you, yourselves, your* are **second person** forms.

sentence a complete 'piece of language'. In writing, a **sentence** begins
  with a capital (big) letter and ends with a full stop (.). A **sentence** is
  usually made of one or more **clauses**.

simple see **progressive**.

singular see **plural**.

stress When we speak, we pronounce some words and parts of words
  higher and louder: we **stress** them. Example: *There's a 'man in the 'garden*.

subject a noun or pronoun that comes before the verb in an affirmative sentence. It often says who or what does an action. Example: *Helen broke another glass today.* See also **direct object**.

subordinate clause see **main clause**.

superlative a form like *oldest, fastest, most intelligent*.

tense *am going, went, will go, have gone* are **tenses** of the verb *go*.

third person *he, him, his, they, goes* are **third person** forms.

verb a word like *ask, play, wake, be, can.* Many **verbs** refer to actions or states.

Phonetic alphabet

Vowels and diphthongs (double vowels)

iː	*sea*t /siːt/, *fee*l /fiːl/	ɜː	*tur*n /tɜːn/, *wor*d /wɜːd/
ɪ	*si*t /sɪt/, *i*n /ɪn/	ə	*a*nother /ə'nʌðə(r)/
e	*se*t /set/, *a*ny /'enɪ/	eɪ	*ta*ke /teɪk/, *wai*t /weɪt/
æ	*sa*t /sæt/, *ma*tch /mætʃ/	aɪ	*mi*ne /maɪn/, *li*ght /laɪt/
ɑː	*mar*ch /mɑːtʃ/, *a*fter /'ɑːftə(r)/ *po*t /pɒt/, *go*ne /gɒn/	ɔɪ	*oi*l /ɔɪl/, *bo*y /bɔɪ/
ɒ	*po*rt /pɔːt/, *la*w /lɔː/	əʊ	*no* /nəʊ/, *o*pen /'əʊpən/
ɔː	*goo*d /gʊd/, *coul*d /kʊd/	aʊ	*hou*se /haʊs/, *no*w /naʊ/
ʊ	*foo*d /fuːd/, *grou*p /gruːp/	ɪə	*hea*r /hɪə(r)/, *dee*r /dɪə(r)/
uː	*mu*ch /mʌtʃ/, *fro*nt /frʌnt/	eə	*whe*re /weə(r)/, *ai*r /eə(r)/
ʌ		ʊə	*tou*r /tʊə(r)/

Consonants

p	*p*ull /pʊl/, *cup* /kʌp/	tʃ	*ch*eap /tʃiːp/, *catch* /kætʃ/
b	*b*ull /bʊl/, *rob* /rɒb/	dʒ	*j*ail /dʒeɪl/, *bridge* /brɪdʒ/
f	*f*erry /'ferɪ/, *cough* /kɒf/	k	*k*ing /kɪŋ/, *case* /keɪs/
v	*v*ery /'verɪ/, *live* /lɪv/	g	*g*o /gəʊ/, *rug* /rʌg/
θ	*th*ink /θɪŋk/, *bath* /bɑːθ/	m	*m*y /maɪ/, *come* /kʌm/
ð	*th*ough /ðəʊ/, *with* /wɪð/	n	*n*o /nəʊ/, *on* /ɒn/
t	*t*ake /teɪk/, *set* /set/	ŋ	*sing* /sɪŋ/, *finger* /'fɪŋgə(r)/
d	*d*ay /deɪ/, *red* /red/	l	*l*ove /lʌv/, *hole* /həʊl/
s	*s*ing /sɪŋ/, *rice* /raɪs/	r	*r*ound /raʊnd/, *carry* /'kærɪ/
z	*z*oo /zuː/, *days* /deɪz/	w	*w*ell /wel/
ʃ	*sh*ow /ʃəʊ/, *wish* /wɪʃ/	j	*y*oung /jʌŋ/
ʒ	*pleasure* /'pleʒə(r)/	h	*h*ouse /haʊs/

' shows which part of a word is stressed. Example: /'lɪmɪt/.

1 abbreviations

1 We usually write abbreviations without full stops in British English.

> *Mr* (NOT *Mr.*) = *Mister*
> *Ltd = Limited (company)*
> *kg = kilogram*
> *the BBC = the British Broadcasting Corporation*
> *the USA = the United States of America*
> *NATO = the North Atlantic Treaty Organization*
> *OPEC = the Organization of Petroleum Exporting Countries*

2 Some abbreviations are made from the first letters of several words. We usually pronounce these with the stress on the last letter.

> *the BBC* /ðə biːbiːˈsiː/   *the USA* /ðə juːesˈeɪ/

Some of these abbreviations are pronounced like one word.
We do not usually use articles with these.

> *NATO* /ˈneɪtəʊ/ (NOT *the NATO*)
> *OPEC* /ˈəʊpek/ (NOT *the OPEC*)

2 about to

> be + about + *to*-infinitive

If you are **about to do something**, you are going to do it very soon.

> *Don't go out now—we're **about to have supper**.*
> *I was **about to go to bed** when the telephone rang.*

▷ For other ways of talking about the future, see 134–140.

3 above and over

1 *Above* and *over* can both mean 'higher than'.

*A is **above/over** B.*

*The snow came up **above/over** our knees.*
*There's a spider on the ceiling just **above/over** your head.*

2 We use *above* when one thing is not directly over another.

> *We've got a little house **above** the lake.*

*A is **above** B.* (NOT *A is over B.*)

3 We use *over* when one thing covers another.

*A is **over** B.*

*There is cloud **over** the South of England.*

And we use *over* when one thing crosses another. (*Across* is also possible.)

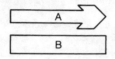

*A is (moving) **over**/**across** B.*

*Electricity cables stretch **over**/**across** the fields.*
*The plane was flying **over**/**across** the Channel.*

4 We usually use *over* to mean 'more than'.

*'How old are you?' '**Over** thirty.'*
*He's **over** two metres tall.*
*There were **over** fifty people at the party.*

But we use *above* in some expressions,
particularly when we are thinking of a vertical scale.

Examples are: ***above** zero* (for temperatures); ***above** sea-level*; ***above** average.*

▷ For the difference between *over* and *across*, see 4.
For other meanings of *over* and *across*, see 4.
For other meanings of *above* and *over*, see a good dictionary.

4 across and over

1 We use both *across* and *over* to mean 'on the other side of' or 'to the other side of'.

*His house is just **over**/**across** the road.*
*Try to jump **over**/**across** the stream.*

OVER

2 We prefer *over* to talk about a movement to the other side of something high.

*Why is that woman climbing **over the wall**?*
(NOT *... climbing **across the wall**?*)

3 We prefer *across* to talk about a movement to the other side of a flat area.

> *It took him six weeks to walk **across the desert**.*
> (NOT ... *to walk over the desert*.)

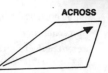
ACROSS

5 across and through

1 The difference between *across* and *through* is like the difference between *on* and *in*. *Across* is used for a movement on a surface.
Through is used for a movement in a three-dimensional space, with things on all sides. Compare:

> *We walked **across the ice**.*
> *I walked **through the wood**.*

> *We drove **across the desert**.*
> *We drove **through several towns**.*

*I walked **across the square** to the café.*

*I walked **through the crowd** to the bar.*

2 People swim, and ships move, *across* rivers, lakes etc.

> *The **river's** too wide to swim **across**.*

▷ For the difference between *across* and *over*, see 4.

6 active verb forms

This is a list of all the affirmative active forms of an English regular verb, with their names. For passive forms, see 238. For questions, see 270. For negatives, see 215. For irregular verbs, see 186.
For more information about the forms and their uses, see the entry for each one. For details of auxiliary and modal auxiliary verbs, see the entry for each one.

future *I will/shall work, you will work, he/she/it will work, we will/ shall work, they will work*

future progressive *I will/shall be working, you will be working,* etc

future perfect simple *I will/shall have worked, you will have worked,* etc

future perfect progressive *I will/shall have been working, you will have been working,* etc

simple present *I work, you work, he/she/it works, we work, they work*

   present progressive *I am working, you are working, etc*

present perfect simple *I have worked, you have worked, he/she/it has worked, etc*

present perfect progressive *I have been working, you have been working, etc*

simple past *I worked, you worked, he/she/it worked, etc*

past progressive *I was working, you were working, etc*

past perfect simple *I had worked, you had worked, he/she/it had worked, etc*

past perfect progressive *I had been working, you had been working, etc*

infinitives *(to) work; (to) be working; (to) have worked; (to) have been working*

participles *working; worked; having worked*

Note: Future tenses can be constructed with *going to* instead of *will* (for the difference, see 136.3).

   I'm going to work; I'm going to be working; I'm going to have worked

7 actual(ly)

1 *Actual* means 'real'; *actually* means 'really' or 'in fact'.
We often use them to correct mistakes and misunderstandings, or when we say something unexpected or surprising.

   *The book says he was 47 when he died, but his **actual** age was 43.*
   *'Hello, John. Nice to see you again.' '**Actually**, my name's Andy.'*
   *'Do you like opera?' 'Yes, I do.' '**Actually**, I've got two tickets ...'*
   *She was so angry that she **actually** tore up the letter.*

2 Note that *actual* and *actually* are 'false friends' for people who speak European languages. They do not mean the same as, for example, *actuel(lement)*, *aktuell*, *attuale/attualmente*. To express these ideas, we say *present, current, up to date; at this moment, now, at present.*

   *What's our **current** financial position?*
   *A hundred years ago, the population of London was higher than it is **now**.* (NOT *... higher than it actually is.*)

8 adjectives ending in **-ly**

1 Many adverbs end in *-ly*—for example *happily, nicely*. But some words that end in *-ly* are adjectives, not adverbs. The most important are *friendly, lovely, lonely, ugly, silly, cowardly, likely, unlikely*.

   *She gave me a **friendly** smile.*   *Her singing was **lovely**.*

There are no adverbs *friendly* or *friendlily*, *lovely* or *lovelily*, etc. We have to use different structures.

> She smiled at me **in a friendly way**. (NOT ~~She smiled at me friendly~~.)
> He gave a **silly** laugh. (NOT ~~He laughed silly~~.)

2 *Daily, weekly, monthly, yearly,* and *early* are both adjectives and adverbs.

> It's a **daily** paper.   It comes out **daily**.
> an **early** train   I got up **early**.

9 adjectives: order

Before a noun, we put adjectives in a fixed order. The exact rules are very complicated (and not very well understood). Here are the most important rules.

1 Adjectives of colour, origin (where something comes from), material (what it is made of) and purpose (what it is for) go in that order.

colour	origin	material	purpose	noun
red	Spanish	leather	riding	boots

> a **Venetian glass** ashtray (NOT ~~a glass Venetian ashtray~~)
> a **brown German** beer-mug (NOT ~~a German brown beer mug~~)

2 Other adjectives come before colour-adjectives etc. Their exact order is too complicated to give rules.

> a **big black** cat (NOT ~~a black big cat~~)
> the **round glass** table (NOT ~~the glass round table~~)

3 *First, last* and *next* usually comes before numbers.

> the **first three** days (NOT ~~the three first days~~)
> my **last two** jobs (NOT ~~my two last jobs~~)

▷ For *and* with adjectives, see 31.3.
For commas with adjectives, see 266.1.

10 adjectives: position

> adjective + noun
> subject + copula verb (*be, seem, look* etc.) + adjective

1 Most adjectives can go in two places in a sentence:

a before a noun

> The **new secretary** doesn't like me.
> She married a **rich businessman**.

b   after a 'copula verb' (*be, seem, look, appear, feel* and some other verbs—see 91)

> *That dress is new, isn't it?*   *He looks rich.*

2   A few adjectives can go before a noun, but not usually after a verb. Examples are *elder, eldest* (see 299.5) and *little* (see 309). After a verb we use *older, oldest* and *small*.

> *My elder brother lives in Newcastle.* (Compare: *He's three years older than me.*)
> *He's a funny little boy.* (Compare: *He looks very small.*)

3   Some adjectives can go after a verb, but not usually before a noun. The most common are *ill* (see 169), *well* (see 359) and *afraid, alive, alone, asleep*. Before nouns we use *sick, healthy, frightened, living, lone, sleeping*.

> *He looks ill.* (Compare: *He's a sick man.*)
> *Your mother's very well.* (Compare: *She's a very healthy woman.*)
> *She's asleep.* (Compare: *a sleeping baby*)

4   In expressions of measurement, the adjective comes after the measurement-noun.

> *two metres high* (NOT *high two metres*)
> *ten years old*   *two miles long*

11 adjectives without nouns

We cannot usually leave out a noun after an adjective.

> *Poor little boy!* (NOT *Poor little!*)

But there are some exceptions:

1   We sometimes leave out a noun when we are talking about a choice between two or three different kinds (of car, milk, cigarette, bread, for example).

> *'Have you got any bread?' 'Do you want white or brown?'*
> *'A pound of butter, please.' 'I've only got unsalted.'*

2   We can use superlative adjectives without nouns, if the meaning is clear.

> *I'm the tallest in my family.*   *'Which one shall I get?' 'The cheapest.'*

3   We can use some adjectives with *the* to talk about people in a particular condition.

> *He's collecting money for the blind.*

Note that this structure has a plural 'general' meaning: the *blind* means 'all blind people', not 'the blind person' or 'certain blind people'. The most common expressions of this kind are:

the dead	the sick	the blind	the deaf	the rich
the poor	the unemployed	the young	the old	
the handicapped	the mentally ill			

(In informal speech, we usually say *old people, young people* etc instead of *the old, the young*.)
These expressions cannot be used with a possessive *'s*.

> *the problems of the poor* OR *poor people's problems*
> (NOT ~~the poor's problems~~)

12 adverbs of manner

1 Adverbs of manner say *how* something happens.
Examples: *happily, quickly, terribly, beautifully, badly, well, fast*.
Don't confuse these adverbs with adjectives (*happy, quick*, etc.) We use adverbs, not adjectives, to modify verbs.

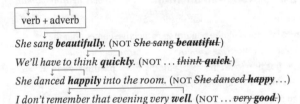

> verb + adverb

> *She sang **beautifully**.* (NOT ~~She sang beautiful.~~)
> *We'll have to think **quickly**.* (NOT ... ~~think quick.~~)
> *She danced **happily** into the room.* (NOT ~~She danced happy~~ ...)
> *I don't remember that evening very **well**.* (NOT ... ~~very good.~~)

2 Adverbs of manner can also modify adjectives, past participles, other adverbs, and adverbial phrases.

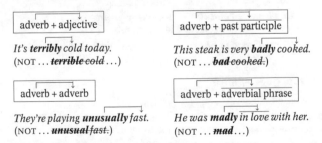

> adverb + adjective

> *It's **terribly** cold today.*
> (NOT ... ~~terrible cold~~ ...)

> adverb + past participle

> *This steak is very **badly** cooked.*
> (NOT ... ~~bad cooked.~~)

> adverb + adverb

> *They're playing **unusually** fast.*
> (NOT ... ~~unusual fast.~~)

> adverb + adverbial phrase

> *He was **madly** in love with her.*
> (NOT ... ~~mad~~ ...)

3 Some adverbs of manner have the same form as adjectives.
Examples are *fast* (see 127), *slow* (see 308), *loud, wide* and *hard* (see 150).

▷ For the use of adjectives with 'copula verbs' like *look* or *seem*, see 91.
For adjectives ending in *-ly*, see 8. For the position of adverbs of manner, see 14.6. For spelling rules, see 327.

13 adverbs: position (general)

Different kinds of adverbs go in different positions in a clause. Here are some general rules: for more details, see 14. (Note: these rules apply both to one-word adverbs and to *adverb phrases* of two or more words.)

1 Verb and object

We do not usually put adverbs between a verb and its object.

| ... adverb + verb + object |
*I **very much** like my job.*

| ~~verb + adverb + object~~ |
(NOT *I like **very much** my job.*)

| ... verb + object + adverb |
*She speaks English **well**.*

(NOT *She speaks **well** English.*)

2 Initial, mid- and end position

There are three normal positions for adverbs:

a. initial position (at the beginning of a clause)

   ***Yesterday morning** something very strange happened.*

b. mid-position (with the verb—for the exact position see 14.2)

   *My brother **completely** forgot my birthday.*

c. end position (at the end of a clause)

   *What are you doing **tomorrow**?*

Most adverb phrases (adverbs of two or more words) cannot go in mid-position. Compare:

   *He got dressed **quickly**.   He **quickly** got dressed.*
   (*Quickly* can go in end or mid-position.)

   *He got dressed **in a hurry**.* (NOT *He **in a hurry** got dressed.*)
   (*In a hurry* cannot go in mid-position.)

3 What goes where?

a initial position

Connecting adverbs (which join a clause to what came before). Time adverbs can also go here (see 14.8).

   ***However**, not everybody agreed.* (connecting adverb)
   ***Tomorrow** I've got a meeting in Cardiff.* (time adverb)

b mid-position

Focusing adverbs (which emphasize one part of the clause); adverbs of certainty and completeness; adverbs of indefinite frequency; some adverbs of manner (see 14.6).

   *He's been everywhere—he's **even** been to Antarctica.* (focusing adverb)

*It will **probably** rain this evening.* (certainty)
*I've **almost** finished painting the house.* (completeness)
*My boss **often** travels to America.* (indefinite frequency)
*He **quickly** got dressed.* (manner)

a   end-position

Adverbs of manner (how), place (where) and time (when) most often go in end-position. (For details, see 14.9.)

*She brushed her hair **slowly**,* (manner)
*The children are playing **upstairs**.* (place)
*I phoned Alex **this morning**.* (time)

14 adverbs: position (details)

(Read section 13 before you read this.)

1 Connecting adverbs

These adverbs **join** a clause to what came before.
Examples: *however, then, next, besides, anyway*
Position: beginning of clause.

*Some of us wanted to change the system; **however**, not everybody agreed.*
*I worked without stopping until five o'clock. **Then** I went home.*
***Next**, I want to say something about the future.*

2 Indefinite frequency

These adverbs say **how often** something happens.
Examples: *always, ever, usually, normally, often, frequently, sometimes, occasionally, rarely, seldom, never*
Position: mid-position (after auxiliary verbs and *am, are, is, was* and *were*; before other verbs).

> auxiliary verb + adverb

*I **have never** seen a whale.*
*You **can always** come and stay with us if you want to.*
***Have** you **ever** played American football?*

> *be* + adverb

*My boss **is often** bad-tempered.*
*I'**m seldom** late for work.*

> adverb + other verb

*We **usually go** to Scotland in August.*
*It **sometimes gets** very windy here.*

When there are two auxiliary verbs, these adverbs usually come after the first.

> We *have never been invited* to one of their parties.
> She *must sometimes have wanted* to run away.

Usually, normally, often, frequently, sometimes and *occasionally* can go at the beginning of a clause for emphasis. *Always, never, rarely, seldom* and *ever* cannot.

> *Sometimes* I think I'd like to live somewhere else.
> *Usually* I get up early.
> (NOT *~~Always I get up early. Never I get up early.~~*)

But *always* and *never* can come at the beginning of imperative clauses.

> *Always* look in your mirror before starting to drive.
> *Never* ask her about her marriage.

For the position of adverbs of definite frequency (for example *daily, weekly*), see 8 below.

3 Focusing adverbs

These adverbs '**point to**' or **emphasize** one part of the clause.
Examples: *also, just, even, only, mainly, mostly, either, or, neither, nor*
Position: mid-position (after auxiliary verbs and *am, are, is, was* and *were*; before other verbs).

| auxiliary verb + adverb |

> He's been everywhere—he*'s even* been to Antartica.
> I'm *only* going for two days.

| be + adverb |

> She's my teacher, but she*'s also* my friend.
> The people at the meeting *were mainly* scientists.

| adverb + other verb |

> Your bicycle *just needs* some oil—that's all.
> She *neither said* thank-you *nor looked* at me.

Too and *as well* are focusing adverbs that go in end-position. (See 28.)
Either goes in end-position after *not*. (See 217.)

4 Adverbs of certainty

We use these adverbs to say **how sure** we are of something.
Examples: *certainly, definitely, clearly, obviously, probably, really*
Position: mid-position (after auxiliary verbs and *am, are, is, was* and *were*; before other verbs).

> auxiliary verb + adverb

*It **will probably** rain this evening.*
*The train **has obviously** been delayed.*

> be + adverb

*There **is clearly** something wrong.*
*She **is definitely** older than him.*

> adverb + other verb

*He **probably thinks** you don't like him.*
*I **certainly feel** better today.*

Maybe and *perhaps* usually come at the beginning of a clause.

> **Perhaps** her train is late.
> **Maybe** I'm right, and maybe I'm wrong.

5 Adverbs of completeness

These adverbs say **how completely** something happens.
Examples: *completely, practically, almost, nearly, quite, rather, partly, sort of, kind of, hardly, scarcely*
Position: mid-position (after auxiliary verbs and *am, are, is, was* and *were*; before other verbs).

> auxiliary verb + adverb

*I **have completely** forgotten your name.*
*Sally **can practically** read.*

> be + adverb

*It **is almost** dark.*
*The house **is partly** ready.*

> adverb + other verb

*I **kind of hope** she wins.*

6 Adverbs of manner

These adverbs say **how, in what way**, something happens or is done.
Examples: *angrily, happily, fast, slowly, suddenly, well, badly, nicely, noisily, quietly, hard, softly*
Position: most often at the end of a clause, especially if the adverb is emphasized. Adverbs in *-ly* can go in mid-position if the adverb is less important than the verb or object. Initial position is also possible.

> end-position

*He drove off **angrily**.*
*You speak English **well**.*
*She read the letter **slowly**.*

> mid-position

*She **angrily** tore up the letter.*
*I **slowly** began to feel better again.*

> initial position

***Suddenly** I had an idea.*

In passive clauses, adverbs of manner often go before the past participle.
This is very common with adverbs that say **how well** something is done
(for example *well, badly*).

> adverb + past participle

*Everything has been **carefully checked**.*
*I thought it was very **well written**.*
*The conference was **badly organized**.*

7 Adverbs of place

These adverbs say **where** something happens.
Examples: *upstairs, around, here, to bed, in London, out of the window*
Position: at the end of a clause. Initial position also possible, especially
in literary writing.

*The children are playing **upstairs**.*
*Come and sit **here**.*
*Don't throw orange peel **out of the window**.*
*She's sitting **at the end of the garden**.*
***At the end of the garden** there was a very tall tree.*

Adverbs of direction (movement) come before adverbs of position.

*The children are running **around upstairs**.*

Here and *there* often begin clauses. Note the word order.

> *Here/There* + verb + subject

***Here** comes your bus.* (NOT ~~Here your bus comes.~~)   ***There**'s Alice.*

Pronoun subjects come directly after *here* and *there*.

*Here **it** comes* (NOT ~~Here comes it.~~)
*There **she** is.* (NOT ~~There is she.~~)

8 Adverbs of time

These adverbs say **when** something happens.
Examples: *today, afterwards, in June, last year, daily, weekly, every
year, finally, before, eventually, already, soon, still, last*

Position: mostly in end-position; initial position also common. Some can
go in mid-position (see below). Adverbs of indefinite frequency
(*often, ever* etc) go in mid-position (see paragraph 2).

*I'm going to London **today**.*
***Today** I'm going to London.*

*She has a new hair style **every week**.*
***Every week** she has a new hair style.*

Time adverbs in *-ly* can also go in mid-position; so can *already,* soon and
last. Still and *just* only go in mid-position.

*So you **finally** got here.*
*I've **already** paid the bill.*
*We'll **soon** be home.*
*When did you **last** see your father?*
*I **still** love you.*
*She's **just** gone out.*

9   Manner, place, time

At the end of a clause, adverbs usually come in the order **manner**, **place**,
time (MPT).

$$\overset{\text{P}}{}\quad\overset{\text{T}}{}$$
I went `there` `at once`. (NOT ~~I went at once there.~~)

$$\overset{\text{P}}{}\quad\overset{\text{T}}{}$$
Let's go `to bed` `early`. (NOT ... ~~early to bed.~~)

$$\overset{\text{M}}{}\quad\overset{\text{T}}{}$$
I worked `hard` `yesterday`.

$$\overset{\text{M}}{}\qquad\overset{\text{P}}{}\qquad\overset{\text{T}}{}$$
She sang `beautifully` `in the town hall` `last night`.

With verbs of movement, we often put adverbs of place before adverbs of
manner.

$$\overset{\text{P}}{}\quad\overset{\text{M}}{}$$
She went `home` `quickly`.

10   Emphatic position

Mid-position adverbs go before emphasized auxiliary verbs or *be*.
Compare:

*She **has certainly** made him angry.*
*She **certainly HAS** made him angry!*

*I'm **really** sorry.*
*I **really AM** sorry.*

*'Polite people **always say** thank-you.'*
*'I **always DO say** thank-you.'*

11 Other positions

Some adverbs can go directly with particular words or expressions that they modify. The most important are *just*, *almost*, *only*, *really*, *even*, *right*, *terribly*.

> *I'll see you in the pub **just before eight o'clock**.*
> *I've read the book **almost to the end**.*
> ***Only you** could do a thing like that.* *I feel **really tired**.*
> *He always wears a coat, **even in summer**.*
> *She walked **right past me**.* *We all thought she sang **terribly badly**.*

15 after (conjunction)

clause + *after* + clause
after + clause, + clause

1 We can use *after* to join two clauses.
We can either say: *B happened **after** A happened*
OR ***After** A happened, B happened.*

The meaning is the same: *A* happened first.
Note the comma (,) in the second structure.

> *I went to America **after** I left school.*
> ***After** I left school, I went to America.*
>
> *He did military service **after** he went to university.*
> (= He went to university first.)
> ***After** he did military service, he went to university.*
> (= He did military service first.)

2 In a clause with *after*, we use a present tense if the meaning is future (see 343).

> *I'll telephone you **after** I **arrive**.* (NOT *... after I will arrive.*)

3 In clauses with *after*, we often use perfect tenses. We can use the present perfect (*have* + past participle) instead of the present, and the past perfect (*had* + past participle) instead of the past.

> *I'll telephone you **after** I've arrived.*
> ***After** I had left school, I went to America.*

There is not usually much difference of meaning between the perfect tenses and the others in this case. Perfect tenses emphasize the idea that one thing was finished before another started.

4 In a formal style, we often use the structure ┌ *after* + *-ing* ┐ .

> ***After** completing this form, return it to the Director's office.*
> *He wrote his first book **after** visiting Mongolia.*

16 **after** (preposition); **afterwards** (adverb)

After is a preposition: it can be followed by a noun or an -*ing* form.

> *We ate in a restaurant **after** the film.*
> ***After seeing** the film, we ate in a restaurant.*

After is not an adverb: we do not use it with the same meaning as *afterwards*, *then* or *after that*.

> *We went to the cinema and **afterwards** (**then**/**after that**) we ate in a restaurant.*
> (NOT ... *and ~~after we ate in a restaurant.~~*)

17 **after all**

1 *After all* gives the idea that one thing was expected, but the opposite happened. It means 'Although we expected something different'.

> *I'm sorry. I thought I could come and see you this evening, but I'm not free **after all**.*
> *I expected to fail the exam, but I passed **after all**.*

Position: usually at the end of the clause.

2 We can also use *after all* to mean 'We mustn't forget that ...' It is used to introduce a good reason or an important argument which people seem to have forgotten.

> *It's not surprising you're hungry. **After all**, you didn't have breakfast.*
> *I think we should go and see Granny. **After all**, she only lives ten miles away, and we haven't seen her for ages.*

Position: usually at the beginning of the clause.

18 **afternoon, evening** and **night**

1 *Afternoon* changes to *evening* when it starts getting dark, more or less. However, it depends on the time of year. In summer, we stop saying *afternoon* by six o'clock, even if it is still light. In winter we can go on saying *afternoon* until at least five o'clock, even if it is dark.

2 *Evening* changes to *night* more or less at bedtime. Note that *Good evening* usually means 'Hello', and *Good night* means 'Goodbye'—it is never used to greet people.

> *A: **Good evening**. Terrible weather, isn't it?*
> *B: Yes, dreadful.*
> *A: Hasn't stopped raining for weeks. Well, I must be going.*
> ***Good night**.*
> *B: **Good night**.*

19 ages

1 We talk about people's ages with $\boxed{be + number}$

> *He **is** thirty-five.*
> *She **will be** twenty-one next year.*

or $\boxed{be + number + years\ old}$.

> *He **is** thirty-five **years old**.*

To ask about somebody's age, say *How old are you?* (*What is your age?* is correct but not usual.)

2 Note the structure $\boxed{be + \dots age}$ (without preposition).

> *When I **was your age**, I was already working.*
> *The two boys **are the same age**.*
> *She's **the same age** as me.*

20 ago

1 Position

$\boxed{expression\ of\ time + ago}$

> *I met her **six weeks ago**. (NOT ... ago six weeks.)*
> *It all happened **a long time ago**.*
> *How **long ago** did you arrive?*

2 *Ago* is used with a past tense, not the present perfect.

> *She **phoned** a few minutes ago. (NOT She **has phoned** ...)*
> *'Where's Mike?' 'He **was working** outside ten minutes ago.'*

3 The difference between *ago* and *for*

Compare:

> *I went to Spain **six weeks ago**. (= six weeks before now)*
> *I went to Germany **for six weeks** this summer. (= I spent six weeks in Germany.)*

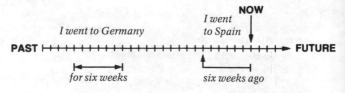

4 The difference between *ago* and *before*

two years ago = two years before now
two years before = two years before then (before a past time)
Compare:

> **Two years ago**, I visited my home town, which I had left **two years before**.

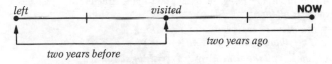

▷ For other uses of *before*, see 61–63.

21 all (of) with nouns and pronouns

1 We can put *all* (*of*) before nouns and pronouns.
Before a noun with a determiner (for example *the*, *my*, *this*), *all* and *all of* are both possible.

> **All (of) my** friends like riding.
> She's eaten **all (of) the** cake.

Before a noun with no determiner, we do not use *of*.

> **All children** can be naughty sometimes. (NOT ~~All of children~~ ...)

Before a personal pronoun, we use *all of*.

> **All of them** can come tomorrow.
> Mary sends her love to **all of us**.

All we, *all they* are not possible.

2 We can put *all* after object pronouns.

> I've invited **them all**.
> Mary sends her love to **us all**.
> I've made **you all** something to eat.

22 all with verbs

All can go with a verb, in 'mid-position', like some adverbs (see 13.2).

1 | auxiliary verb + *all*
am/are/is/was/were + *all* |

> We **can all** swim.
> They **have all** finished.
> We **are all** tired.

2 | *all* + other verb |

> My family **all like** travelling.
> You **all look** tired.

23 all, everybody and everything

1 We do not usually use *all* alone to mean 'everybody'.
Compare:

> *All the people stood up.*
> *Everybody stood up.* (NOT ~~All stood up.~~)

2 *All* can mean *everything*, but usually only in the structure *all* + relative
clause (= *all (that)* ...). Compare:

> *All (that) I have is yours.* (OR *Everything* ...)
> *Everything is yours.* (NOT ~~All is yours.~~)
>
> *She lost all she owned.* (OR ... *everything she owned.*)
> *She lost everything.* (NOT ~~She lost all.~~)

This structure often has a rather negative meaning: 'nothing more' or 'the
only thing(s)'.

> *This is all I've got.*
> *All I want is a place to sleep.*

Note the expression *That's all* (= 'It's finished').

24 all and every

1 *All* and *every* have similar meanings. (*Every* means 'all without
exception'.)
They are used in different structures:

all + plural	every + singular
All children need love.	*Every child needs love.*
All cities are noisy.	*Every city is noisy.*

2 We can use *all*, but not *every*, before a determiner (for example *the, my,
this*).

all + determiner + plural	every + singular
Please switch off all the lights.	*Please switch off every light.*
I've written to all my friends.	*I've written to every friend I have.*
	(NOT ... *every my friend.*)

3 We can use *all*, but not *every*, with uncountable nouns.

> *I like all music.* (NOT ... *every music.*)

We can use *all* with some singular countable nouns, to mean 'every part
of', 'the whole of'. Compare:

> *She was here all day.* (= from morning to night)
> *She was here every day.* (= Monday, Tuesday, Wednesday ...)

4   At the beginning of negative sentences, we use these structures:

> *Not all/every* + noun + affirmative verb

***Not all** Scottish people drink whisky.*
***Not every** student passed the exam.*

> *No* + noun + affirmative verb
> *None of* + determiner + noun + affirmative verb

***No** Scottish people work in our office.*
***None of the** students passed the exam.*

For the use of *no* and *none*, see 221.

5   We do not usually use *all* and *every* alone without nouns. Instead, we say *all of it/them* and *every one*.

> *'She's eaten all the cakes.' 'What, **all of them**?' 'Yes, **every one**.'*

▷   For the difference between *all* and *whole*, see 25.
For more rules about *all*, see 21–23.
For the difference between *every* and *each*, see 104.

25   **all** and **whole**

> *all* + determiner + noun
> determiner + *whole* + noun

1   *Whole* means 'complete', 'every part of'. *All* and *whole* can both be used with singular nouns. They have similar meanings, but the word order is different. Compare:

> *Julie spent **all the summer** at home.*   ***all my** life*
> *Julie spent **the whole summer** at home.*   ***my whole** life*

2   *Whole* is more common than *all* with singular countable nouns.

> *She wasted **the whole lesson**.* (More common than . . . *all the lesson*.)

3   We usually use *all*, not *whole*, with uncountable nouns.

> *She's drunk **all the milk**.* (NOT . . . *the whole milk*.)

There are some exceptions: for example *the whole time*; *the whole truth*.

4   *The whole of* or *all (of)* is used before proper nouns, pronouns and determiners.

> ***The whole of/All of** Venice was under water.* (NOT *Whole Venice* . . .)
> *I've just read **the whole of** 'War and Peace'.*
> (OR . . . ***all of** 'War and Peace'*.)
> *I didn't understand **the whole of/all of it**.*

26 all right

We usually write *all right* as two separate words in British English.
(*Alright* is possible in American English.)

> *Everything will be **all right**.*

27 almost and nearly

1 There is not usually much difference between *almost* and *nearly*, and we
can often use both with the same meaning.

> *I've **nearly** finished.*   *I've **almost** finished.*

Sometimes *almost* is a little 'nearer' than *nearly*.

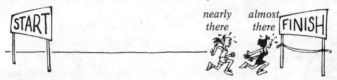

2 We do not usually use *nearly* with negative words: *never, nobody,
no-one, nothing, nowhere, no* and *none.*
Instead, we use *almost*, or we use *hardly* with *ever, anybody*, etc. (See
150.2.)

> *almost never* (NOT ~~nearly never~~)   *hardly ever*
> *almost nobody*   *hardly anybody*
> *almost no money*   *hardly any money*

28 also, as well and too

| clause + *as well* |
| clause + *too* |

| subject + *also* + verb ... |
| subject + *be* + *also* + complement |

1 *As well* and *too* usually come at the end of a clause. They mean the same.

> *She not only sings; she plays the piano **as well**.*
> *We all went to Brighton yesterday. John came **too**.*

As well and *too* can refer to ('point to') different parts of the sentence,
depending on the meaning. Consider the sentence: *We have meetings
on Sundays as well*. This can mean three different things:

a *(Other people have meetings on Sundays, and)*

  we have meetings on Sundays *as well.*

b *(We go for walks on Sundays, and)*

we have meetings on Sundays ‾*as well.*‾

c *(We have meetings on Tuesdays, and)*

we have meetings on Sundays ‾*as well.*‾

When we speak, we show the exact meaning by stressing the word that *as well* or *too* refers to.

*'We have meetings on **Sundays** as well.'*

2 *Too* and *as well* are often used in 'short answers'.

> *'She's nice.' 'I think so **too**.'*
> *'I've got a headache.' 'I have **as well**.'*

In very informal speech, we often use *Me too* as a short answer.

> *'I'm going home.' '**Me too**.'*

In a more formal style, we would say *I am too*, or *So am I* (see 312).

3 We usually put *also* before the verb (for the exact position when there are auxiliary verbs, see 14.3).

> *I don't like him. I **also think** he's dishonest.*
> *She sings, and she **also plays** the piano.*

Also comes after *am, is, are, was* and *were*.

> *I'm hungry, and I'**m also** very tired.*

Also can refer to any part of the sentence, like *as well* and *too*.
We do not use *also* in short answers.

> *'I'm hungry.' 'I am too.'/'So am I.'/'Me too.'/'I am as well.'*
> (NOT *'I also.'*)

4 | *Also* + comma (,) | can be used at the beginning of a sentence, to refer to the whole sentence.

> *It's a nice house, but it's very small. **Also**, it needs a lot of repairs.*

5 We do not usually use *also, as well* and *too* in negative sentences.
Instead, we use structures with *not ... either, neither* or *nor*. (See 217.)
Compare:

> *He's there too. – He is**n't** there **either**.*
> *I like you as well. – I do**n't** like you **either**.*
> *I do too. – **Nor** do I.*

▷ For the difference between *also* and *even*, see 114.3.
For *as well as*, see 51.

29 although and though

(al)though + clause, + clause clause, + (al)though + clause
clause + though

1 Both these words can be used as conjunctions. They mean the same. *Though* is informal.

> *(Al)though I don't agree with him, I think he's honest.*
> *She went on walking, (al)though she was terribly tired.*
> *I'll talk to him, (al)though I don't think it'll do any good.*

We use *even though* to emphasize a contrast. (*Even although* is not possible.)

> *Even though I didn't understand the words, I knew what he wanted.*

2 We can use *though* to mean 'however'. It usually comes at the end of a sentence in informal speech.

> *'Nice day.' 'Yes. Bit cold, though.'*

▷ For the difference between *even* and *even though*, see 114.4.
For *even though* and *even so*, see 114.4, 5. For *as though*, see 49.

30 among and between

1 We say that somebody/something is *between* two or more clearly separate people or things.
We use *among* when somebody/something is in a group, a crowd or a mass of people or things, which we do not see separately. Compare:

> *She was standing between Alice and Mary.*
> *She was standing among a crowd of children.*

> *Our house is between the wood, the river and the village.*
> *His house is hidden among the trees.*

BETWEEN

AMONG

2 We use *between* to say that there are things (or groups of things) on two sides.

> *a little valley between high mountains*
> *I saw something between the wheels of the car.*

3   We say *divide between* and *share between* before singular nouns.
Before plural nouns, we can say *between* or *among*.

> He **divided** his money **between** his wife, his daughter and his sister.
> I **shared** the food **between**/ **among** all my friends.

31 and

> A and B
> A, B and C
> A, B, C and D

1   When we join two or more expressions, we usually put *and* before the
last. (For rules about commas, see 266.1.)

> bread **and** cheese
> We drank, talked **and** danced.
> I wrote the letters, Peter addressed them, George bought the stamps
> **and** Alice posted them.

2   In two-word expressions, we often put the shortest word first.

> young and pretty   cup and saucer

Some common expressions with *and* have a fixed order which we cannot
change.

> hands and knees (NOT ~~knees and hands~~)
> knife and fork   bread and butter
> men, women and children   fish and chips

3   We do not usually use *and* with adjectives before a noun.

> Thanks for your **nice long** letter. (NOT ... ~~your nice and long letter.~~)
> a **tall dark handsome** cowboy

But we use *and* when the adjectives refer to different parts of the same
thing.

> red **and** yellow socks   a metal **and** glass table

▷   Note: *and* is usually pronounced /ənd/, not /ænd/. (See 358.)
For ellipsis (leaving words out) with *and*, in expressions like *the bread
and (the) butter*, see 108.2. For *and* after *try, wait, go, come* etc, see 32.

32 and after **try, wait, go** etc

1   We often use *try and ...* instead of *try to ...*
This is informal.

> **Try and** eat something—you'll feel better if you do.
> I'll **try and** phone you tomorrow morning.

We only use this structure with the simple form *try*. It is not possible with *tries*, *tried*, or *trying*.

Compare:

> ***Try and*** *eat something.*
> *I **tried to** eat something.* (NOT *I ~~tried and ate something.~~*)

We usually say *wait and see*, not *wait to see*.

> *'What's for lunch?' '**Wait and see**.'*

2   We often say *come and*, *go and*, *run and*, *hurry up and*, *stay and*. This has the same meaning as *come*, *go* etc + infinitive of purpose (see 178).

> ***Come and*** *have a drink.*   ***Stay and*** *have dinner.*
> ***Hurry up and*** *open the door.*

We can use this structure with forms like *comes*, *came*, *going*, *went* etc.

> *He often **comes and** spends the evening with us.*
> *She **stayed and** played with the children.*

33 another

---
another + singular noun
another + *few*/number + plural noun
---

1   *Another* is one word.

> *He's bought **another** car.* (NOT *... ~~an other car.~~*)

2   Normally, we only use *another* with singular countable nouns. Compare:

> *Would you like **another** potato?*
> *Would you like **some more** meat?* (NOT *... ~~another meat?~~*)
> *Would you like **some more** peas?* (NOT *... ~~another peas?~~*)

3   But we can use *another* before a plural noun in expressions with *few* or a number.

> *I'm staying for **another few weeks**.*
> *We need **another three chairs**.*

▷   For information about *one another*, see 105.
    For more information about *other*, see 231.

34 any (= 'it doesn't matter which')

Any can mean 'it doesn't matter which'; 'whichever you like'.

> *'When shall I come?' '**Any** time.'*
> *'Could you pass me a knife?' 'Which one?' 'It doesn't matter. **Any** one.'*

We can use *anybody*, *anyone*, *anything* and *anywhere* in the same way.

> *She goes out with **anybody** who asks her.*
> *'What would you like to eat?' 'It doesn't matter. **Anything** will do.'*
> *'Where can we sit?' '**Anywhere** you like.'*

▷ For the use of *any* and *no* as adverbs, see 35.
  For other uses of *any* (and *some*), see 314.

35 any and no: adverbs

> *any/no* + comparative
> *any/no different*
> *any/no good/use*

1 *Any* and *no* can modify (= change the meaning of) comparatives (see also 86.2).

> *You don't look **any older** than your daughter.*
> (= *You don't look at all older ...*)
> *I can't go **any further**.*
> *I'm afraid the weather's **no better** than yesterday.*

2 We also use *any* and *no* with *different*.

> *This school isn't **any different** from the last one.*
> *'Is John any better?' '**No different**. Still very ill.'*

3 Note the expressions *any good/use* and *no good/use*.

> *Was the film **any good**?*   *This watch is **no use**. It keeps stopping.*

36 appear

1 *Appear* can mean 'seem'. In this case, it is a 'copula verb' (see 91), and is followed by an adjective or a noun.
We often use the structure *appear to be*, especially before a noun.

> subject + *appear (to be)* + adjective

> *He **appeared** very angry.* (NOT *... very angrily.*)

> subject + *appear to be* + noun

> *She **appears to be** a very religious person.*

2 *Appear* can also mean 'come into sight' or 'arrive'. In this case, it is not followed by an adjective or noun, but it can be used with adverbs.

> subect (+ adverb) + *appear* (+ adverb/adverb phrase)

> *A face suddenly **appeared** at the window.*
> *Mary **appeared** unexpectedly this morning and asked me for some money.*

▷ For *seem*, see 291.

37 (a)round and about

1   We usually use *round* for movement or position in a circle, or in a curve.

>*We all sat **round** the table.*
>*I walked **round** the car and looked at the wheels.*
>*'Where do you live?' 'Just **round** the corner.'*

2   We also use *round* when we talk about going
to all (or most) parts of a place, or giving things
to everybody in a group.

>*We walked **round** the old part of the town.*
>*Can I look **round**?*
>*Could you pass the cups **round**, please?*

3   We use *around* or *about* to express movements or positions that are not
very clear or definite: 'here and there', 'in lots of places', 'in different parts
of', 'somewhere near' and similar ideas.

>*The children were running **around/about** everywhere.*
>*Stop standing **around/about** and do some work.*
>*'Where's John?' 'Somewhere **around/about**.'*

We also use these words to talk about time-wasting or silly activity.

>*Stop **fooling around/about**. We're late.*

And *around/about* can mean 'approximately', 'not exactly'.

>*There were **around/about** fifty people there.*
>*'What time shall I come?' '**Around/about** eight.'*

▷   Note: In American English, *around* is generally used for all of these
meanings.

38 articles: introduction

The correct use of the articles (*a/an* and *the*) is one of the most difficult
points in English grammar. Fortunately, most article mistakes do not
matter too much. Even if we leave all the articles out of a sentence, it is
usually possible to understand it.

>*Please can you lend me pound of butter till end of week?*

However, it is better to use the articles correctly if possible. Sections 39 to
45 give the most important rules and exceptions.
Most Western European languages have article systems very like English.
You do not need to study sections 39 to 41 in detail if your language is
one of these: French, German, Dutch, Danish, Swedish, Norwegian,
Icelandic, Spanish, Catalan, Galician, Italian, Portuguese, Greek,
Romanian. If your language is not one of these, you should study all of
the sections 39 to 45.
To understand the rules for the articles, you need to know about
countable and uncountable nouns. Read 92 if you are not sure of this.

articles: **a/an**

1 A noun like *house, engineer, girl, name* refers to a whole class of people or things.

We use *a/an* with a noun to talk about just one member of that class. (*A/an* means 'one'.)

> *She lives in **a** nice big house.*
> *My father is **an** engineer.* (NOT ~~My father is engineer.~~)
> ***A** girl phoned this morning.*   *Tanaka is **a** Japanese name.*

2 We use *a/an* when we define or describe people or things (when we say what class or kind they belong to).

> *He's **a** doctor.*   *She's **a** beautiful woman.*
> *'What's that?' 'It's **a** calculator.'*

3 We do not use *a/an* with a plural or uncountable noun (see 92), because *a/an* means 'one'.

> *My parents are **doctors**.* (NOT ... ~~a doctors.~~)
> *Would you like **some** salt?* (NOT ... ~~a salt.~~)

We do not use *a/an* with an adjective alone (without a noun). Compare:

> *She's **a** very good engineer.*
> *She's very good.* (NOT ~~She's a very good.~~)

We do not use *a/an* together with another determiner (for example *my, your*).

> *He's **a** friend of mine.* (NOT ~~He's a my friend.~~)

4 Note that we write *another* in one word.

> *Would you like **another** drink?* (NOT ... ~~an other drink?~~)

▷ For the exact difference between *a* and *an*, see 44.
For the difference between *a/an* and *the*, see 41.
For the use of *some* with plural and uncountable nouns, see 316.

40 articles: **the**

1 *The* means something like 'you know which one I mean'. It is used with uncountable (see 92), singular and plural nouns.

> ***the** water* (uncountable)   ***the** table* (singular countable)
> ***the** stars* (plural countable)

We use *the*:

a. to talk about people and things that we have already mentioned.

> *She's got two children: a girl and a boy. **The** boy's fourteen and **the** girl's eight.*

b. when we are saying which people or things we mean.

> *Who's **the** girl in **the** car over there with John?*

c. when it is clear from the situation which people or things we mean.

*Could you close **the** door?* (Only one door is open.)
*'Where's Ann?' 'In **the** kitchen.'*   *Could you pass **the** salt?*

2 We do not use *the* with other determiners (for example *my*, *this*, *some*).

*This is **my** uncle.* (NOT ... ~~**the my** uncle.~~)
*I like **this** beer.* (NOT ... ~~**the this** beer.~~)

We do not usually use *the* with proper names (there are some exceptions—see 45).

Mary lives in Switzerland. (NOT ~~The Mary lives in the Switzerland.~~)

We do not usually use *the* to talk about things in general—*the* does not mean 'all'. (See 42.)

Books are expensive. (NOT ~~The books are expensive.~~)

▷ For the pronunciation of *the*, see 44.

41 articles: the difference between **a/an** and **the**

Very simply:

a/an just means 'one of a class'
the means 'you know exactly which one'.

Compare:

A doctor must like people. (= *any doctor, any one of that profession*)
*My brother's **a** doctor.* (= *one of that profession*)
*I'm going to see **the** doctor.* (= *you know which one: my doctor*)
*I live in **a** small flat at **the** top of **an** old house near **the** town hall.*
(**a** *small flat*: there might be two or three at the top of the house—it could be any one of these.
an *old house*: there are lots near the town hall—it could be any one.
the *top*: we know which top: it's the top of the house where the person lives—a house only has one top.
the *town hall*: we know exactly which town hall is meant: there's only one in the town.)

42 articles: talking in general

1 We do not use *the* with uncountable or plural nouns (see 92) to talk about things in general—to talk about all books, all people or all life, for example. *The* never means 'all'. Compare:

*Did you remember to buy **the** books?* (= *particular books which I asked you to buy*)
Books are expensive. (NOT ~~The books are expensive. We are talking about books in general—all books.~~)

*I'm studying **the life** of Beethoven. (= one particular life)*
***Life** is hard.* (NOT ~~The life~~ .... This means 'all life'.)

*'Where's **the cheese**?' 'I ate it.'*
***Cheese** is made from milk.*

*Could you put **the light** on?*
***Light** travels at 300,000 km a second.*

2 Sometimes we talk about things in general by using a singular noun as an example. We use *a/an* with the noun (meaning 'any').

> *A **baby deer** can stand as soon as it is born.*
> *A **child** needs plenty of love.*

We can also use *the* with a singular countable noun in generalizations (but not with plural or uncountable nouns—see 1 above). This is common with the names of scientific instruments and inventions, and musical instruments.

> *Life would be quieter without **the telephone**.*
> ***The violin** is more difficult than **the piano**.*

3 These common expressions have a general meaning: *the town, the country, the sea, the seaside, the mountains, the rain, the wind, the sun(shine)*.

> *I prefer **the mountains** to **the sea**.* *I hate **the rain**.*
> *Would you rather live in **the town** or **the country**?*
> *We usually go to **the seaside** for our holidays.*
> *I like lying in **the sun(shine)**.* *I like the noise of **the wind**.*

43 articles: countable and uncountable nouns

A singular countable noun (see 92) normally has an article or other determiner with it. We can say *a cat, the cat, my cat, this cat, any cat, either cat* or *every cat*, but not just *cat*. (There are one or two exceptions—see 45.) Plural and uncountable nouns can be used without an article or determiner, or with *the*. They cannot be used with *a* (because it means 'one').

	a/an	*the*	no article
singular countable *cat*	*a cat*	*the cat*	
plural countable *cats*		*the cats*	*cats*
uncountable *water*		*the water*	*water*

▷ See diagram overleaf

44 articles: **a** and **an**; pronunciation of **the**

1 We do not usually pronounce /ə/ before a vowel (*a, e, i, o, u*). So before a vowel, the article *a* (/ə/) changes to *an*, and *the* changes its pronunciation from /ðə/ to /ði:/. Compare:

a rabbit   **an** *elephant*   **the** *sea* /ðə 'si:/   **the** *air* /ði: 'eə/

2 We use *an* and *the* /ði:/ before a vowel *sound*—a pronounced vowel— even if it is written as a consonant.

an hour / ən 'aʊə/   *the hour* /ði: 'aʊə/
(the *h* in *hour* is not pronounced)
an MP /ən em'pi:/   *the MP* /ði: em'pi:/
(the name of the letter *M* is pronounced /em/)

We use *a* and *the* /ðə/ before a consonant *sound*, even if it is written as a vowel.

a university /ə ju:nɪ'vɜ:səti/   *the university* /ðə ju:nɪ'vɜ:səti/
a one-pound note

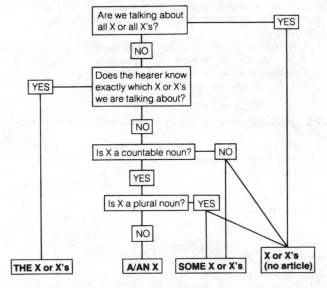

▷   For the difference between *X* and *some X*, see 316.
      For exceptions, see 45.

45 articles: special rules and exceptions

1 **Common expressions without articles**

Articles are not used in these expressions:

> *to school   at school   from school   to/at/from university/college*
> *to/at/in/into/from church   to/in/into/out of bed/prison/hospital*
> *to/at/from work   to/at sea   to/in/from town   at/from home*
> *for/at/to breakfast/lunch/dinner/supper   at night*
> *by car/bus/bicycle/plane/train/tube/boat*
> *on foot   go to sleep   watch television (TV)   on TV*

2 **Possessives**

A noun that is used after a possessive (like *John's, America's*), has no article.

> *John's coat* (NOT ~~the John's coat~~)
> *America's economic problems*
> (NOT ~~the America's economic problems~~)

3 **Musical instruments**

We usually use the article *the* when we talk in general about a musical instrument. (See 42.2.)

> *I'd like to learn **the** piano.*

But *the* is not used when we talk about jazz or pop music.

> *This recording was made with Miles Davis **on trumpet**.*

4 *all* and *both*

We sometimes leave out *the* after *both*, and after *all* when there is a number.

> ***Both (the) children** are good at maths.*
> ***All (the) eight** students passed the exam.*

We can say *all day, all night, all week, all summer/winter, all year*, without *the*.

> *I've been waiting for you **all day**.*

5 **Seasons**

We can say *in spring* or *in the spring, in summer* or *in the summer*, etc. There is little difference.

6 **Jobs and positions**

We use the article with the names of jobs.

> *My sister is **a doctor**.* (NOT ~~My sister is doctor.~~)

But *the* is not used in titles like *Queen Elizabeth, President Lincoln*.

7 Exclamations

We use *a/an* in exclamations after *what*, with singular countable nouns.

> **What a** *lovely dress!* (NOT ~~What lovely dress!~~)

8 Nature

We often use *the* with the words *town*, *country*, *sea*, *seaside* and *mountains*, even when we are talking in general. The same happens with *wind*, *rain*, *snow* and *sun(shine)*. (See 42.3.)

> *Do you prefer **the town** or **the country**?*
> *I love **the mountains**.*
> *I like the noise of **the wind**.*
> *She spends her time lying in **the sun**.*

9 Place-names

We usually use *the* with these kinds of place-names:

> seas (***the** Atlantic*)
> mountain groups (***the** Himalayas*)
> island groups (***the** West Indies*)
> rivers (***the** Rhine*)
> deserts (***the** Sahara*)
> hotels (***the** Grand Hotel*)
> cinemas and theatres (***the** Odeon,* ***the** Playhouse*)
> museums and art galleries (***the** British Museum,* ***the** Tate*)

We usually use no article with:

> continents, countries, states, counties, departments etc
> (*Africa, Brazil, Texas, Berkshire, Westphalia*)
> towns (*Oxford*)
> streets (*New Street*)
> lakes (*Lake Michigan*)

Exceptions: countries whose name contains a common noun like *republic, state(s), union* (***the** People's **Republic** of China,* ***the** USA*). Note also ***the** Netherlands*, and its seat of government ***the** Hague*.

We do not usually use *the* with the names of the principal buildings of a town.

> *Oxford University* (NOT ~~the Oxford University~~)
> *Oxford Station* (NOT ~~the Oxford Station~~)
> *Salisbury Cathedral*
> *Birmingham Airport*
> *Bristol Zoo*

Names of single mountains vary—some have articles, some do not (*Everest,* ***the** Matterhorn*).

10 Newspapers

The names of newspapers usually have *the*.

> *The* Times *The* Washington Post

Most names of magazines do not have *the*.

> *Punch New Scientist*

11 Special styles

We leave out articles in some special ways of writing.

newspaper headlines	*MAN KILLED ON MOUNTAIN*
notices, posters etc	*SUPER CINEMA, RITZ HOTEL*
telegrams	*WIFE ILL MUST CANCEL TODAY*
instructions	*Open packet at other end*
dictionary entries	**palm** *inner surface of hand between wrist and fingers*
lists	*take car to garage; buy buttons; pay phone bill*
notes	*J. thinks company needs new office*

▷ For the use of articles with abbreviations (*NATO, **the** USA*), see 1.
For the use of *the* in double comparatives (***the** more, **the** better*), see 85.4.
For *a* with *few* and little, see 129.
For *a* with *hundred, thousand* etc. see 227.8.

46 as ... as ...

| as + adjective + as
as + adverb + as | + noun/pronoun/clause |

1 We use *as ... as ...* to say that two things are the same in some way.

> *She's **as** tall **as** her brother.*
> *Can a man run **as** fast **as** a horse?*
> *It's not **as** good **as** I expected.*

2 We can use object pronouns (*me, him* etc) after *as*, especially in an informal style. (See 331.4.)

> *She doesn't sing as well **as me**.*

In a formal style, we use subject + verb.

> *She doesn't sing as well **as I do**.*

3 After *not*, we can use *as ... as ...* or *so ... as ...*

> *She's **not as/so pretty as** her sister.*

4 Note the structure *half as ... as ...* ; *twice as ... as ...* ; *three times as ... as ...* ; etc.

> *The green one isn't **half as good as** the blue one.*
> *A colour TV is **twice as expensive as** a black and white.*

▷ For *as much/many as ...* , see 50.
For *as soon as ...* , see 343.1.
For *as well as ...* , see 51.

47 as, because and since (reason)

> *as/because/since* + clause + clause
> clause + *as/because/since* + clause

1 *Because* is used when we give the reason for something.

> ***Because I was ill** for six months I lost my job.*

If the reason is the most important idea, we put it at the end of the sentence.

> *Why am I leaving? I'm leaving **because I'm fed up**!*

2 *As* and *since* are used when the reason is not the most important idea in the sentence, or when it is already known. *Since* is more formal. *As-* and *since*-clauses often come at the beginning of the sentence.

> ***As it's raining again**, we shall have to stay at home.*
> ***Since he had not paid his bill**, his electricity was cut off.*

48 as and like

1 Similarity

We can use *like* or *as* to say that things are similar.

a *Like* is a preposition. We use *like* before a noun or pronoun.

> *like* + noun/pronoun

> *You look **like your sister**. (NOT ... ~~as your sister~~.)*
> *He ran **like the wind**. It's **like a dream**.*
> *She's dressed just **like me**.*

We use *like* to give examples.

> *He's good at some subjects, **like mathematics**.*
> *(NOT ... ~~as mathematics~~.)*
> *In mountainous countries, **like Switzerland**, ...*

b *As* is a conjunction. We use *as* before a clause, and before an expression beginning with a preposition.

> *as* + clause
> *as* + preposition phrase

> *Nobody knows her **as I do**.*
> *We often drink tea with the meal, **as they do** in China.*
> *In 1939, **as in 1914**, everybody wanted war.*
> *On Friday, **as on Tuesday**, the meeting will be at 8.30.*

In informal English *like* is often used instead of *as*.
This is very common in American English.

> *Nobody loves you **like I do**.*

For *like = as if*, see 49.3.
For *as ... as*, see 46. For *the same as*, see 288.

2 Function

We use *as*, not *like*, to say what function a person or thing has—what jobs people do, what things are used for, etc.

> *He worked **as a waiter** for two years.* (NOT *... like a waiter.*)
> *Please don't use your plate **as an ashtray**.*

49 **as if** and **as though**

> *as if/though* + subject + present/past verb
> *as if/though* + subject + past verb with present meaning

1 *As if* and *as though* mean the same.
We use them to say what a situation seems like.

> *It looks **as if/though** it's going to rain.*
> *I felt **as if/though** I was dying.*

2 We can use a past tense with a present meaning after *as if/though*. This means that the idea is 'unreal'.
Compare:

> *He looks as if **he's** rich.* (Perhaps he is rich.)
> *She talks as if **she was** rich.* (But she isn't.)

We can use *were* instead of *was* when we express 'unreal' ideas after *as if/though*. This is common in a formal style.

> *She talks as if **she were** rich.*

3 *Like* is often used instead of *as if/though*, especially in American English. This is very informal.

> *It looks **like** it's going to rain.*

50 as much/many ... as ...

We use *as much ... as ...* with a singular (uncountable) noun, and *as many ... as ...* with a plural. Compare:

*We need **as much** time **as** possible.*
*We need **as many** cars **as** possible.*

As much/many can be used without a following noun.

*I ate **as much** as I wanted.   Rest **as much** as possible.*
*'Can I borrow some books?' 'Yes, **as many** as you like.'*

51 as well as

> noun/adjective/adverb + *as well as* + noun/adjective/adverb
> clause + *as well as* -*ing* ...
> *As well as* -*ing* ... + clause

1 *As well as* has a similar meaning to 'not only ... but also'.

*He's got a car **as well as** a motorbike.*
*She's clever **as well as** beautiful.*

2 When we put a verb after *as well as*, we use the -*ing* form.

*Smoking is dangerous, **as well as making** you smell bad.*
***As well as breaking** his leg, he hurt his arm.*
(NOT *As well as he broke his leg ...*)

Note the difference between:

*She sings **as well as playing** the piano.* (= She not only plays, but also sings.)
*She sings **as well as she plays** the piano.*)= Her singing is as good as her playing.)

52 as, when and while (things happening at the same time)

1

> *As/When/While A was happening, B happened.*
> *B happened as/when/while A was happening.*

As/When/While A was happening

| AAAAAAAAAAAAAAAAAAAAAA (B) AAAAAAAAAAAAAAAAAAAAAA |

B happened

We can use *as*, *when*, or *while* to say that a longer action or event was going on when something else happened.

We usually use the past progressive tense (*was/were* + ... *-ing*) for the longer action or event (see 242).

> ***As I was walking*** down the street I saw Joe driving a Porsche.
> The telephone rang ***when I was having*** a bath.
> ***While they were playing*** cards, somebody broke into the house.

As, *when* and *while* can be used in the same way with present tenses.

> Please don't interrupt me ***when I'm speaking***.
> I often get good ideas ***while I'm shaving***.

2

> While A was happening, B was happening.
> While A happened, B happened.

While A was happening/happened

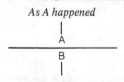

B was happening/happened.

We usually use *while* to say that two long actions or events went on at the same time.

We can use the past progressive or the simple past.

> ***While you were reading*** the paper, I ***was working***.
> John ***cooked*** supper ***while I watched*** TV.

Present tenses are also possible.

> After supper, I ***wash up while*** Mary ***puts*** the children to bed.

3

> As A happened, B happened.
> B happened, as A happened.

As A happened

A

B

B happened.

We can use *as* to say that two short actions or events happened at the same time.

> ***As I opened*** my eyes I heard a strange voice.
> The doorbell rang just ***as I picked*** up the phone.

53 ask

1

> *Ask for*: ask somebody to give something
> *Ask* without *for*: ask somebody to tell something

> *Don't **ask** me **for** money.* (NOT *Don't ask me money.*)
> *Don't **ask** me my name.* (NOT *Don't **ask** me **for** my name.*)
> ***Ask for** the menu.*
> ***Ask** the price.*

2 When there are two objects, the indirect object (the person) comes first, without a preposition.

>   1   2
> *I'll ask **that man** the time.*
> (NOT *I'll ask the time **to that man**.*)

3 We can use *ask* with just one object (direct or indirect).

> *Ask **him**.*   *Ask **his name**.*

4 We can use infinitive structures after *ask*.

> *ask* + infinitive

> *I asked **to go** home.* (= I said I wanted to go home.)

> *ask* + object + infinitive

> *I asked **John to go** home.* (= I said I wanted John to go home.)

> *ask* + *for* + noun/pronoun + passive infinitive

> *I asked **for the parcel to be sent** to my home address.*

54 at, in, and on (place)

1 *At* is used to talk about position at a point.

> *It's very hot **at** the centre of the earth.*
> *Turn right **at** the next traffic-lights.*

Sometimes we use *at* with a larger place, if we just *think* of it as a point: a point on a journey, a meeting place, or the place where something happens.

> *You have to change trains **at** Didcot.*
> *The plane stops for an hour **at** Frankfurt.*
> *Let's meet **at** the station.*
> *There's a good film **at** the cinema in Market Street.*

2 *On* is used to talk about position on a line.

> *His house is **on** the way from Aberdeen*
> *to Dundee.*
> *Stratford is **on** the River Avon.*

On is also used for position on a surface.

> *Come on—supper's **on** the table!*
> *I'd prefer that picture **on** the other wall.*
> *There's a big spider **on** the ceiling.*

3 *In* is used for position in a three-dimensional space (when something is surrounded on all sides).

> *I don't think he's **in** his office.*
> *Let's go for a walk **in** the woods.*
> *I last saw her **in** the car park.*

4 We say *on* (and *off*) for buses, planes and trains.

> *He's arriving **on** the 3.15 train.*
> *There's no room **on** the bus; let's get **off** again.*

5 In addresses, we use *at* if we give the house number.

> *She lives **at** 73 Albert Street.*

We use *in* if we just give the name of the street.

> *She lives **in** Albert Street.*

We use *on* for the number of the floor.

> *She lives in a flat **on** the third floor.*

6 Learn these expressions:

> ***in** a picture*   ***in** the sky*   ***on** a page*
> ***in** bed/hospital/prison/church*
> ***at** home/school/work/university/college*

▷ Note that *at* is usually pronounced /ət/, not /æt/. (See 358.)

55 at, in and on (time)

> *at* + exact time
> *in* + part of day
> *on* + particular day
> *at* + weekend, public holiday
> *in* + longer period

1 Exact times

> *I usually get up **at** six o'clock.*   *I'll meet you **at** 4.15.*
> *Phone me **at** lunch time.*

In informal English, we say *What time...?*
(*At what time...?* is correct, but unusual.)

> *What time does your train leave?*

2 Parts of the day

> *I work best in the morning.*
> *three o'clock in the afternoon*
> *We usually go out in the evening.*

Exception: *at night.*

We use *on* if we say which morning/afternoon/etc we are talking about,
or if we describe the morning/afternoon/etc.

> *See you on Monday morning.*
> *It was on a cold afternoon in early spring, ...*

3 Days

> *I'll phone you on Tuesday.*
> *My birthday's on March 21st.*
> *They're having a party on Christmas Day.*

In informal speech we sometimes leave out *on*. (This is very common in
American English.)

> *I'm seeing her Sunday morning.*

Note the use of plurals (*Sundays, Mondays* etc) when we talk about
repeated actions.

> *We usually go to see Granny on Sundays.*

4 Weekends and public holidays

We use *at* to talk about the whole of the holidays at Christmas, New Year,
Easter and Thanksgiving (US).

> *Are you going away at Easter?*

We use *on* to talk about one day of the holiday.

> *It happened on Easter Monday.*

British people say *at the weekend*; Americans use *on*.

> *What did you do at the weekend?*

5 Longer periods

> *It happened in the week after Christmas.*
> *I was born in March.*
> *Kent is beautiful in spring.*
> *He died in 1616.*
> *Our house was built in the 15th Century.*

6 Expressions without preposition

Prepositions are not used in expressions of time before *next*, *last*, *this*, *one*, *any*, *each*, *every*, *some*, *all*.

> See you **next week**.   Are you free **this morning**?
> Let's meet **one day**.   Come **any time**.
> I'm at home **every evening**.   We stayed **all day**.

Prepositions are not used before *yesterday*, *the day before yesterday*, *tomorrow*, *the day after tomorrow*.

> What are you doing **the day after tomorrow**?

▷ Note that *at* is usually pronounced /ət/, not /æt/ (see 358).

56 at all

1 We often use *at all* to emphasize a negative.

> I **don't** like her **at all**. (= I don't like her even a little.)
> This restaurant is **not at all** expensive.

2 We also use *at all* with *hardly*; in questions; and after *if*.

> She **hardly** eats anything **at all**.
> Do you sing **at all**? (= . . . even a little?)
> I'll come in the morning **if** I come **at all**. (= Perhaps I won't come.)

3 We can say *Not at all* as a polite answer to *Thank you*. (See 249.4.)

57 be with auxiliary do

---

do + be + adjective/noun
don't + be + adjective/noun

---

1 *Don't be* . . . is used to give people advice or orders.

> **Don't be** afraid.   **Don't be** a fool!

In affirmative sentences, we usually just use *Be* . . .

> **Be** careful!

But *Do be* . . . is used for emphasis.

> **Do be** careful, please!!!
> **Do be** quiet, for God's sake!

2 In other cases, we do not use *do* with *be*.

> I am not often lonely. (NOT ~~I do not often be lonely.~~)

58 be + infinitive

> *I am to ...   you are to ...* etc

1 We use this structure in a formal style to talk about plans and
arrangements, especially when they are official.

> *The President **is to visit** Nigeria next month.*
> *We **are to get** a 10 per cent wage rise in June.*

2 We also use the structure to give orders. Parents often use it to children.

> *You **are to eat** all your supper before you watch TV.*
> *She can go to the party, but she's **not to be** back late.*

3 You can often see *be* + passive infinitive in notices and instructions.

> (noun + *is*) + passive infinitive (= *to be* + past participle)

> *(This form is) **to be filled in** in ink.*

Sometimes *be* is omitted.

> ***To be taken*** *three times a day after meals.* (on a medicine bottle)

▷ For other ways of talking about the future, see 134–140

59 be: progressive tenses

> *I am being/you are being* etc + adjective/noun

We can use this structure to talk about what people are/were doing, but
not usually to say how they are/were feeling. Compare:

> *You**'re being** stupid.* (= *You're doing stupid things.*)
> *I **was being** very careful.* (= *I was doing something carefully.*)

> *I**'m happy** just now.* (NOT ~~I'm being happy just now.~~)
> *I **was** very depressed when you phoned.*
> (NOT ~~I was being very depressed ...~~)

▷ For the use of *am being* etc in passive verb forms, see 238.

60 because and because of

> clause + *because* + clause
> *because* + clause, + clause
>
> *because of* + noun/pronoun

Because is a conjunction. It joins two clauses together.

> *I was worried **because** Mary was late.*
> ***Because** I was tired, I went home.*

Because of is a preposition (used before a noun or a pronoun).

> *I was late **because of** the rain.*

61 **before** (adverb)

1   We can use *before* to mean 'at any time before now'. We use it with a present perfect tense (*have* + past participle).

> ***Have*** *you* ***seen*** *this film* ***before****?*
> *I'****ve never been*** *here* ***before****.*

Before can also mean 'before then', 'before the past time that we are talking about'. We use a past perfect tense (*had* + past participle).

> *She realized that she* ***had seen*** *him* ***before****.*

2   In expressions like *three days before, a year before, a long time before*, the meaning is 'before then'. We use a past perfect tense. (See 20.4 for an explanation of the difference between *before* and *ago* in these expressions.)

> *When I went back to the school that I* ***had left eight years before****, everything was different.*

62 **before** (conjunction)

> clause + *before* + clause
> *before* + clause, + clause

1   We can use *before* to join two clauses.
We can either say: *A happened* ***before*** *B happened*
          OR ***Before*** *B happened, A happened.*

The meaning is the same: A happened first.
Note the comma (,) in the second structure.

> *I bought a lot of new clothes* ***before*** *I went to America.*
> ***Before*** *I went to America, I bought a lot of new clothes.*

> *He did military service* ***before*** *he went to university.*
> *(= He did military service first.)*
> ***Before*** *he did military service, he went to university.*
> *(= He went to university first.)*

2   In a clause with *before*, we use a present tense if the meaning is future. (See 343.)

> *I'll telephone you* ***before*** *you* ***leave****.*
> (NOT ... ***before*** ~~*you will leave*~~.)

3   In a formal style, we often use the structure *before* + *-ing*.

> *Please put out all lights* ***before leaving*** *the office.*
> ***Before beginning*** *the book, he spent five years on research.*

63 before (preposition) and in front of

> before: time
> in front of: place

Compare:

> *I must move my car **before nine o'clock.***
> *It's parked **in front of the post office.***
> (NOT ... ***before** the post office.*)

We do not use *in front of* for things
which are on opposite sides of a
road, river, room etc. Use
opposite or *facing*.

> *There's a pub **opposite** my house.*
> (NOT ... *in front of my house.*)
> *We stood **facing** each other
> across the train.*
> (NOT ... *in front of each other.*)

in front of   opposite

64 begin and start

1   There is not usually any difference between **begin** and **start**.

> *I **started/began** teaching when I was twenty-four.*
> *If John doesn't come soon, let's **start/begin** without him.*

We prefer *start* when we talk about an activity that happens regularly,
with 'stops and starts'.

> *It's **starting** to rain.*
> *What time do you **start** teaching tomorrow morning?*

We prefer *begin* when we talk about long, slow activities, and when we
are using a more formal style.

> *Very slowly, I **began** to realize that there was something wrong.*
> *We will **begin** the meeting with a message from the President.*

2   *Start* (but not *begin*) is used to mean:

a   'start a journey'

> *I think we ought to **start** at six, while the roads are empty.*

b   'start working' (for machines)

> *The car won't **start**.*

c   'make (machines) start'

> *How do you **start** the washing machine?*

▷   For the use of the infinitive and the *-ing* form after *begin* and *start*, see
182.11.

65 big, large, great and tall

1 We use *big* mostly in an informal style.

> *We've got a **big** new house.*
> *Get your **big** feet off my flowers.*
> *That's a really **big** improvement.*
> *You're making a **big** mistake.*

In a more formal style, we prefer *large* or *great*.
Large is used with concrete nouns (the names of things you can see, touch, etc).
Great is used with abstract nouns (the names of ideas etc).

> *It was a **large house**, situated near the river.*
> *I'm afraid my daughter has rather **large feet**.*
> *Her work showed **a great improvement** last year.*

With uncountable nouns, only *great* is possible.

> *There was **great confusion** about the dates.*
> (NOT ... ~~big confusion~~ ...)
> *I felt **great excitement** as the meeting came nearer.*

2 *Tall* is used to talk about vertical height (from top to bottom). It is mostly used for people; sometimes for buildings and trees. (See also 339: **tall** and **high**.)

> *'How **tall** are you?' 'One metre ninety-one.'*

a tall man   a big man

3 We also use *great* to mean 'famous' or 'important'.

> *Do you think Napoleon was really a **great** man?*
> *Newton was probably the **greatest** scientist who ever lived.*

4 We sometimes use *great* to mean 'wonderful' (very informal).

> *I've had a **great** idea!*
> *'How's the new job?' **'Great.'***
> *It's a **great** car.*

5 Note that *large* is a 'false friend' for people who speak some European languages. It does not mean the same as *wide*.

> *The river is a hundred metres **wide**.* (NOT ... ~~metres large~~.)

66 born

To be born is passive.

> *Hundreds of children **are born** deaf every year.*

To talk about somebody's date or place of birth, use the simple past tense *was/were* born.

> *I **was born** in 1936. (NOT I am born in 1936.)*
> *My parents **were** both **born** in Scotland.*

67 borrow and lend

> borrow something from somebody
>
> lend something to somebody
> lend somebody something

Borrow is like *take*. You borrow something *from* somebody.

> *I **borrowed** a pound **from** my son.*   *Can I **borrow** your bicycle?*

Lend is like *give*. You lend something *to* somebody, or lend somebody something (the meaning is the same).

> *I **lent** my coat **to** a friend of my brother's, and I never saw it again.*
> ***Lend** me your comb for a minute, will you?*

▷ For *lend* in passive structures, see 356.4.

68 both (of) with nouns and pronouns

1 We can put *both (of)* before nouns and pronouns.
Before a noun with a determiner (for example: *the, my, these*), *both* and *both of* are both possible.

> ***Both (of) my** parents like riding.*   *She's eaten **both (of) the** chops.*

We can also use *both* without a determiner.

> *She's eaten **both** chops. (= ... **both of the** chops.)*

Only *both of* is possible before a personal pronoun (*us, you, them*).

> ***Both of them** can come tomorrow.*
> *Mary sends her love to **both of us**.*

2 We can put *both* after object pronouns.

> *I've invited **them both**.*   *Mary sends **us both** her love.*
> *I've made **you both** something to eat.*

3 Note: we do not put *the* before *both*.

> ***both** children (NOT the both children)*

69 both with verbs

Both can go with a verb, in 'mid-position', like some adverbs (see 13.2).

1

> auxiliary verb + *both*
> am/are/is/was/were + *both*

> *We **can both** swim.*
> *They **have both** finished.*
> *We **are both** tired.*

2

> *both* + other verb

> *My parents **both like**
> travelling.*
> *You **both look** tired.*

70 both ... and ...

> *both* + adjective + *and* + adjective
> *both* + noun + *and* + noun
> *both* + clause + *and* + clause

We usually put the same kind of words after *both* and *and*.

> *She's both **pretty** and **clever**.* (adjectives)
> *I spoke to both **the Director** and **his secretary**.* (nouns)
> (NOT *I both **spoke to** the Director and **his secretary**.*)
> *She both **plays** the piano and **sings**.* (verbs)
> (NOT *She both **plays** the piano and **she sings**.*) (verb, clause)

▷ See also *either ... or* (107) and *neither ... nor* (218).

71 bring and take

1 We use *bring* for movements to the place where the speaker or hearer is.
We use *take* for movements to other places.

Compare:

> *This is a nice restaurant. Thanks for **bringing** me here.*
> (NOT *... Thanks for **taking** me here.*)
> *Let's have another drink, and then I'll **take** you home.*
> (NOT *... and then I'll **bring** you home.*)
> (on the phone) *Can we come and see you next weekend? We'll **bring**
> a picnic.*
> *Let's go and see the Robinsons next weekend. We can **take** a picnic.*

2 We can use *bring* for a movement to a place where the speaker or listener was or will be. Compare:

> '*Where are those papers I asked for?*' '*I **brought** them to you when you were in Mr Allen's office. Don't you remember?*'
> *I **took** the papers to John's office.*

> *Can you **bring** the car to my house tomorrow?*
> *Can you **take** the car to the garage tomorrow?*

▷ The difference between *come* and *go* is similar. (See 83.)
For other uses of *take*, see 337; 338.

72 (Great) Britain, the United Kingdom, the British Isles and England

Britain (or *Great Britain*) and *the United Kingdom* (or *the UK*) include England, Scotland, Wales and Northern Ireland. (Sometimes *Britain* or *Great Britain* is used just for the island which includes England, Scotland and Wales, without Northern Ireland.)
The British Isles is the name for England, Scotland, Wales, the whole of Ireland, and all the islands round about.
Note that *England* is only one part of Britain. Scotland and Wales are not in England, and Scottish and Welsh people do not like to be called 'English'.

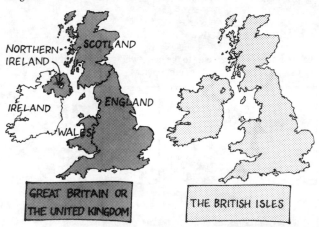

73 British and American English

These two kinds of English are very similar. There are a few differences of grammar and spelling, and rather more differences of vocabulary. Pronunciation is sometimes very different, but most British and American speakers can understand each other.

1 **Grammar**

US	GB
*He just **went** home.*	*He's just **gone** home.* (See 243.)
***Do you have** a problem?*	***Have you got** a problem?* (See 153.2.)
*I've never really **gotten** to know him.*	*I've never really **got** to know him.*
*It's important that he **be** told.*	*It's important that he **should be** told.* (See 332.1.)
(on the telephone) *Hello, is **this** Harold?*	*Hello, is **that** Harold?* (See 341.4.)
*It looks **like** it's going to rain.*	*It looks **as if** it's going to rain.* (See 49.3.)
*He looked at me **real strange**.* (informal)	*He looked at me **really** strangely.* (See 275.)

2 **Vocabulary**

There are very many differences. Sometimes the same word has different meanings (GB *mad* = 'crazy'; US *mad* = 'angry'). Often different words are used for the same idea (GB *lorry*; US *truck*).
Here are a few examples:

US	GB	US	GB
apartment	flat	second floor	first floor
cab	taxi	french fries	chips
can	tin	garbage *or* trash	rubbish
candy	sweets		
check	bill (*in a restaurant*)	gas(oline)	petrol
closet *or* cabinet	cupboard	highway	main road
		intersection	crossroads
cookie	biscuit	mad	angry
corn	maize	mail	post
crazy	mad	motor	engine
elevator	lift	movie	film
fall	autumn	one-way	single (ticket)
first floor	ground floor	pants	trousers

US	GB	US	GB
pavement	road surface	store	shop
potato chips	crisps	subway	underground
railroad	railway	truck	lorry
round-trip	return (ticket)	vacation	holiday(s)
sidewalk	pavement	zipper	zip

Expressions with prepositions and particles:

US	GB
check something **out**	check something
do something **over**	do something **again**
fill **in/out** a form	fill **in** a form
meet **with** somebody	meet somebody
visit **with** somebody	visit somebody
Monday **through** Friday	Monday **to** Friday
home	**at** home
Mondays	**on** Mondays

3 Spelling

US	GB	US	GB
aluminum	aluminium	jewelry	jewellery
analyze	analyse	labor	labour
catalog	catalogue	pajamas	pyjamas
center	centre	practice	practise (*verb*)
check	cheque (*from a bank*)	program	programme
color	colour	theater	theatre
defense	defence	tire	tyre (*on car*)
honor	honour	traveler	traveller

Many verbs end in *-ize* in American English, but in *-ise* or *-ize* in British English. For example: US *realize*/GB *realise* or *realize*.

74 broad and wide

Wide is used for the physical distance from one side of something to the other.

    *We live in a very **wide** street.*   *The car's too **wide** for the garage.*

Broad is mostly used in abstract expressions. Some examples:

    ***broad** agreement* (= agreement on most points)
    ***broad**-minded* (= tolerant)   ***broad** daylight* (= full, bright daylight)

Broad is also used in the expression **broad** *shoulders* (= wide strong shoulders), and in descriptions of landscape in a formal style.

> *Across the **broad** valley, the mountains rose blue and mysterious.*

75 but = except

1 We use *but* to mean 'except' after *all, none, every, any, no* (and *everything, everybody, nothing, nobody, anywhere* etc).

> *He eats **nothing but** hamburgers. **Everybody**'s here **but** George.*
> *I've finished **all** the jobs **but** one.*

We usually use object pronouns (*me, him* etc) after *but*.

> *Nobody **but her** would do a thing like that.*

2 We use the infinitive without *to* after *but*.

> *That child does nothing **but watch** TV.*
> (NOT ... *nothing **but watching** TV*.)

3 Note the expressions *next but one, last but two* etc.

> *My friend Jackie lives **next door but one**.*
> (= *two houses from me.*)
> *Liverpool are **last but one** in the football league.*

▷ For *except*, see 118; 119.

76 by: time

By can mean 'not later than'.

> *I'll be home **by** five o'clock.* (= *at or before five*)
> *'Can I borrow you car?' 'Yes, but I must have it back **by** tonight.'*
> (= *tonight or before*)
> *I'll send you the price list **by** Thursday.*

▷ For the difference between *by* and *until*, see 351.

77 can and could: forms

1 *Can* is a 'modal auxiliary verb' (see 202).
There is no *-s* in the third person singular.

> *She **can** swim very well.* (NOT *She ~~cans~~* ...)

Questions and negatives are made without *do*.

> ***Can** you swim?* (NOT *~~Do you can swim?~~*)
> *I **can't** swim.* (NOT *~~I don't can swim.~~*)

After *can*, we use the infinitive without *to*.

> *I **can speak** a little English.* (NOT *~~I can to speak~~* ...)

2 *Can* has no infinitive or participles. When necessary, we use other words.

> *I'd like **to be able** to stay here.* (NOT *... **to can** stay ...*)
> *You'll **be able** to walk soon.* (NOT *You'll **can** ...*)
> *I've always **been able** to play games well.* (NOT *I've always **could** ...*)
> *I've always **been allowed** to do what I liked.*
> (NOT *I've always **could** ...*)

3 *Could* is the 'past tense' of *can*. But we use *could* to talk about the past, present or future (see 78–80).

> *I **could** read when I was four.   You **could** be right.*
> ***Could** I see you tomorrow evening?*

Could also has a conditional use.

> *I **could** marry him if I wanted to.*
> (= *It would be possible for me to marry him ...*)

4 Contracted negative forms (see 90) are *can't* (/kɑːnt/) and *couldn't* (/'kʊdnt/).
Cannot is written as one word.
For 'weak' and 'strong' pronunciations of *can*, see 358.

5 *Can* and *could* are used in several ways. The main uses are:

a   to talk about ability
b   to talk about possibility
c   to ask, give and talk about permission
d   to make offers and requests, and to tell people what to do.

For details, see the following sections.

78 can and could: ability

1 Present

We use *can* to talk about present or 'general' ability.

> *Look! I **can** do it! I **can** do it!   I **can** read Italian, but I **can't** speak it.*

2 Future

We use *will be able to* to talk about future ability.

> *I'**ll be able to** speak good English in a few months.*
> *One day people **will be able to** go to the moon on holiday.*

We use *can* if we are deciding now about the future.

> *I haven't got time today, but I **can** see you tomorrow.*
> ***Can** you come to a party on Saturday?*

3 Past

We use *could* for 'general ability'—to say that we could do something at any time, whenever we wanted. (*Was/were able to* is also possible.)

> *She **could** read when she was four.* (NOT *She was able to …*)
> *My father **could** speak ten languages.*

We do not use *could* to say that we did something on one occasion. We use *managed to, succeeded in … -ing,* or *was able to.*

> *How many eggs **were you able to** get?*
> (NOT *… **could** you get?*)
> *I **managed to** find a really nice dress in the sale yesterday.*
> (NOT *I **could** find …*)
> *After six hours' climbing we **succeeded in** getting to the top of the mountain.* (NOT *… we **could** get to the top …*)

But we can use *couldn't* to say that we did *not* succeed in doing something on one occasion.

> *I **managed to** find the street, but I **couldn't** find her house.*

4 Conditional

We can use *could* to mean 'would be able to'.

> *You **could** get a better job if you spoke a foreign language.*

5 *could have …*

We use a special structure to say that we had the ability to do something, but did not try to do it.

> | *could have* + past participle |
> | --- |

> *I **could have married** anybody I wanted to.*
> *I was so angry I **could have killed** her!*
> *You **could have helped** me—why didn't you?*

79 can: possibility and probability

1 Possibility

We use *can* to say that situations and events are possible.

> *Scotland **can** be very warm in September.*
> *'Who **can** join the club?' 'Anybody who wants to.'*
> *There are three possibilities: we **can** go to the police, we **can** talk to a lawyer, or we **can** forget all about it.*
> *'There's the doorbell.' 'Who **can** it be?' 'Well, it **can't** be your mother. She's in Edinburgh.'*

We use *could* to talk about past possibility.

> *It **could** be quite frightening if you were alone in our big old house.*

2 Probability

We do not usually use *can* when we are talking about the chances that something is true, or that something will happen. For this idea (probability), we prefer *could*, *may* or *might* (see 199).

> *'Where's Sarah?' 'She **may**/**could** be at Joe's place.'*
> (NOT *'She **can be** ...'*)
> *We **may** go camping this summer.* (NOT *We **can go** ...*)

3 *could have ...*

We use a special structure to say that something was possible, but did not happen.

> | *could have* + past participle |

> *That was a bad place to go skiing—you **could have broken** your leg.*
> *Why did you throw the bottle out of the window? It **could have hit** somebody.*

80 can: permission, offers, requests and orders

1 Permission

We use *can* to ask for and give permission.

> *'**Can** I ask you something?' 'Yes, of course you **can**.'*
> ***Can** I have some more tea?   You **can** go now if you want to.*

We also use *could* to ask for permission. This is more polite or formal.

> ***Could** I ask you something, if you're not too busy?*

May and *might* are also possible in formal and polite requests for permission. (See 200.)

> ***May** I have some more tea?*

2 Past permission

We use *could* to say that we had 'general' permission to do something at any time.

> *When I was a child, I **could** watch TV whenever I wanted to.*

But we don't use *could* to talk about permission for one particular past action.

> *I **was allowed** to see her yesterday evening.* (NOT *I **could see** ...*)

(This is like the difference between *could* and *was able to*. See 73.3.)

3 Offers

We use *can* when we offer to do things for people.

> *'**Can** I carry your bag?' 'Oh, thanks very much.'*
> *'I **can** baby-sit for you this evening if you like.' 'No, it's all right, thanks.'*

4 Requests

We can ask people to do things by saying *Can you . . . ?* or *Could you . . . ?* (more polite); or *Do you think you could . . . ?*

> '*Can you* put the children to bed?' 'Yes, all right.'
> '*Could you* lend me five pounds until tomorrow?' 'Yes, of course.'
> '*Do you think you could* help me for a few minutes?' 'Sorry, I'm afraid I'm busy.'

5 Orders

We can use *you can/could* to tell people to do things.

> When you've finished the washing up **you can** clean the kitchen. Then **you could** iron the clothes, if you like.

81 can with remember, understand, speak, play, see, hear, feel, taste and smell

1 *remember, understand, speak, play*

These verbs usually mean the same with or without *can*.

> I *(can) remember* London during the war.
> She *can speak* Greek/She *speaks* Greek.
> I *can't/don't understand*.
> *Can/Do you play* the piano?

2 *see, hear, feel, smell, taste*

We do not use these verbs in progressive tenses when they refer to perception (receiving information through the eyes, ears etc). To talk about seeing, hearing etc at a particular moment, we often use *can see, can hear* etc.

> I *can hear* Susan coming. (NOT *I'm seeing* . . .)
> I *can hear* somebody coming up the stairs.
> What did you put in the stew? I *can taste* something funny.

82 close and shut

1 *Close* and *shut* can often be used with the same meaning.

> Open your mouth and **close/shut** your eyes.
> I can't **close/shut** the window. Can you help me?

The past participles *closed* and *shut* can be used as adjectives.

> The post office is **closed/shut** on Saturday afternoon.

Shut is not usually used before a noun.

> a **closed** door (NOT *a shut door*)
> **closed** eyes (NOT *shut eyes*)

2 We prefer *close* for slow movements (like flowers closing at night), and *close* is more common in a formal style. Compare:

> *As we watched, he **closed** his eyes for the last time.*
> ***Shut** your mouth!*

3 We *close* roads, railways etc (channels of communication).
We *close* (= *end*) letters, bank accounts, meetings etc.

83 come and go

1 We use *come* for movements to the place where the speaker or hearer is. We use *go* for movements to other places.

> *'Maria, would you **come** here, please?' 'I'm **coming**.'*
> (NOT ... *'I'm going.'*)
> *When did you **come** to live here?*
> *Can I **come** and sit on your lap?*

> *I want to **go** and live in Greece.*
> *Let's **go** and see Peter and Diane.*
> *In 1577, he **went** to study in Rome.*

2 We can use *come* for a movement to a place where the speaker or listener was or will be. Compare:

> *What time did I **come** to see you in the office yesterday? About ten, was it?*
> *I **went** to your office yesterday, but you weren't in.*

> *Will you **come** and visit me in hospital?*
> *He's **going** into hospital next week.*

▷ The difference between *bring* and *take* is similar. (See 71.)

84 comparison: comparative and superlative adjectives

1 Short adjectives

(adjectives with one syllable; adjectives with two syllables ending in -y)

ADJECTIVE	COMPARATIVE	SUPERLATIVE	
old	old**er**	old**est**	Most adjectives:
tall	tall**er**	tall**est**	+ -er, -est.
cheap	cheap**er**	cheap**est**	
late	late**r**	late**st**	Adjectives ending
nice	nice**r**	nice**st**	in -e: + -r, -st.
fat	fa**tt**er	fa**tt**est	One vowel +
big	bi**gg**er	bi**gg**est	one consonant:
thin	thi**nn**er	thi**nn**est	double consonant.
happ**y**	happ**ier**	happ**iest**	Change y to i.
eas**y**	eas**ier**	eas**iest**	

Note the pronunciation of:

younger /ˈjʌŋgə(r)/   *longer* /ˈlɒŋgə(r)/   *stronger* /ˈstrɒŋgə(r)/
youngest /ˈjʌŋgɪst/   *longest* /ˈlɒŋgɪst/   *strongest* /ˈstrɒŋgɪst/

2 Irregular comparatives and superlatives

ADJECTIVE	COMPARATIVE	SUPERLATIVE
good	better	best
bad	worse	worst
far	farther/further	farthest/furthest (see 126)
old	older/elder	oldest/eldest (see 299.5)

The determiners *little* and *much/many* have
irregular comparatives and superlatives:

little	less	least
much/many	more	most

3 Longer adjectives

(adjectives with two syllables not ending in -y, adjectives with three or
more syllables)

ADJECTIVE	COMPARATIVE	SUPERLATIVE
tiring	**more** tiring	**most** tiring
cheerful	**more** cheerful	**most** cheerful
handsome	**more** handsome	**most** handsome
intelligent	**more** intelligent	**most** intelligent
practical	**more** practical	**most** practical

Some two-syllable adjectives have two comparatives and superlatives: for example *commoner/more common*; *politest/most polite*. We usually prefer the forms with *more* and *most*.

▷ For information about how to use comparatives and superlatives, see 85.

How to make Comparative Adjectives

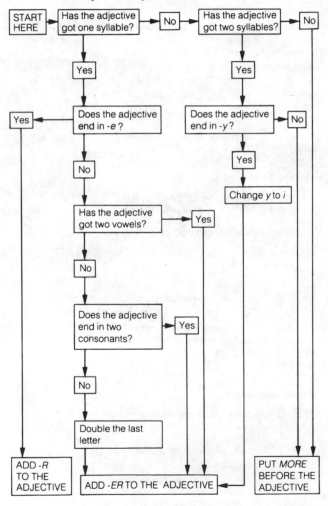

85 comparison: using comparatives and superlatives

1 **The difference between comparatives and superlatives**

We use the comparative to compare one person or thing with (an)other
person(s) or thing(s).
We use the superlative to compare one person or thing with his/her/its
whole group.
Compare:

> *Mary's **taller** than her three sisters.*
> *Mary's **the tallest** of the four girls.*

> *Your accent is **worse** than mine.*
> *Your accent is **the worst** in the class.*

> *Paul is **older** than Charles. Sally is **younger** than Paul. Albert is*
> ***older** than Sally. Charles is **younger** than Sally. Paul is **younger** than*
> *Eric. Eric is **older** than Albert. Who is **the oldest**? Who is **the youngest**?*

Mary's taller than her three sisters.   *Mary's the tallest of the four girls.*

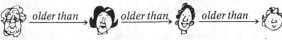

the   *older than* → *older than* → *older than* → *the*
oldest   *youngest*

2 We use *than* after comparatives.

> *The weather's better **than** yesterday.*
> (NOT ... *better **as** yesterday* OR *better **that** yesterday*.)
> *You sing better **than** me.* (OR ... *than I do.*)

(For *I* and *me* etc *than*, see 331.4.)

3 We can use double comparatives to say that something is changing.

> adjective + *-er and* adjective + *-er*
> *more and more* + adjective/adverb

*I'm getting **fatter and fatter**.*
*We're going **more and more slowly**.*
(NOT . . . *more slowly and more slowly*.)

4 We can use comparatives with *the . . . the . . .* to say that two things change or vary together.

> *the* + comparative + subject + verb,
>   *the* + comparative + subject + verb

***The older** I get, **the happier** I am.* (NOT *Older I get . . .*)
***The more dangerous** it is, **the more** I like it.*
(NOT *The more it is dangerous, . . .*)
***The more** I study, **the less** I learn.*

5 After superlatives, we do not usually use *of* to refer to a place.

> *I'm the happiest man **in** the world.* (NOT . . . *of the world.*)

6 Don't leave out *the* with superlatives.

> *It's **the best** book I've ever read.* (NOT *It's **best** book . . .*)

7 We can use superlatives without nouns (see 11.2).

> *You're **the nicest** of all.*
> *Which one do you think is **the best**?*

86 comparison: **much, far** etc with comparatives

1 We cannot use *very* with comparatives. Instead, we use *much* or *far*.

> *My boyfriend is **much/far older** than me.*
> (NOT . . . *very older than me.*)
> *Russian is **much/far more difficult** than Spanish.*

2 We can also modify comparatives with *very much, a lot, lots, any, no, rather, a little, a bit.*

> ***very much** nicer*
> ***a lot** happier*
> ***rather** more quickly*
> ***a little** less expensive*
> ***a bit** easier*
> *Is your mother **any** better?*
> *She looks **no** older than her daughter.*

87 comparison: comparative and superlative adverbs

Most comparative and superlative adverbs are made with *more* and *most*.

*Could you talk **more quietly**?* (NOT ... ***quietlier**?*)

A few adverbs have comparatives and superlatives with *-er* and *-est*. The most common are: *fast, soon, early, late, hard, long, well* (*better, best*), *far* (*farther/further, farthest/furthest*, see 126), *near*; and in informal English *slow, loud* and *quick*.

*Can't you drive any **faster**?*
*Can you come **earlier**?*
*She sings **better** than you do.*
*Talk **louder**.*

88 conditional

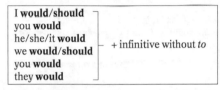

I **would/should**
you **would**
he/she/it **would**   + infinitive without *to*
we **would/should**
you **would**
they **would**

Contractions: *I'd, you'd, he'd* etc; *wouldn't/shouldn't*

1 Structures

> *would/should* + infinitive without *to*

*I **would like** a drink.*

> *would/should* + *be* + *-ing*   (progressive conditional)

*If I was at home now **I would be watching** TV.*

> *would/should* + *have* + past participle   (perfect conditional)

*If it hadn't been so expensive I **would have bought** it.*

> *would/should* + *be* + past participle   (passive conditional)

*I knew that the letter **would be opened** by his secretary.*

We can use *would* or *should* after *I* and *we*. They mean the same in conditional structures. After *you, he, she, it* and *they*, and nouns, we only use *would*. Compare:

*I **would/should** buy it if I had enough money.*
*John **would** buy it if he had enough money.*

2 Use

a   In sentences with *if*, and similar words (see 165).

> *I **wouldn't go** there if I didn't have to.*
> *Suppose there was a war, what **would you do**?*

b   In reported speech (see 283.3), to show that somebody said *shall* or *will*.

> *I said that I **should need** help. ('I **shall need** help.')*
> *He told me everything **would be** all right.*

c   For 'future in the past'.

> *I was late. I **would have** to run to catch the train.*

d   With *like*, *prefer* etc. in polite requests and offers.

> *I **would like** some tea.   **Would you prefer** meat or fish?*

3   After some conjunctions we use a past tense instead of a conditional. (See 343.)

> *If I was rich I would do **what I liked**.* (NOT *... **what I would like**.*)

4   Note that the word *conditional* can have another meaning. It is used not only for the structure *would/should* + infinitive (as here), but also for a kind of clause or sentence with *if* (see 164–165).

▷   For other uses of *should*, see 294. For other uses of *would*, see 369.

89 conjunctions

> clause + conjunction + clause
> conjunction + clause, + clause

1   A conjunction joins two clauses.

> *I'm tired **and** I want to go to bed.*
> *I tried hard **but** I couldn't understand.*
> *His father died, **so** he had to stop his studies.*
> *I know **that** you don't like her.*
> *I'll sell it to you cheap **because** you're a friend of mine.*
> *She married him **although** she didn't love him.*
> *We'll start at eight o'clock **so that** we can finish early.*
> *I'd tell you **if** I knew.*

And, but, so and *that* go between two clauses.
Most other conjunctions can also go at the beginning of a sentence.

> ***Because** you're a friend of mine, I'll sell it to you cheap.*
> ***Although** she didn't love him, she married him.*
> ***So that** we can finish early, we'll start at eight o'clock.*
> ***If** I knew, I'd tell you.*

When a conjunction begins a sentence, there is usually a comma (,) between the two clauses.

2 We do not usually write the two clauses separately, with a full stop (.) between them.

> *It was late **when** I got home.* (NOT ~~It was late. When I got home.~~)

But we can sometimes separate the two clauses in order to emphasize the second, especially with *and, but, so, because* and *although*.

> *James hated Mondays. **And** this Monday was worse than usual.*

And we separate clauses in conversation (when two different people say them).

> *'John's late.' '**Because** he was doing your shopping.'*

3 One conjunction is enough to join two clauses. Don't use two.

> ***Although** she was tired, she went to work.*
> *She was tired, **but** she went to work.*
> (NOT ~~Although she was tired, but she went to work.~~)
>
> ***Because** I liked him, I tried to help him.*
> *I liked him, **so** I tried to help him.*
> (NOT ~~Because I like him, so I tried to help him.~~)
>
> ***As** you know, I work very hard.*
> *You know **that** I work very hard.*
> (NOT ~~As you know, that I work very hard.~~)

4 Relative pronouns (*who, which* and *that*—see 277) join clauses like conjunctions.

> *There's the girl **who** works with my sister.*

A relative pronoun is the subject or object of the verb that comes after it. So we do not need another subject or object.

> *I've got a friend **who** works in a pub.* (NOT *... **who he works** ...*)
> *The man (**that**) she married was an old friend of mine.*
> (NOT ~~The man (that) she married him ...~~)
> *She always says thank-you for the money (**that**) I give her.*
> (NOT *... ~~for the money (that) I give it her.~~*)

90 contractions

1 Sometimes we make two words into one: for example
I've /aɪv/ (= *I have*); *don't* /dəʊnt/ (= *do not*).
These forms are called 'contractions'. There are two kinds:

pronoun + auxiliary verb	auxiliary verb + *not*
I've you'll he'd	*aren't isn't hadn't*
we're they've it's	*don't won't* (= *will not*)

The forms *'ve, 'll, 'd,* and *'re* are only written after pronouns, but we write *'s* (= *is/has*) after nouns and question-words as well.

> *My **father's** a gardener.   **Where's** the toilet?*

The apostrophe (') goes in the same place as the letters that we leave out: *has not = hasn't* (NOT *ha'snt*).

Contractions are common in informal speech and writing; they are not used in a formal style.

2 Sometimes an expression can have two possible contractions. For *she had not*, we can say *she'd not* or *she hadn't*; for *he will not*, we can say *he'll not* and *he won't*.

In Southern British English, the forms with *n't* are more common in most cases (for example *she hadn't*; *he won't*).

We do not use double contractions: *she'sn't* is impossible.

3 Contractions are unstressed. When an auxiliary verb is stressed (for example, at the end of the clause), a contraction is not possible. Compare:

> *You're late. Yes, you are.* (NOT *Yes, you're.*)
> *I've forgotten. Yes, I have.* (NOT *Yes, I've.*)

However, negative contractions are stressed, and we can use them at the ends of clauses.

> *No, you aren't.*   *No, you haven't.*

Contractions: pronunciation and meaning

I'm	/aɪm/	I am
I've	/aɪv/	I have
I'll	/aɪl/	I will/shall
I'd	/aɪd/	I had/would/should
you're	/jɔː(r)/	you are
you've	/juːv/	you have
you'll	/juːl/	you will
you'd	/juːd/	you had/would
he's	/hiːz/	he is/has
he'll	/hiːl/	he will
he'd	/hiːd/	he had/would
she's	/ʃiːz/	she is/has
she'll	/ʃiːl/	she will
she'd	/ʃiːd/	she had/would
it's	/ɪts/	it is/has
it'll	/ɪtl/	it will
it'd	/ɪtəd/	it had/would (not often written)
we're	/wɪə(r)/	we are
we've	/wiːv/	we have
we'll	/wiːl/	we will/shall
we'd	/wiːd/	we had/would
they're	/ðeə(r)/	they are
they've	/ðeɪv/	they have
they'll	/ðeɪl/	they will
they'd	/ðeɪd/	they had/would

aren't	/ɑːnt/	are not
can't	/kɑːnt/	cannot
couldn't	/'kʊdnt/	could not
daren't	/deənt/	dare not
didn't	/'dɪdnt/	did not
doesn't	/'dʌznt/	does not
don't	/dəʊnt/	do not
hasn't	/'hæznt/	has not
haven't	/'hævnt/	have not
hadn't	/'hædnt/	had not
isn't	/'ɪznt/	is not
mightn't	/'maɪtnt/	might not
mustn't	/'mʌsnt/	must not
needn't	/'niːdnt/	need not
oughtn't	/'ɔːtnt/	ought not
shan't	/ʃɑːnt/	shall not
shouldn't	/'ʃʊdnt/	should not
wasn't	/wɒznt/	was not
weren't	/wɜːnt/	were not
won't	/wəʊnt/	will not
wouldn't	/wʊdnt/	would not

Notes

a   *Am not* is contracted to *aren't* (/ɑːnt/) in questions.

   *I'm late, **aren't** I?*

b   In non-standard English, *ain't* is used as a contraction of *am not, are not, is not, have not* and *has not*.

c   Do not confuse *it's* and *its*. (See 299.8.)

d   For the contraction *let's*, see 191.

91 'copula' verbs

We use some verbs to join an adjective to the subject. These can be called 'copulas' or 'copula verbs'.
Compare:

   The car went fast. (*Fast* is an adverb. It tells you about the movement.)

   *The car **looks** fast.* (*Fast* is an adjective. It tells you about the car itself—rather like saying *The car **is** fast. Look* is a copula verb.)

Common copula verbs are:

   be   look   seem   appear   sound   smell   taste   feel

   *She **is** nice.   She **looks** nice.   She **seems** nice.   Her perfume **smells** nice.   Her voice **sounds** nice.   Her skin **feels** nice.*

Some copula verbs are used to talk about change. The most common are *become*, *get*, *grow*, *go* and *turn*.

> *It's **becoming** colder.*   *It's **getting** colder.* (informal)
> *It's **growing** colder.* (literary)
> *The leaves are **turning** brown.* (formal)
> *The leaves are **going** brown.* (informal—see 146)

Other copula verbs are used to say that things do not change. The most common are *stay*, *remain* and *keep*.

> *How does she **stay** so young?*
> *I hope you will always **remain** so charming.*
> ***Keep** calm.*

92 countable and uncountable nouns

1 Countable nouns are the names of separate objects, people, ideas etc which we can count.
We can use numbers and *a/an* with countable nouns; they have plurals.

> *a cat   three cats   a newspaper   two newspapers*

Uncountable nouns are the names of materials, liquids, and other things which we do not see as separate objects. We cannot use *a/an* or numbers with uncountable nouns; they have no plurals.

> *water* (NOT *a water; two waters*)
> *wool* (NOT *a wool; two wools*)
> *weather* (NOT *a weather; two weathers*)

countable   uncountable

2 We cannot usually put *a/an* with an uncountable noun even when there is an adjective.

> *My father enjoys very good **health**.* (NOT *... a very good health.*)
> *We're having terrible **weather**.* (NOT *... a terrible weather.*)
> *He speaks good **English**.* (NOT *... a good English.*)

3 Usually it is easy to see if a noun is countable or uncountable. Obviously *house* is a countable noun, and *air* is not. But sometimes things are not so clear. For instance, *travel* and *journey* have very similar meanings, but *travel* is uncountable (it means 'travelling in general') and *journey* is countable (it means 'one movement from one place to another'). Also, different languages see the world in different ways. For example *hair* is uncountable in English, but plural countable in many languages; *grapes* are plural countable in English, but uncountable in some languages. Here are some more nouns which are uncountable in English, but countable in some other languages, together with related singular countable expressions.

Uncountable	Countable
accommodation	a place to live or stay (NOT ~~an accommodation~~)
advice	a piece of advice (NOT ~~an advice~~)
bread	a loaf; a roll
furniture	a piece of furniture
grass	a blade of grass; a lawn
information	a piece of information
knowledge	a fact
lightning	a flash of lightning
luggage	a piece of luggage; a case, a trunk
money	a note; a coin; a sum
news	a piece of news
progress	a step forward
research	a piece of research; an experiment
rubbish	a piece of rubbish
spaghetti	a piece of spaghetti
thunder	a clap of thunder
toothache	an aching tooth
travel	a journey; a trip
work	a job; a piece of work

Note: *A headache* is countable.

4 Many nouns have both countable and uncountable uses.
Compare:

> *I'd like some white **paper**.* (uncountable)
> *I'm going out to buy **a paper**.* (= *a newspaper*—countable)

> *The window's made of unbreakable **glass**.* (uncountable)
> *Would you like **a glass** of water?* (countable)

> *Could I have some **coffee**?* (uncountable)
> *Could we have **two coffees**, please?* (= *cups of coffee*—countable)

*She's got red **hair**.*   *I've got two white **hairs**.*
(uncountable)   (countable)

▷ For more information about particular nouns, look in a good dictionary.

93 country

1 *Country* (countable) = 'nation', 'land'.

> *Scotland is a cold **country**.*
> *France is the **country** I know best.*
> *How many **countries** are there in Europe?*

2 *The country* (uncountable) = 'open land without many buildings' (the opposite of *the town*).
With this meaning, we cannot say *a country* or *countries* (see 92 for the use of uncountable nouns).

> *My parents live in **the country** near Edinburgh.*
> *Would you rather live in the town or **the country**?*

94 dare

1 *Dare* is used in two ways:

a as an ordinary verb, followed by the infinitive with *to*:

> *He **dares to** say what he thinks.*
> *She **didn't dare to** tell him.*

b as a modal auxiliary verb (see 202)

> ***Dare** she tell him?*
> *I **daren't** say what I think.*
>
> (question and negative without *do*;
> third person without -*s*;
> following infinitive without *to*.)

2 In modern English, we usually use *dare* as an ordinary verb. It is most common in negative sentences.

> *She **doesn't dare to** go out at night.*
> *They **didn't dare to** open the door.*

We can use the modal auxiliary form *daren't* to say that somebody is afraid to do something at the moment of speaking.

> *I **daren't** look.*

3 *I dare say* = 'I think probably', 'I suppose'.

> *I **dare say** it'll rain tomorrow.*
> *I **dare say** you're ready for a drink.*

95 dates

1 Writing

A common way to write the day's date is like this:

> *30 March 1993   27 July 1984*

There are other possibilities:

30th March, 1993   March 30(th) 1993   March 30(th), 1993   30.3.93

British and American people write 'all-figure' dates differently: British people put the day first, Americans put the month first.

6.4.77 = 6 April in Britain, June 4 in the USA.

For the position of dates in letters, see 192.

2 Speaking

30 March 1993 = (British) *'March the thirtieth, nineteen ninety-three'* OR
'The thirtieth of March, nineteen ninety-three'
(American) *'March thirtieth, nineteen ninety-three'*

▷   For the use of prepositions in dates, see 55; 256.2, 3.

96 determiners

1   Determiners are words like *the, my, this, some, either, every, enough, several.*
Determiners come at the beginning of noun phrases, but they are not adjectives.

the moon   *a* nice day   *my* fat old cat   *this* house
every week   *several* young students

We cannot usually put two determiners together. We can say *the* house, *my* house or *this* house, but not ~~the my house~~ or ~~the this house~~ or ~~this my house.~~

2   There are two groups of determiners:

Group A

| a/an the |
| my your his her its our your their one's whose |
| this these that those |

Group B

| some any no |
| each every either neither |
| much many more most little less least |
| few fewer fewest enough several |
| all both half |
| what whatever which whichever |

3 If we want to put a group B determiner before a group A determiner, we have to use *of*.

> group B determiner + *of* + group A determiner

> **some of** the people
> **each of** my children
> **neither of** these doors
> **most of** the time
> **which of** your records
> **enough of** those remarks

Before *of* we use *none*, not *no*, and *every one*, not *every*.

> **none of** my friends   **every one** of these books

We can leave out *of* after *all*, *both* and *half*.

> **all (of)** his ideas   **both (of)** my parents

4 We can use group B determiners alone (without nouns). We can also use them with *of* before pronouns.

> *'Do you know Orwell's books?' 'Yes, I've read* **several**.*'*
> *'Would you like some water?' 'I've got* **some**, *thanks.'*

> **neither of** them   **most of** us   **which of** you

▷ The index will tell you where to find more information about particular determiners.

97 discourse markers

Discourse means 'pieces of language longer than a sentence.' Some words and expressions are used to show how discourse is constructed. They can show the connection between something we have said and something we are going to say; or they can show the connection between what somebody else has said and what we are saying; or they can show what we think about what we are saying; or why we are talking. Here are some common examples of these 'discourse markers'.

1 *by the way*

We use *by the way* to introduce a new subject of conversation.

> *'Nice day.' 'Yes, isn't it?* **By the way**, *have you heard from Peter?'*

2 *talking about ...*

We use this to join one piece of conversation to another.

> *'I played tennis with Mary yesterday.' 'Oh, yes.* **Talking about Mary**, *do you know she's going to get married?'*

3 *firstly, secondly, thirdly; first of all; to start with*

We use these to show the structure of what we are saying.

Firstly, *we need somewhere to live.* *Secondly*, *we need to find work.*
And *thirdly*, ...
'What are you going to do?' *'Well,* *to start with* *I'm going to buy a*
newspaper.'

4 *all the same, yet, still, on the other hand, however*

These show a contrast with something that was said before.

'She's not working very well.' *'All the same*, *she's trying hard.'*
He says he's a socialist, and *yet* *he's got two houses and a Rolls*
Royce.
It's not much of a flat. *Still*, *it's home.*
'Shall we go by car or train?' *'Well, it's quicker by train.* *On the other*
hand, *it's cheaper by car.'*
Jane fell down the stairs yesterday. *However*, *she didn't really hurt*
herself.

5 *anyway, anyhow, at any rate*

These can mean 'what was said before is not important—the main point
is: ...'

I'm not sure what time I'll arrive: maybe half past seven or a quarter
to eight. *Anyway*, *I'll be there before eight.*
What a terrible experience! *Anyhow*, *you're all right—that's the main*
thing.

6 *mind you*

To introduce an exception to what was said before.

I don't like the job at all, really. *Mind you*, *the money's good.*

7 *I mean*

We say this when we are going to make things clearer, or give more
details.

It was a terrible evening. *I mean*, *they all sat round and talked*
politics for hours.

8 *kind of, sort of*

To show that we are not speaking very exactly.

I *sort of* *think we ought to start going home, perhaps, really.*

9 *let me see, well*

To give the speaker time to think.

'How much are you selling it for?' *'Well, let me see*, ...'

10 *well*

To make agreement or disagreement 'softer', less strong.

> '*Do you like it?*' '***Well***, *yes, it's all right.*'
> '*Can I borrow your car?*' '***Well***, *no, I'm afraid you can't.*'

11 *I suppose*

To make a polite enquiry.

> ***I suppose*** *you're not free this evening?*

To show unwilling agreement.

> '*Can you help me?*' '***I suppose*** *so.*'

12 *I'm afraid*

To say that one is sorry to give bad news.

> '*Do you speak German?*' '***I'm afraid*** *I don't.*'

▷ Most of these expressions have more than one meaning.
For full details, see a good dictionary. For *after all*, see 17. For *actually*, see 7.

98 do: auxiliary verb

The auxiliary verb *do* is used in a lot of ways.

1 We use *do* to make questions with ordinary verbs, but not with auxiliary verbs. (See 270.) Compare:

> ***Do you like*** *football?* (NOT *Like you football?*)
> ***Can you*** *play football?* (NOT *Do you can play football?*)

2 We use *do* to make negative sentences with ordinary verbs, but not with auxiliary verbs. (See 214.) Compare:

> *I* ***don't like*** *football.* (NOT *I like not football.*)
> *I* ***can't*** *play football.* (NOT *I don't can play football.*)

3 We use *do* instead of repeating a complete verb or clause. (See 108.3.)

> *She doesn't like dancing, but I* ***do***. (= ... *but I like dancing.*)
> *Ann thinks there's something wrong with Bill, and so* ***do*** *I.*
> *You play bridge,* ***don't*** *you?*

4 We use *do* in an affirmative clause for emphasis. (See 110.1.)

> ***Do*** *sit down.*   *She thinks I don't love her, but I* ***do*** *love her.*

5 We can use the auxiliary verb *do* together with the ordinary verb *do*—so that we have *do* twice in the same verb phrase.

> *What* ***do*** *you* ***do*** *in the evenings?*
> '*My name is Robinson.*' '*How* ***do*** *you* ***do***?'

99 do + -ing

We often use *do* with *-ing* to talk about activities that take some time, or that are repeated.
There is usually a 'determiner' (see 96) before the *ing* form—for example *the*, *my*, *some*, *much*.

> I **do my shopping** at weekends.   Have you **done the washing up**?
> I **did a lot of running** when I was younger.
> I think I'll stay at home and **do some reading** tonight.

▷   For *go -ing*, see 147.

100 do and make

These words are very similar, but there are some differences.

1   We use *do* when we do not say exactly what activity we are talking about—for example with *something*, *nothing*, *anything*, *everything*, *what*.

> **Do** something!   I like **doing** nothing.
> What shall we **do**?   Then he **did** a very strange thing.

2   We use *do* when we talk about work, and in the structure *do -ing* (see 99).

> I'm not going to **do** any work today. I'm going to **do** some reading.
> I dislike **doing** housework. I hate **doing** the cooking and shopping.
> Would you like to **do** my job?

3   We often use *make* to talk about constructing, building, creating, etc.

> I've just **made** a cake.   Let's **make** a plan.
> My father and I once **made** a boat.

4   Learn these expressions:

> **do** good / harm / business / one's best / a favour
> **make** an offer / arrangements / a suggestion / a decision /
> an attempt / an effort / an excuse / an exception / a mistake / a noise /
> a journey / a phone call / money / a profit / love / peace / war / a bed

▷   For other expressions, look in a dictionary to see if *do* or *make* is used.

101 during and for

During says *when* something happens; *for* says *how long* it lasts.
Compare:

> My father was in hospital **during** the summer.
> My father was in hospital **for** six weeks. (NOT ... **during six weeks.**)
> It rained **during** the night **for** two or three hours.
> I'll call in and see you **for** a few minutes **during** the afternoon.

102 **during** and **in**

1 We use both *during* and *in* to say that something happens inside a
particular period of time.

> *We'll be on holiday **during/in** August.*
> *I woke up **during/in** the night.*

2 We prefer *during* when we stress that we are talking about the whole of
the period.

> *The shop's closed **during the whole of August**.*
> (NOT ... ***in the whole of August.***)

3 We use *during*, not *in*, when we say that something happens between the
beginning and end of an *activity* (not a period of time).

> *He had some strange experiences **during** his military service.*
> (NOT ... ***in his military service.***).
> *I'll try to phone you **during** the meeting.* (NOT ... ***in the meeting.***)

103 **each**: grammar

1 We use *each* before a singular noun.

> | *each* + singular noun |

> ***Each* new *day** is different.*

2 We use *each of* before a pronoun or a determiner (for example *the, my,
these*). The pronoun or noun is plural.

> | *each of us/you/them*
> *each of* + determiner + plural noun |

> *She bought a different present for **each of us**.*
> *I write to **each of my children** once a week.*

After *each of* ... a verb is usually singular, but it can be plural in an
informal style.

> *Each of them **has** his own way of doing things.*
> (More informal: *Each of them **have** their own way ...*)

3 *Each* can come after an indirect object (but not usually a direct object).

> | indirect object + *each* |

> *I bought **the girls each** an ice-cream.*
> *She sent **them each** a present.*

4 We can use *each* without a noun, but *each one* is more common.

> *I've got five brothers, and **each (one)** is quite different from the others.*

5 *Each* can go with a verb, in 'mid-position', like some adverbs (see 13.2).

> auxiliary verb + *each*
> *be* + *each*

*They **have each** got their own rooms.*
*We **are each** going on a separate holiday this year.*
*You **are each** right in a different way.*

> *each* + other verb

*We **each think** the same.*
*They **each want** to talk all the time.*

▷ For *each* and *every*, see 104.

104 each and every

1 We use *each* to talk about two or more people or things.
We use *every* to talk about three or more. (Instead of 'every two' we say *both*.)

2 We say *each* when we are thinking of people or things separately, one at a time.
We say *every* when we are thinking of people or things together, in a group. (*Every* is closer to *all*.)
Compare:

*We want **each** child to develop in his or her own way.*
*We want **every** child to be happy.*

***Each** person in turn went to see the doctor.*
*He gave **every** patient the same medicine.*

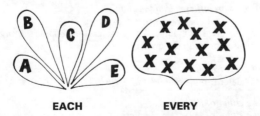

EACH   **EVERY**

The difference is not always very great, and often both words are possible.

*You look more beautiful **each/every** time I see you.*

▷ For the difference between *every* and *all*, see 24.
For the grammar of *each*, see 103.
For the grammar of *every*, see 117.

105 each other and one another

1 *Each other* and *one another* mean the same.

> *Mary and I write to **each other/one another** every day.*
> *They sat without looking at **each other/one another**.*

2 There is a possessive *each others/one another's*.

> *We often borrow **each other's** clothes.*
> *They stood looking into **one another's** eyes.*

Each other/one another are not used as subjects.

> *We must each listen carefully to what the other says.*
> (NOT ~~We must listen carefully to what **each other** say.~~)

3 Note the difference between *each other/one another* and
ourselves/yourselves/themselves. Compare:

> *They are looking at **each other**.*
> (= *Each person was looking at the other*.)
> *They were looking at **themselves**.*
> (= *Each person was looking at him-*
> *or herself*.)

A ⇄ B each other

A ⇆ B themselves

106 either: determiner

1 We use *either* before a singular noun to mean 'one or the other'.

> | *either* + singular noun |

> *Come on Tuesday or Thursday. **Either day** is OK.*

Sometimes *either* can mean 'both' (especially before *side* and *end*). The
noun is singular.

> *There are roses on **either side** of the door.*

2 We use *either of* before a pronoun or a determiner (for example *the*, *my*,
these). The pronoun or noun is plural.

> | *either of us/you/them*
> *either of* + determiner + plural noun |

> *I don't like **either of them**.*
> *I don't like **either of my maths teachers**.*

3 We can use *either* without a noun.

> *'Would you like tea or coffee?' 'I don't mind. **Either**.'*

4 *Either* is pronounced /'aɪðə(r)/ or /'iːðə(r)/ (in American English usually
/'iːðər/).

▷ For *either . . . or . . .* see 107. For *not either, neither* and *nor*, see 217.

107 either ... or ...

We use *either ... or ...* to talk about a choice between two possibilities (and sometimes more than two).

> *You can **either** have tea **or** coffee.*
> *I don't speak **either** French **or** German.*
> *You can **either** come with me now **or** walk home.*
> ***Either** you leave this house **or** I'll call the police.*
> *If you want ice-cream, you can have **either** lemon, coffee **or** vanilla.*

▷ For pronunciation see 106.
For *either* as a determiner (with a noun) see 106.
For *not either*, *neither* or *nor*, see 217.

108 ellipsis (leaving words out)

We often leave words out when the meaning is clear without them.

1 At the beginning of a sentence

In an informal style, we often leave out articles (*the*, *a/an*), possessives (*my*, *your* etc), personal pronouns (*I*, *you* etc) and auxiliary verbs (*am*, *have* etc) at the beginning of a sentence.

> *Car's running badly.* (= ***The** car's ...*)
> *Wife's on holiday.* (= ***My** wife's ...*)
> *Couldn't understand a word.* (= ***I** couldn't understand ...*)
> *Seen Joe?* (= ***Have you** seen Joe?*)

2 With *and, but* and *or*

If the same word comes in two expressions that are joined by *and*, *but* or *or*, we can usually leave out the word once.

> *He sang and (he) played the guitar.*
> *Would you like some tea or (some) coffee?*
> *young boys and (young) girls*
> *in France and (in) Germany*
> *He opened his eyes once, but (he) didn't wake up.*

We can leave out more than one word.

> *She washed (her jeans) and ironed her jeans.*
> *You could have come and (you could have) told me.*

3 After auxiliary verbs

We can use an auxiliary verb instead of a complete verb, or even instead of a whole clause, if the meaning is clear. The auxiliary verb usually has a 'strong' pronunciation (see 358).

> *'Get up.' 'I **am** /æm/.'* (= *'I am getting up.'*)
> *He said he'd write, but he **hasn't**.* (= *... hasn't written*)
> *I can't see you today, but I **can** tomorrow.*

> *'You're getting better at tennis.' 'Yes, I **am**.'*
> *'I've forgotten the address.' 'So **have** I.'*
> *'You wouldn't have won if I hadn't helped you.' 'Yes I **would**.'*

In clauses without an auxiliary verb, we can use *do* instead of repeating a verb or clause.

> *She likes walking in the mountains, and I **do** too.*

4 After *as* and *than*

We can leave out words after *as* and *than*, if the meaning is clear.

> *The weather isn't as good **as** last year.* (= ... as good as it was ...)
> *I found more blackberries **than** you.* (= ... than you found.)

5 Infinitives

We can use *to* instead of repeating a whole infinitive.

> *'Are you and Gillian getting married?' 'We hope **to**.'*
> *I don't dance much now, but I used **to** a lot.*

To is not necessary after | conjunction + *want/like* | .

> *Come when you want.*   *I'll do what I like.*
> *Stay as long as you like.*

109 else

1   *Else* means 'other'.

> *If you can't help me I'll ask somebody **else**.* (= ... some other person.)

We use *else* after:
somebody, someone, something, somewhere; *anybody, anyone* etc;
everybody, everyone etc; *nobody, no-one* etc;
who, what, where, how, why;
little and *(not) much*.

> *Would you like **anything else**?*
> *'Harry gave me some perfume for Christmas.' 'Oh, lovely. **What else** did you get?'*
> ***Where else** did you go besides Madrid?*
> *We know when Shakespeare was born, and when he died, but we don't know **much else** about his life.*

2   *Else* has a possessive *else's*.

> *You're wearing somebody **else's** coat.*

There is no plural structure with *else*. The plural of *somebody else* is *(some) other people*.

3   *Or else* means 'otherwise', 'if not'.

> *Let's go, **or else** we'll miss the train.*

110 emphasis

We can emphasize an idea (make it seem more important) in several ways.

1 We can pronounce some words louder and with a higher intonation. In writing, we can show this by using CAPITAL LETTERS or by <u>underlining</u>. In printing, *italics* or **bold type** are used.

Mary, I'm IN LOVE! Please don't tell anybody.

This is the *last* opportunity.
He lived in **France**, not Spain.

Changes in emphasis can change the meaning. Compare:

> ***Jane*** *phoned me yesterday.* (*Not somebody else.*)
> *Jane **phoned** me yesterday.* (*She didn't come to see me.*)
> *Jane phoned **me** yesterday.* (*She didn't phone you.*)
> *Jane phoned me **yesterday**.* (*Not today.*)

We often emphasize auxiliary verbs. This makes the sentence 'stronger', or it expresses a contrast. When we stress auxiliary verbs, they change their pronunciation (see 358).

> *It **was** a nice party!*
> *You **have** grown!*
> *I **am** telling the truth—you **must** believe me!*

In sentences without auxiliary verbs, we can add *do* for emphasis.

> ***Do*** *sit down.*
> *You're wrong—she **does** like you.*

When auxiliary verbs are stressed, the word order can change (see 14.10). Compare:

> *You have certainly grown.*
> *You certainly **have** grown!* (emphatic)

2 We can use special words to show emphasis; for example *so*, *such*, *really*.

> *Thank you **so** much. It was **such** a lovely party. I **really** enjoyed myself.*

3 We can also use special structures, including repetition, to make some parts of the sentence more important.

> ***That film***—*what did you think of it?*
> ***Asleep**, then, were you?*
> *It was **John** who paid for the drinks.*
> ***What*** *I need is **a drink**.*
> *She looks **much, much** older.*

For details of some of these structures, see 111.

111 emphatic structures with **it** and **what**

We can use structures with *it* and *what* to 'point out' or emphasize particular ideas.

1 | *It is/was ... that ...* |

Compare:

> *My secretary sent the bill to Mr Harding yesterday.*
> *It was my secretary that sent the bill to Mr Harding yesterday.*
> (not somebody else)
> *It was the bill that my secretary sent to Mr Harding yesterday.*
> (not something else)
> *It was Mr Harding that my secretary sent the bill to yesterday.*
> (not to somebody else)
> *It was yesterday that my secretary sent the bill to Mr Harding.*
> (not another day)

2 | *What* (+ subject) + verb + *be ...* |

Compare:

> *My left leg hurts.*
> *What hurts is my left leg.*
>
> *I like her sense of humour.*
> *What I like is her sense of humour.*

3 We can emphasize a verb by using *what* with *do* and an infinitive. Compare:

> *She screamed.*
> *What she did was (to) scream.*

112 enjoy

| *enjoy* + noun |
| *enjoy* + pronoun |
| *enjoy ... -ing* |

Enjoy always has an object. When we talk about having a good time, we can use *enjoy myself/yourself* etc.

> *'Did you enjoy the party?' 'Yes, I enjoyed it very much.'*
> *I really enjoyed myself when I went to Rome.*
> (NOT *I really enjoyed when I went ...*)

Enjoy can be followed by *... -ing*.

> *I don't enjoy looking after children.* (NOT *... enjoy to look ...*)

113 enough

1 *Enough* comes after adjectives (without nouns) and adverbs.

| adjective/adverb + *enough* |

*Is it **warm enough** for you?* (NOT ... ~~enough warm~~ ...)
*You're not driving **fast enough**.*

2 *Enough* comes before nouns.

| *enough* (+ adjective) + noun |

*Have you got **enough milk**?* (NOT ... ~~enough of milk.~~)
*There isn't **enough blue paint** left.*

We use *enough of* before pronouns and determiners (for example *the, my, this*).

| *enough of* + pronoun |

*We didn't buy **enough of them**.*

| *enough of* + determiner (+ adjective) + noun |

*The exam was bad. I couldn't answer **enough of the questions**.*
*Have we got **enough of those new potatoes**?*

3 We can use an infinitive structure after *enough*.

| ... *enough* ... + infinitive |

*She's old **enough to do** what she wants.*
*I haven't got **enough** money **to buy** a car.*

| ... *enough* ... + *for* + object + infinitive |

*It's late **enough for us to stop** work.*

114 even

1 We can use *even* to talk about surprising extremes—when people 'go too far', or do more than we expect, for example. *Even* usually goes in 'mid-position' (see 13.2).

| auxiliary verb + *even*
be + *even* |

*She has lost half her clothes. She **has even** lost two pairs of shoes.*
(NOT ... ~~Even she has lost~~ ...)
*She is rude to everybody. She **is even** rude to the police.*
(NOT ~~Even she is rude~~ ...)

| *even* + other verb |

*They do everything together. They **even brush** their teeth together.*
*He speaks lots of languages. He **even speaks** Eskimo.*

Even can go in other positions when we want to emphasize a particular expression.

> *Anybody can do this. **Even a child** can do it.*
> *He eats anything—**even raw potatoes**.*
> *I work every day, **even on Sundays**.*

2 We use *not even* to say that we are surprised because something has not happened, is not there, etc.

> *He ca**n't even** write his own name.*
> *I haven't written to anybody for months—**not even** my parents.*
> *She did**n't even** offer me a cup of tea.*

3 *Also* is not used to talk about surprising extremes.

> *Everybody got up early. **Even George**.* (NOT *Also George.*)

4 *Even* is not used as a conjunction, but we can use *even* before *if* and *though*.

> ***Even if** I become a millionaire, I shall always be a socialist.*
> (NOT *Even I become ...*)
> ***Even though** I didn't know anybody at the party, I had a good time.*

5 *Even so* means 'however'.

> *He seems nice. **Even so**, I don't really like him.*

115 eventual(ly)

Eventual and *eventually* mean 'final(ly)', 'in the end'. We use them when we say that something happened after a long time, or a lot of work.

> *The chess game lasted for three days. Androv was the **eventual** winner.*
> *The car didn't want to start, but **eventually** I got it going.*

Eventual(ly) is a 'false friend' for students who speak some European languages. We do not use it to talk about possibilities—things that might happen. For this meaning, use *possible, perhaps, if, may, might* etc.

> *In our new house, I'd like to have a spare bedroom for **possible** visitors.* (NOT *... eventual visitors.*)
> *I'm not sure what I'll do next year. I **might** go to America if I can find a job.* (NOT *... Eventually I'll go to America ...*)

116 ever

1 *Ever* means 'at any time'. Compare:

> *Do you **ever** go to Ireland on holiday?* (= 'at any time')
> *We **always** go to Ireland on holiday.* (= 'every time')
> *We **never** have holidays in England.* (= 'at no time')

2 *Ever* is used mostly in questions. We also use *ever* in affirmative sentences after *if*, and with words that express a negative idea (like *nobody*, *hardly* or *stop*).

> ***Do you ever*** *go to pop concerts?*
> *I **hardly ever** see my sister.*
> *Come and see us **if** you are **ever** in Manchester.*
> ***Nobody ever*** *visits them.*
> *I'm going to **stop** her **ever** doing that again.*

3 When *ever* is used with the present perfect tense (see 243.4) it means 'at any time up to now'. Compare:

> ***Have you ever*** *been to Greece?*
> ***Did you ever*** *go to Naples when you were in Italy?*
> (= at a particular time in the past)

4 Note the structure ⌐ comparative + *than ever* ⌐ .

> *You're looking **lovelier than ever**.*

5 In *forever* (or *for ever*) and *ever since*, *ever* means 'always'.
> *I shall love you **forever**.*   *I've loved you **ever since** I met you.*

6 Don't confuse *ever* with *yet* and *already*.
Yet and *already* are used for things which happen around the present—events which are expected.

> *Has Aunt Mary come **yet**?*
> *Good heavens! Have you finished the washing up **already**?*

Ever means 'at any time in the past'.

> *Have you **ever** been to Africa?*

▷ For *who ever*, *what ever* etc, see 364. For *whoever*, *whatever* etc, see 365.

117 **every** and **every one**

1 We use *every* before a singular noun.

> ⌐ *every* + singular noun ⌐

> *I see her **every day**.* (NOT *... every days.*)
> ***Every room*** *is being used.*

2 We use *every one of* before a pronoun or determiner (for example *the*, *my*, *these*). The pronoun or noun is plural.

> ⌐ *every one of us/you/them*
> *every one of* + determiner + plural noun ⌐

> *His books are wonderful. I've read **every one** of them.*
> ***Every one*** *of the plates is broken.*

3 We can use *every one* without a noun.

> *Every one* is broken.
> I've read *every one*.

4 *Every* is used with a plural noun in expressions like *every three days*, *every six weeks*.

> I go to Italy *every six weeks*.

5 *Everybody*, *everyone* and *everything* are used with singular verbs, like *every*.

> *Everybody has* gone home.
> (NOT *Everybody have* ...)
> *Everything is* ready.

▷ For *he or she* etc or *they* etc after *every*, *everybody*, see 307.
For *each* and *every* (meaning), see 104.

118 except

> *except* + infinitive without *to*
> *except* + *me*/*him* etc

1 When we put a verb after *except*, we usually use the infinitive without *to*.

> We can't do anything *except wait*.
> He does nothing *except eat* all day.

2 After *except*, we put object pronouns (*me*, *him* etc), not subject pronouns.

> Everybody understands *except me*.
> We're all ready *except her*.

▷ *But* (meaning 'except') is used in the same way. See 75.
For the difference between *except* and *except for*, see 119.

119 except and except for

1 We can use *except* or *except for* after *all*, *any*, *every*, *no*, *anything*/*body*/*one*/*where*, *everything*/*body*/*one*/*where*, *nothing*/*body*/*one*/*where*, and *whole*—that is to say, words which suggest the idea of a *total*.
In other cases we usually use *except for*, but not *except*.
Compare:

> He ate *everything* on his plate *except (for)* the beans.
> He ate the *whole* meal *except (for)* the beans.
> He ate the meal *except for* the beans.
> (NOT ... *except the beans*.)

*I've cleaned all the rooms **except (for)** the bathroom.*
*I've cleaned the whole house **except (for)** the bathroom.*
*I've cleaned the house **except for the bathroom**.*
(NOT *... except the bathroom.*)

*We're all here **except (for)** John and Mary.*
***Except for** John and Mary, we're all here.*
(NOT *Except John and Mary, ...*)

2 We use *except*, not *except for*, before prepositions and conjunctions.

*It's the same everywhere **except in** Scotland.*
*She's beautiful **except when** she smiles.*

120 exclamations

1 With *how* (rather formal)

how + adjective

*Strawberries! **How nice!***

how + adjective/adverb + subject + verb

***How cold** it is!* (NOT *How it is cold!*)
***How beautifully** you sing!* (NOT *How you sing beautifully!*)

how + subject + verb

***How** you've grown!*

2 With *what*

what a/an (+ adjective) + singular countable noun

***What a** rude man!* (NOT *What rude man!*)
***What a** nice dress!* (NOT *What nice dress!*)
***What a** surprise!*

what (+ adjective) + uncountable/plural noun

***What** beautiful weather!* (NOT *What a beautiful weather!*)
***What** lovely flowers!*

3 Negative questions

***Isn't** the weather nice!*
***Hasn't** she grown!*

In American English, ordinary (non-negative) question forms are often
used in exclamations.

***Am I** hungry!   **Did she** make a mistake!*

121 excuse me, pardon and sorry

1 We usually say *excuse me* before we interrupt or disturb somebody; we say *sorry* after we disturb or trouble somebody. Compare:

> ***Excuse me***, *could I get past? … Oh,* ***sorry***, *did I step on your foot?*
> ***Excuse me***, *could you tell me the way to the station?*

I beg your pardon is a more formal way of saying sorry.

> ***I beg your pardon***. *I'm afraid I didn't realize this was your seat.*

2 If we do not hear or understand what people say, we usually say *Sorry? What?* (informal) or *(I beg your) pardon?*
Americans also say *Pardon me?*

> *'Mike's on the phone.'* ***'Sorry?'*** *'I said, "Mike's on the phone." '*
> *'See you tomorrow.'* ***'What?'*** *'I said, "See you tomorrow." '*
> *'You're going deaf.'* ***'I beg your pardon?'***

122 expect, hope, look forward, wait, want and wish

1 Meaning

expect
Expecting is a kind of thinking: it is not an emotion. If I *expect* something, I have good reason to think that it will happen.

> *We* ***expect*** *to leave here in three years.*
> *I'm* ***expecting*** *a phone call from John today.*

hope
Hoping is more emotional. If I *hope* for something, I want it to happen, but I am not sure that it will happen, and I can nothing about it.

> *I* ***hope*** *she writes to me soon.*
> *I* ***hope*** *they find that poor woman's child.*
> *I* ***hope*** *we don't have a war.*

look forward

Looking forward is an emotion about something that is certain to happen. If I *look forward* to something, I know it will happen, I feel happy about it, and I would like the time to pass quickly so that it will happen soon.

> *He's **looking forward** to his birthday.*
> *I'm **really looking forward** to going to Morocco in June.*
> *I **look forward** to hearing from you.* (common formula at the end of a letter)

wait

Waiting happens when something is late, or when you are early for something. I *wait* for something that will probably happen soon; I am conscious of the time passing (perhaps not quickly enough); I may be angry or impatient.

> *I hate **waiting** for buses.*
> *It's difficult **to wait** for things when you're three years old.*
> *'What's for supper?' '**Wait** and see.'*

want

Wanting is emotional, like *hoping*. But if I *want* something to happen, I may be able to do something about it.

> *What do you **want** to do when you leave school?*
> *I'm going to start saving money. I **want** a better car.*

wish

Wishing is wanting something that is impossible, or that doesn't seem probable—being sorry that things are not different.

> *I **wish** I could fly.*
> *I **wish** I had more money.*
> *I **wish** she would stop singing.*

Wish + infinitive can also be used like *want* (but *wish* is more formal).

> *I **wish** to see the manager.*

2 Some comparisons

> *I'm **expecting** a phone call from Mary.*
> *I've been **waiting** all day for Mary to phone—what does she think she's doing?*

> *I **expect** it will stop raining soon.* (= I think it will stop.)
> *I **hope** it stops raining soon.* (= It may stop or it may not; I would like it to stop.)
> *I **wish** it would stop raining.* (= It doesn't look as if it's going to stop; I feel sorry about that.)

> *I **hope** you have a good time in Ireland.* (I can't do anything about it.)
> *I **want** you to have a good time while you're staying with us.* (I'll do what I can to make things nice for you.)

> *I **expected** her at ten, but she was late.*
> *I **waited** for her until eleven, and then I went home.*

3 Structures

> *expect* + object
> *expect* (+ object) + infinitive
> *expect* + *that*-clause
> *expect so*

I'm expecting a phone call.
I expect to see her on Sunday.
I'm expecting him to arrive soon.
I expect (that) he'll be here soon.
'Is Lucy coming?' 'I expect so.' (See 311.1.)

> *hope for* + object
> *hope* + infinitive
> *hope* + *that*-clause
> *hope so*

I'm hoping for a letter from Eric.
I hope to go to America next month.
I hope that they get here soon. (See 162.)
'Are the shops open tomorrow?' 'I hope so.' (See 311.1.)

> *look forward to* + object
> *look forward to . . . -ing*

I'm looking forward to the holidays.
I look forward to hearing from you. (See 181.)

> *wait*
> *wait and . . .*
> *wait for* + object
> *wait* + infinitive
> *wait for* + object + infinitive

'Can I go now?' 'Wait.'
'What's for supper?' 'Wait and see.'
I'm waiting for a phone call.
I'm waiting to hear from John.
I'm waiting for John to phone.

> *want* + object
> *want* (+ object) + infinitive

I want a new car.
I want to go home.
I want him to go home.

> *wish* (+ object) + infinitive
> *wish* + clause

I wish to see the manager. (formal)
I wish him to look at this. (formal)
I wish I had more money. (See 367.)

123 explain

After *explain*, we use *to* before an indirect object.

> *I explained my problem **to her**.* (NOT ~~I explained her my problem.~~)
> *Can you explain(**to me**) how to get to your house?*
> (NOT ~~Can you explain me...?~~)

124 fairly, quite, rather and pretty

not	*fairly*	*quite*	*rather/pretty*	*very*
nice	*nice*	*nice*	*nice*	*nice*

1 *Fairly* modifies adjectives and adverbs. It is not very strong: if you say that somebody is 'fairly nice' or 'fairly clever', she will not be very pleased.

> *'How was the film?' '**Fairly** good. Not the best one I've seen this year.'*
> *I speak Greek **fairly** well—enough for most everyday purposes.*

2 *Quite* is a little stronger than *fairly*.

> *'How was the film?' '**Quite** good. You ought to go.'*
> *He's been in Greece for two years, so he speaks Greek **quite** well.*

Quite can modify verbs.

> *It was a good party. I **quite enjoyed** myself.*

3 *Rather* is stronger than *quite*. It can mean 'more than is usual', 'more than was expected' or 'more than is wanted'.

> *'How was the film?' '**Rather** good—I was surprised.'*
> *Maurice speaks Greek **rather** well. People often think he's Greek.*
> *I think I'll put the heating on. It's **rather** cold.*

Rather can modify verbs.

> *I **rather** like gardening.*

4 *Pretty* is similar to *rather*. It is only used in informal English.

> *'How are you feeling?' '**Pretty** tired. I'm going to bed.'*

5 Note:

a The exact meaning of these words may depend on the intonation used.

b *Quite* is not used very much in this way in American English.

c We put *quite* and *rather* before *a/an*.

> *It was **quite a** nice day.   I'm reading **rather an** interesting book.*

d For other meanings of *quite*, see 274. For other meanings of *rather*, see 370.

125 far and a long way

Far is most common in questions and negative sentences, and after *too* and *so*.

> **How far** did you walk?
> I **don't** live **far** from here.
> You've gone **too far**.
> 'Any problems?' 'Not **so far**.' (= Not up to now.)

In affirmative sentences, we usually use *a long way*.

> We walked **a long way**. (We walked **far** is possible, but not usual.)
> She lives **a long way** from here.

Much, *many* and *long* (for time) are also more common in questions and negative sentences. (See 205 and 194.)

126 farther and further

1 We use both *farther* and *further* to talk about distance. There is no difference of meaning.

> Edinburgh is **farther/further** away than York.

(Only *farther* is used in this sense in American English.)

2 We can use *further* (but not *farther*) to mean 'extra', 'more advanced', 'additional'.

> For **further** information, see page 277.
> College of **Further** Education.

127 fast

Fast can be an adjective or an adverb.

> I've got a **fast** car. (adjective)   It goes **fast**. (adverb)

128 feel

Feel has several meanings.

1 'to touch something'

> **Feel** the car seat. It's wet.

Progressive tenses are possible.

> 'What are you doing?' 'I'**m feeling** the shirts to see if they are dry.'

2 'to receive physical sensations'

> I suddenly **felt** something on my leg.

We do not use progressive tenses, but we often use *can feel* to talk about a present sensation.

>   I **can feel** something biting me!

3 'to think, have an opinion'

Progressive tenses are not used.

>   I **feel** that you're making a mistake. (NOT ~~I'm feeling~~ ...)

4 copula verb (see 91), used with adjectives

>   Your hands **feel** cold on my skin.   I **feel** fine.   Do you **feel** happy?

Progressive forms can be used to talk about one's 'inside' feelings.

>   I'**m feeling** fine.   How **are** you **feeling**?

129 (a) few and (a) little

1 We use *few* with plural nouns, and *little* with singular (uncountable) nouns. Compare:

>   **Few** politicians are really honest.   I have **little** interest in politics.

2 There is a difference between *a few* and *few*, and between *a little* and *little*. *Few* and *little* are rather negative: they mean 'not much/many'. *A few* and *a little* are more positive: their meaning is more like 'some'. Compare:

>   His ideas are very difficult, and **few** people understand them.
>   (= not many people; hardly any people)
>   His ideas are very difficult, but **a few** people understand them.
>   (= some people—better than nothing)

>   Cactuses need **little** water.   Give the roses **a little** water every day.

3 *Few* and *little* (without *a*) are rather formal. In conversation, we prefer *not many*, *not much*, *only a few* or *only a little*.

>   **Only a few** people speak a foreign language perfectly.
>   Come on! We have**n't** got **much** time!

130 fewer and less

Fewer is the comparative of *few* (used before plural nouns).
Less is the comparative of *little* (used before uncountable nouns, which are singular).

>   **few** problems   **fewer** problems   **little** money   **less** money

>   I've got **fewer** problems than I used to have.
>   I earn **less** money than a postman.

In informal English, some people use *less* with plural words.

>   I've got **less problems** than I used to have.

131 **for**: purpose

1 We use *for* before a noun to talk about a purpose, or reason for doing something.

> *We went to the pub **for a drink**.*   *I went to London **for an interview**.*

We do not use *for* before a verb to talk about purpose.

> *I went to the pub **to have** a drink.* (NOT ... *for (to) have a drink.*)
> *I went to London **to see** about a job.*

2 We can use *for ... -ing* to talk about the purpose of a thing—the reason why we use it.

> *We use an altimeter **for measuring** height.*
> *'What's that stuff **for**?' '**Cleaning** leather.'*

132 **for** + object + infinitive

1 We use this structure after certain adjectives. Some common examples are: *usual, unusual, common, normal, rare, important, essential, necessary, unnecessary, anxious, delighted.*

> adjective + *for* + object + *to*-infinitive

> *Is it usual **for John to be** so late?*
> *It's unusual **for the weather to be** bad in July.*
> *It's important **for the meeting to start** at eight.*
> *It's unnecessary **for all of us to go**—one will be enough.*
> *I'm anxious **for Peter to go** to a good school.* (= I want him to go ...)
> *I'd be delighted **for you to come** and stay with us.*

We could often use a *that*-clause instead (for example: *It's important **that the meeting should start** at eight*). A *that*-clause is usually more formal.

2 We use a *for*-structure after *too* (see 348.1) and *enough* (see 113.3).

> *It's **too** heavy **for you to lift**.*
> *It's warm **enough for the snow to melt**.*

3 We can use the same structure after some nouns. Examples: *idea, time.*

> *His **idea** is **for us to travel** in separate cars.*
> *It's **time for everybody to go** to bed.*

4 Common verbs that are followed by *for* + object + infinitive: *ask, hope, arrange, pay, wait, take* (time).

> *She asked **for the car to be** ready by five o'clock.*
> *I was hoping **for somebody to come** and help me.*
> *Can you arrange **for the car to be** ready this evening?*
> *He paid **for her to see** the best doctors.*
> *I'm waiting **for it to get** dark.*
> *It takes five days **for a letter to go** from London to New York.*

133 for, since, from ago and before

1 *For, since* and *from* 'point forwards' in time.
Ago and *before* 'point backwards' in time.

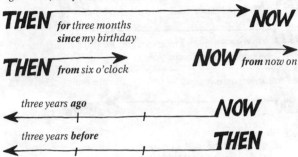

For details of the use of *ago* and *before*, see 20.4.

2 We use *for* to say how long something lasts.

> for + period of time

> *I once studied the guitar **for three years**.*
> *That house has been empty **for six weeks**.*
> *We go away **for three weeks** every summer.*
> *My boss will be in Italy **for the next ten days**.*

When we talk about a period of time up to the present, we use *for* with the present perfect tense (*have* + past participle).

> ***I've known her** for a long time.* (NOT ~~I know her ...~~)

A present progressive with *for* often refers to the future.

> *How long **are you staying** for?* (= *Until when* ...)

We can leave out *for* with *How long* ...?

> *How long are you staying?*   *How long have you been waiting?*

3 *From* and *since* give the starting point of an action or state: they say when something begins or began.

> from / since + starting point

> *I'll be here **from three o'clock** onwards.*   *I work **from nine** to five.*
> ***From now on**, I'm going to go running every day.*
> ***From his earliest childhood** he loved music.*
> *I've been waiting **since ten o'clock**.*
> *I've known her **since January**.*

Since gives the starting point of actions and states that continue up to the present; *from* gives the starting point of other actions and states.

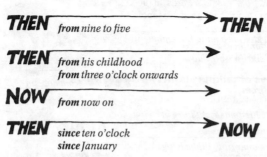

4 *For* and *since* can both be used with the present perfect (*have* + past participle). They are not the same.

for + period		*since* + starting point

*I've known her **for three days**.*   *I've known her **since Tuesday**.*
*I've been here **for a month**.*   *I've been here **since July**.*
*I've had my car **for ages**.*   *I've had my car **since 1980**.*

134 future: introduction

There are several ways to talk about the future in English.

1 Present tenses

When we talk about future events which are already decided *now*, or which we can see *now* 'are on the way', we often use present tenses.

There are two possibilities: the present progressive | *I am . . . -ing* | ,

and a structure with the present progressive of *go* | *I am going to . . .* | .

    ***I'm seeing** John tomorrow.*   ***She's going to** have a baby.*

For more details, see 135.
We can sometimes use the simple present to talk about the future, but only in certain cases. See 138.

2 *shall/will*

When we are predicting future events which are *not* already decided or obviously 'on the way', we usually use | *shall/will* + infinitive | .

    *Nobody **will** ever **know** what happened to her.*
    *I think Liverpool **will win**.*

For more details, see 136.

3 We can also use $\boxed{shall \text{ or } will + \text{infinitive}}$ to express 'interpersonal'
meanings: when we are offering, making requests, promising or
threatening.

> ***Shall*** *I open the window?*   ***I WILL*** *stop smoking!*
> ***Will*** *you give me a hand for a moment?*   ***You'll*** *be sorry!*

For more details, see 137.

4 Other ways of talking about the future

future perfect (see 139)

> *By next Christmas **we'll have been here** for eight years.*

future progressive (see 140)

> *This time tomorrow **I'll be lying** on the beach.*

about to (see 2)

> *I think the plane's **about to** take off.*

be to (see 58)

> *The President **is to** visit Beijing.*

135 future: present progressive and **going to**

We use these two present tenses to talk about future actions and events
which are already decided *now*: they are planned, or they are starting to
happen: we can see them coming.

1 Present progressive

We often say that something *is happening* in the future. We talk like this
about actions that are already planned; we often give the time or date.

> *What **are you doing** this evening?*
> *We're going to Mexico next summer.*
> *I'm having dinner with Larry on Saturday.*

2 *going to*

We can also say that something is *going to happen* in the future.

a We can use *going to* in the same way as the present progressive: to talk about plans and arrangements.

> ***I'm going to get** a new car soon.*
> ***John's going to call** in this evening.*
> *When **are you going to get** your hair cut?*

b We can also use *going to* to say that a future action or event is 'on the way'—we can see it coming; it is starting to happen.

> ***She's going to have** a baby.   **It's going to rain.***
> ***He's going to fall!***

Present   **Future**

*She's **going to have** a baby.*

*It's **going to rain**.*

*He's **going to fall**!*

▷ For a comparison between the present forms and *shall/will*, see 136.3.

136 future: **shall/will** (predictions)

1 Forms

> *I shall/will*
> *you will*
> *he/she/it will* ⎤ + infinitive without *to*
> *we shall/will*
> *they will* ⎦
>
> questions: *shall/will I*; *will you*; *will he/she/it*, etc
> negatives: *I will/shall not*; *you will not*, etc
> contractions: *I'll, you'll, he'll* etc; *shan't, won't*.

In modern English, *I shall* and *I will*, *we shall* and *we will* are used with
the same meaning to talk about the future. We prefer *I will* in promises
and threats, and *shall I* in offers: see 137.

2 Meaning

We say that things *will happen* when they are not already planned or
obviously on the way.

> *Who do you think **will win** on Saturday?*
> *Tomorrow **will be** warm, with some cloud in the afternoon.*
> *One day **I shall/I will/I'll** be rich.*

3 Present tenses and *shall/will*: a comparison

When I say that something *is happening*, or *is going to happen* in the
future, I probably have *outside evidence* for what I say—for example I
can show you a page in a diary, black clouds in the sky, a person who is
going to fall.
When I say that something *will happen*, I do not have outside evidence to
show you. I am telling you what I know, or believe, or have calculated,
and I am asking you to *believe what I say*. Compare:

He's not very good.   *He's **going to** fall.*
He'll fall.

*I reckon **it'll** cost about*   *The builder's just sent his estimate.*
£7,000 to repair the roof.   ***It's going to** cost £9,000 to repair the roof.*

137 future: **shall** and **will** (interpersonal uses)

We can use *shall* and *will* to express our intentions and attitudes towards other people.

1 Decisions

We use *will* at the moment of making a decision.

> *'The phone's ringing.' '**I'll** answer it.'* (NOT ~~I'm going to answer it.~~)
> *'I'm going out for a drink.' 'Wait a moment and **I'll** come with you.'*
> (NOT *... I come with you.*)

We use *shall* to ask what decision we should make.

> *What **shall** I do?   **Shall** we tell her?*

2 Threats and promises

> *I'll hit you if you do that again.*
> *I promise I **won't** smoke again.* (NOT ~~I promise I don't ...~~)
> *I'll give you a teddy bear for your birthday.*
> *I'll phone you tonight.* (NOT ~~I phone you ...~~)

3 Offers and requests

We use *Shall I ...?* when we offer to do things.

> ***Shall I** carry your bag?*

We can use *Will you ...?* to ask people to do things.

> ***Will you** get me a newspaper when you're out?*

138 future: simple present

1 We can sometimes use the simple present to talk about the future. This is common when we are talking about events which are on a timetable, or something similar.

> *What time **does the train arrive** at Paddington?*
> *When **is** the next bus for Warwick?*
> ***Are you** on duty next weekend?*
> *The summer term **starts** on April 10th.*

2 The simple present is often used with a future meaning after conjunctions. For details, see 343.

> *I'll phone you when I **arrive**.*

3 In other cases, we usually use a different tense to talk about the future.

> ***I'm seeing** John tomorrow.* (NOT ~~I see John tomorrow.~~)
> ***I'll phone** you this evening.* (NOT ~~I phone you this evening.~~)

▷ For more information about the simple present, see 261.

139 future perfect

> *shall/will have* + past participle

We use the future perfect to say that something will have been completed by a certain time in the future.

> *I'll **have been here** for seven years next Friday.*
> *The painters say **they'll have finished** the downstairs rooms by Tuesday.*

A progressive form is possible.

> *I'll **have been teaching** for twenty years this summer.*

140 future progressive

> *shall/will + be + ... -ing*

We can use the future progressive to say that something will be going on at a particular moment in the future.

141 gender (masculine and feminine language)

English does not have many problems of grammatical gender: people are *he* or *she* and things are *it*.
Note the following points:

1 Animals, cars and countries

People sometimes call animals *he* or *she*, especially pet animals like cats, dogs and horses.

> *Go and find the cat and put **him** out.*

Some people use *she* for cars, motorbikes etc; sailors often use *she* for boats and ships.

> *'How's your new car?' 'Terrific. **She's** running beautifully.'*

We can use *she* for countries, but *it* is more common.

> *He loves Spain—**its** culture, **its** history and **its** civilization.*
> (OR ... **her** culture, **her** history ...)

2 *he or she*

We can use *he or she*; *him or her*; *his or her* to refer to people like *a student* or *a politician* (who can be men and women).

> *If a student is ill, **he or she** must send **his or her** medical certificate to the College Office.*

This is heavy, and most people use *he/him/his* instead of *he or she* etc.

> *A politician has to do what **his** party tells **him**.*

After *anybody, somebody, nobody* and some other expressions (see 307), we often use *they/them/their* (with a singular meaning) instead of *he or she* etc.

> *If anybody phones, tell **them** I'm out.*

3 *actor* and *actress* etc

Some jobs and positions have different words for men and women.

Man	Woman	Man	Woman	Man	Woman
actor	actress	host	hostess	steward	stewardess
duke	duchess	monk	nun	waiter	waitress
bridegroom	bride	prince	princess	widower	widow

Some words ending in -*man* have a feminine form (for example *policeman/policewoman*).
Others do not: for example, the *chairman* of a committee can be a man or a woman. Many people prefer to use words ending in -*person* for these cases (for example *chairperson, spokesperson*).

142 *get* + noun, adjective, adverb particle or preposition

Get is a very common word in spoken English. It is usually informal, and structures with *get* are not so common in writing.
Get has different meanings—it depends what kind of word comes after it.

1 *get* + noun/pronoun

Before a noun or pronoun, *get* usually means 'receive', 'fetch', 'obtain' or something similar.

> *I **got a letter** from Lucy this morning.*
> *Can you come and **get me** from the station when I arrive?*
> *I'm going out to **get some bread**.*

For the structure *I have got*, see 153.

2 *get* + adjective

Before an adjective, *get* usually means 'become'.

> *As you **get old** your memory **gets worse**.*   *My feet are **getting cold**.*

We can use ⟨ *get* + object + adjective ⟩ (= 'make something become ...').

> *I can't **get my hands warm**.*
> *We must **get the house clean** before Mother arrives.*

For *go* + adjective (*go green, go blind* etc), see 146.

3 *get* + adverb particle or preposition

Before an adverb particle (like *up, away, out*) or a preposition, *get* nearly always refers to a movement.

> *I often **get up** at five o'clock.*
> *I went to see him, but he told me to **get out**.*
> *Would you mind **getting off** my foot?*

We can use the structure with an object, to talk about making somebody/something move.

> *You can't **get her out of** the bathroom in the morning.*
> *Would you mind **getting your papers off** my desk?*
> *Have you ever tried to **get toothpaste back into** the tube?*

▷ For structures with ⟨ *get* (+ object) + verb ⟩, see 143.

143 *get* (+ object) + verb form

1 After *get*, we can use an object with an infinitive or *-ing* form.

⟨ *get* + object + infinitive ⟩

> *I can't **get the car to start**.*

⟨ *get* + object + *-ing* form ⟩

> *Don't **get him talking** about his illnesses, please.*

We often use the structure with the infinitive to talk about persuading somebody to do something.

> ***Get John to help us**, if you can.*   *I can't **get that child to go** to bed.*

2 We can use ⟨ *get* + object + past participle ⟩ with a passive meaning.
to talk about arranging for jobs to be done.

> *I must **get my hair cut**.*
> *You ought to **get your watch repaired**.*

3 We can use *get* instead of *be* to make passive structures. We often do this when we are talking about things that happen by accident or unexpectedly.

> *My watch **got broken** while I was playing with the children.*
> *He **got caught** by the police driving at 160km an hour.*

▷ For similar structures with *have*, see 155.

144 **get** and **go**: movement

Get is used for the end of a movement—the arrival.
Go is used for the whole movement. Compare:

> *I **go** to work by car and Lucy goes by train.   I usually **get** there first.*
>
> *I **went** to Bristol yesterday.   I **got** to Bristol at about eight o'clock.*

We often use *get* when there is some difficulty in arriving.

> *It wasn't easy to **get** through the crowd.*
> *I don't know how we're going to **get** over the river.*
> *Can you tell me how to **get** to the police station?*

145 **go**: **been** and **gone**

1   If somebody has *gone to* a place, he or she is there now, or on the way.

> *'Is Lucy here?' 'No, she**'s gone** to London.'*

If somebody has *been to* a place, he or she has travelled there and come back.

> *I**'ve been** to London six times this week.*
> ***Have** you ever **been** to Northern Ireland?*

Been is also used to mean 'come (and gone away again)'.

> *She**'s been** to see us twice since Christmas.*

2   We can use *be* with *gone* to say that something has disappeared, or that there is no more.

> ***Is** the butter all **gone**?   When I came back my car **was gone**.*

146 **go** meaning 'become'

We use *go* to mean 'become' before some adjectives.

1   This happens with colour words.

> *Leaves **go** brown in autumn.*
> *People **go** red, pale or white with anger; blue with cold; green with seasickness.*
> *If you faint, everything **goes** black.*

In a formal style, we use *turn* instead of *go* in these cases.

2   We use *go* with some other adjectives to talk about things changing for the worse. Some common expressions:

> *People **go** mad, crazy, deaf, blind, grey, bald.*
> *Machines **go** wrong, iron **goes** rusty, meat **goes** bad, milk **goes** sour, bread **goes** stale.*

147 go . . . -ing

We often use the structure *go* . . . *-ing*, especially to talk about sports and free-time activities.

> *Let's **go climbing** next weekend.*
> *Did you **go dancing** last Saturday?*

Common expressions:

go climbing	*go dancing*	*go fishing*
go hunting	*go riding*	*go sailing*
go shooting	*go shopping*	*go skiing*
go swimming	*go walking*	

148 had better

1 We use *had better* to give advice, or to tell people what to do. The meaning is present or future, not past, but we always use *had*, not *have*. After *had better*, we use the infinitive without *to*.

> *It's late—**you'd better hurry** up.*
> (NOT . . . *you ~~have better~~* . . .)
> (NOT . . . *you had better ~~hurrying/to hurry~~ up.*)

We make the negative with *better not* + infinitive.

> *You'd **better not** wake me up when you come in.*
> (NOT *You ~~hadn't better wake me~~* . . .)

We can 'tell ourselves what to do' by using *I'd better*.

> *It's seven o'clock. **I'd better** put the meat in the oven.*

2 We do not use *had better* in polite requests.

> *Could you help me, if you've got time?*
> (NOT *~~You'd better help me.~~* This would sound like an order.)

149 half (of)

1 We can use *half* or *half of* before a noun.

> ***Half (of)** my friends live abroad.*
> *She spends **half (of)** her time travelling.*

Of is not used in expressions of measurement and quantity.

> *I live **half a mile** from here.* (NOT . . . *~~half of a mile~~* . . .)
> *How much is **half a bottle** of whisky?*
> (NOT . . . *~~half of a bottle~~* . . .)

We use *half of* before pronouns.

> *'Did you like the books?' 'I've only read **half of them**.'*
> ***Half of us** are free on Tuesdays, and the other half on Thursdays.*

2 We only use *the* with *half* if we are saying which half we mean. Compare:

> *I've bought some chocolate. You can have **half**.*
> (NOT ... ~~the half~~.)
> *You can have **the big half**.*

3 *One and a half* is plural.

> *I've been waiting for **one and a half hours**.* (NOT ... ~~hour~~.)

150 **hard** and **hardly**

1 *Hard* can be an adjective or an adverb.

> *It's a **hard** job.* (adjective)
> *This is very **hard** bread.* (adjective)
>
> *You have to work **hard**.* (adverb)
> (NOT ~~You have to work hardly~~.)
> *Hit it **hard**.* (adverb)

2 *Hardly* is an adverb. It means 'almost no' or 'almost not'.

> *He **hardly** works at all.* (= *He does very little work.*)
> *I've got **hardly** any money.*
> *He knows **hardly** anything about geography.*

Note that *hardly, hardly any, hardly ever* etc are much more common than *almost not, almost no, almost never* etc.

*He works **hard**.*

*He **hardly** works at all.*

151 **have**: introduction

We can use *have* in several different ways.

a auxiliary verb

> ***Have** you heard about Peter and Corinne?*

b to talk about possession, relationships, and other states:

> *I've **got** a new car.*
> ***Have** you **got** any brothers or sisters?*
> *Do you often **have** headaches?*

c to talk about actions:

> *I'm going to **have** a bath.*
> *We're **having** a party next weekend.*

d to talk about obligation (like *must*):

> *I **had** to work last Saturday.*

e to talk about causing things to happen:

> *He soon **had** everybody laughing.*
> *I must **have** my shoes repaired.*

The grammar is not the same for all of these different meanings of *have*. For details, see the next five sections.

▷ For contractions (*I've*, *haven't* etc), see 90.
For 'weak forms' (/əv/ etc), see 358.

For | *had better* + infinitive | , see 148.

152 have: auxiliary verb

| *have* + past participle |

1 We use *have* as an auxiliary verb to make 'perfect' verb forms.

> ***Have** you **heard** about Peter and Corinne?*
> (present perfect: see 243; 244)
> *I realized that I **had met** him before.*
> (past perfect: see 245)
> *We'll **have been living** here for two years next Sunday.*
> (future perfect: see 139)
> *I **would have told** you, but I didn't see you.*
> (perfect conditional: see 88)
> *I'd like **to have lived** in the eighteenth century.*
> (perfect infinitive: see 175)
> *You **should have written** to me.*
> (modal auxiliary with perfect infinitive: see 202.3)
> ***Having been** there before, he knew what to expect.*
> (perfect participle)

2 Like all auxiliary verbs, *have* makes questions and negatives without *do*.

> ***Have** you **heard** the news? (NOT ~~Do you have heard~~ ...?)*
> *I **haven't** seen them. (NOT ~~I don't have seen them.~~)*

153 have (got): possession, relationships etc

1 We can use *have* to talk about possession, relationships, illnesses, and the characteristics of people and things (for example in descriptions). We can use *do* in questions and negatives.

> They hardly **have** enough money to live on.
> **Do you have** any brothers or sisters?
> The Prime Minister **had** a bad cold.
> My grandmother **didn't have** a very nice character.

2 In British English, we often use the structure *I have got* to talk about possession, relationships etc. *I have got* means exactly the same as *I have*—it is a present tense, not a present perfect.
Questions and negatives are made without *do*.

> They've hardly **got** enough money to live on.
> **Have you got** any brothers or sisters?   **I haven't got** much hair.

Got-forms are used mostly in the present: *I had got* is unusual. They are informal: we use them very often in conversation, but less often in, for example, serious writing.
We do not use *got*-forms to talk about repetition or habit. Compare:

> **I've got** toothache.
> I **often have** toothache. (NOT ~~I've often got toothache.~~)

> We **haven't got** any beer today, I'm afraid.
> We **don't often have** beer in the house.

3 Note that we do not use progressive forms of *have* for these meanings.

> **I have** a headache. OR **I've got** a headache.
> (NOT ~~I'm having a headache.~~)

154 have: actions

We often use *have* + object to talk about actions. (For example: *have a drink*; *have a rest*.) In these expressions, *have* can mean 'eat', 'drink', 'take', 'do', 'enjoy', 'experience' or other things—it depends on the noun. Common expressions:

> have breakfast / lunch / tea / dinner / a meal / a drink / coffee / a beer / a glass of wine
>
> have a bath / a wash / a shave / a shower / a rest / a lie-down / a sleep / a dream
>
> have a holiday / a day off / a good time / a nice evening / a bad day
>
> have a talk / a chat / a conversation / a disagreement / a row / a quarrel / a fight / a word with somebody
>
> have a swim / a walk / a ride / a game of tennis, football etc
>
> have a try / a go

have a baby (= 'give birth')

have difficulty in ... -ing   have trouble ... -ing

have a nervous breakdown

In these structures, we make questions and negatives with *do*. *Got* is not used. Progressive forms are possible. Contractions of *have* are not used.

Did you have a good holiday?

'What are you doing?' '**I'm having** a bath.'

I **have** lunch at 12.30 most days. (NOT ~~I've lunch~~ ...)

155 have + object + verb form

1 We often use the structure | *have* + object + verb form |

It's nice to **have people smile** at you in the street.

We'll soon **have your car going**.

We use | *I won't have* + object + verb form | to say that we refuse to allow or accept something.

I **won't have you telling** me what to do.

I **won't have people talk** to me like that.

2 We use | *have* + object + past participle | with a passive meaning, to talk about jobs which are done for us by other people.

I must **have my shoes repaired**.

Lucy **had her eyes tested** yesterday, and she needs glasses.

▷ For similar structures with *got*, see 143.

156 have (got) to

We use | *have (got)* + infinitive | to talk about obligation.

The meaning is similar to *must*.

Sorry, **I've got to go** now.

Do you often have to travel on business?

The forms with *got* are common in an informal style in present-tense verb forms. (See 153.2.) Compare:

I've got to go to London tomorrow.

I had to go to London yesterday. (NOT ~~I had got to~~ ...)

We do not use *got*-forms to talk about habits or repeated obligations. Compare:

I've got to write a financial report tomorrow.

I have to write financial reports at the end of every month.

▷ For the difference between *have (got) to* and *must*, and between *haven't got to*, *don't have to*, *mustn't* and *needn't*, see 209.

157 hear and listen (to)

1 *Hear* is the ordinary word to say that something 'comes to our ears'.

>*Suddenly I **heard** a strange noise.*
>*Can you **hear** me?*
>*Did you **hear** the Queen's speech yesterday?*

Hear is not used in progressive tenses (see 225). When we want to say that we hear something at the moment of speaking, we often use *can hear*. (See 81.)

>*I **can hear** somebody coming.* (NOT *I am hearing* ...)

2 We use *listen (to)* to talk about concentrating, paying attention, trying to hear as well as possible. Compare:

>*I **heard** them talking in the next room, but I didn't really **listen to** what they were saying.*
>*'**Listen** carefully, please.' 'Could you speak a bit louder? I can't **hear** you very well.'*

We use *listen* when there is no object, and *listen to* before an object. Compare:

>*Listen!* (NOT *Listen to!*)
>*Listen **to** me!* (NOT *Listen me!*)

▷ The difference between *hear* and *listen (to)* is similar to the difference between *see* and *look (at)*. See 196.

For | *hear* + infinitive or *-ing* form | see 182.6.

158 help

We can use | object + infinitive | after *help*.

>*Can you **help** me to **find** my ring?*

In an informal style, we often use the infinitive without *to*.

>*Can you **help** me **find** my ring?*
>***Help** me **get** him to bed.*

We can also use | *help* + infinitive | without an object.

>*Would you like to **help peel** the potatoes?*

159 here and there

We use *here* for the place where the speaker is, and *there* for other places.

>*(on the telephone) 'Hello, is Tom **there**?' 'No, I'm sorry, he's not **here**.'*
>*(NOT ... he's not **there**.)*

*Don't stay **there** in the corner by yourself. Come over **here** and talk to us.*

160 **holiday** and **holidays**

We use the singular *holiday* for a short period of, say, one or two days.

> *We've got **a holiday** next Tuesday.*
> *We get five days' Christmas **holiday** this year.*

We often use *holidays* for the 'big holiday' of the year.

> *Where are you going for your summer **holiday(s)**?*

We always use the singular in the expression *on holiday*. (Note the preposition.)

> *I met her **on holiday** in Norway.* (NOT ... *in holidays* ...)

Americans use the word *vacation* for a long holiday.

161 **home**

We do not use *to* before *home*.

> *I think I'll go **home**.*   *She came **home** late.*
> (NOT ... *to home*.)

In American English, *home* is often used to mean *at home*.

> *Is anybody **home**?*

162 **hope**

1 After *I hope*, we often use a present tense with a future meaning.

> *I hope she **likes** (= will like) the flowers.*
> *I hope the bus **comes** soon.*

2 In negative sentences, we usually put *not* with the verb that comes after *hope*.

> *I **hope** she **doesn't** wake up.*
> (NOT *I **don't hope** she **wakes** up.*)

3 We can use *I was hoping* to introduce a polite request.

> *I **was hoping** you could lend me some money . . .*

I had hoped is used to talk about hopes that were not realized—hopes for things that did not happen.

> *I **had hoped** that Jennifer would become a doctor, but she wasn't good enough at science.*

▷ For *I hope so / not*, see 311.
For the difference between *hope*, *want*, *expect*, *wish*, *look forward to* and *wait*, see 122.

163 how and what . . . like?

1 We use *how* to ask about things that change—for example people's moods and health.
We use *what . . . like* to ask about things that do not change—for example, people's appearance and character. Compare:

> *'**How's** Ron?' 'He's very well.'*
> *'**What's** Ron **like**?' 'He's tall and dark, and a bit shy.'*
>
> *'**How** does he look?' 'Surprised.'*
> *'**What** does he look **like**?' 'Nice.'*

2 We often use *how* to ask about people's reactions to their experiences.

> *'**How** was the film?' 'Great.'*
> *'**How's** your steak?*
> *'**How's** the new job?'*

3 Don't confuse the preposition *like* (in *What . . . like?*) with the verb *like*. Compare:

> *'What **is** she like?' 'Lovely.'*
> *'What **does** she like?' 'Dancing and fast cars.'*

164 if: ordinary tenses

> *if* + clause, + clause
> clause + *if* + clause

1 An *if*-clause can come at the beginning or end of the sentence.

> *If **you eat too much**, you get fat.   You get fat if **you eat too much**.*

2   We can use the same tenses with *if* as with other conjunctions.

> *If you **want** to learn a musical instrument, you **have** to practise.*
> *If that **was** Mary, why **didn't** she stop and say hello?*
> *If you **don't** like hot weather, **you'll be** unhappy in Texas.*

3   In the *if*-clause, we usually use a present tense to talk about the future. (This happens after most conjunctions—see 343.)

> ***If I have** enough time tomorrow, I'll come and see you.*
> (NOT ***If I will have** enough time* ...)
> *I'll give her your love **if I see** her.*
> (NOT ... ***if I will see her.***)

4   We can use $\boxed{if + will}$ in polite requests, but the meaning is not really future.

> ***If you will** come this way, I'll take you to the **manager's office**.*
> (= ***If you are willing** to come this way,* ...)

▷   For $\boxed{if + will}$ in reported speech (for example *I don't know **if I'll be** here tomorrow*), see 343.2.
For *If not* and *unless*, see 350.
For the use of special tenses with *if*, see 165.

165 *if*: special tenses

We use 'special' tenses with *if* when we are talking about 'unreal' situations—things that will probably not happen, present or future situations that we are imagining, or things that did not happen. (For example, we can use past tenses to talk about the future.)

1   Present and future situations

To talk about 'unreal' or improbable situations now or in the future, we use a past tense in the *if*-clause, and a conditional (see 88) in the other part of the sentence.

> if + past, conditional
> conditional *if* + past

> *If I **knew** her name, I **would tell** you.*
> (NOT ***If I would know** ... NOT ... **I will tell you**.*)
> *If you **came** tomorrow, I **would have** more time to talk.*
> *I **would be** perfectly happy if I **had** a car.*
> *What **would you do** if you **lost** your job?*

We often use *were* instead of *was* after *if*, especially in a formal style.

> *If I **were** rich, I would spend all my time travelling.*

2 Special tenses and ordinary tenses compared

The difference between *if I get* and *if I got*, or *if I have* and *if I had*, is not a difference of time. They can both refer to the present or future. After *if*, the past tense suggests that the situation is less probable, or impossible, or imaginary. Compare:

> *If I **become** President, I'll . . .* (said by a candidate in an election)
> *If I **became** President, I'd . . .* (said by a schoolboy)

> *If I **win** this race, I'll . . .* (said by the fastest runner)
> *If I **won** this race, I'd . . .* (said by the slowest runner)

3 Past situations

To talk about past situations that did not happen, we use a past perfect tense (with *had*) in the *if*-clause, and a perfect conditional (see 88) in the other part of the sentence.

> *if* + past perfect, perfect conditional
> perfect conditional *if* + past perfect

> *If you **had worked** harder, you **would have passed** your exam.*
> *If you **had asked** me, I **would have told** you.*
> *I'd have been in bad trouble if Jane **hadn't helped** me.*

166 if-sentences with could and might

In *if*-sentences, we can use *could* to mean 'would be able to' and *might* to mean 'would perhaps' or 'would possibly'.

> *If I had another £500, I **could** buy a car.*
> *(= . . . I would be able to buy a car.)*
> *If you asked me nicely, I **might** buy you a drink.*

167 if only

We can use *If only . . . !* to say that we would like things to be different. It means the same as *I wish* (see 367), but is more emphatic. We use the same tenses after *if only* as after *I wish*:

a. past to talk about the present

> *If only I **knew** more people!*
> *If only I **was** better-looking!*

In a formal style, we can use *were* instead of *was*.

> *If only I **were** better-looking!*

b. *would* to refer to the future

> *If only it **would** stop raining!*
> *If only somebody **would** smile!*

c. past perfect ($\boxed{had + \text{past participle}}$) to refer to the past

> If only she **hadn't** told the police, everything would have been all right.

168 **if so** and **if not**

We can use these expressions instead of repeating a verb that has already been mentioned.

> Are you free this evening? **If so**, let's go out for a meal.
> (= ... If you are ...)
> I might see you tomorrow. **If not**, then it'll be Saturday.
> (= ... If I don't ...)

169 **ill** and **sick**

1 *Ill* means 'unwell'.

> I'm sorry I didn't answer your letter. I've been **ill**.

We do not use *ill* before a noun. Instead, we can use *sick*.

> She spent years looking after her **sick** mother.

2 We can use *be sick* (in British English) to mean 'bring food up from the stomach'. If you *feel sick*, you want to do this.

> I **was sick** three times in the night.
> I **feel sick**. Where's the bathroom?
> She's never **sea-sick**.

In American English *be sick* means 'be ill'.

170 imperative

1 When we say *Have a drink*, *Come here* or *Sleep well*, we are using *imperative* verb forms: *have*, *come* and *sleep*.
Imperatives have exactly the same form as the infinitive without *to*. We use them, for example, for telling people what to do, making suggestions, giving advice, giving instructions, encouraging people, and offering things.

> **Look** in the mirror before you drive off.
> **Tell** him you're not free this evening.
> **Try** again—you nearly did it!
> **Have** some more tea.

Negative imperatives are made with *don't* or *do not*.

> **Don't worry**—everything will be all right.
> **Do not lean** out of the window.

We can make an emphatic imperative with *do*. This is common in polite requests, complaints and apologies.

> ***Do sit*** *down.*   ***Do try*** *to make less noise.*
> ***Do forgive*** *me—I didn't mean to interrupt.*

2   The imperative does not usually have a subject, but we can use a noun or pronoun to make it clear who we are speaking to.

> ***Mary come*** *here—everybody else stay where you are.*
> ***Somebody answer*** *the phone!*

3   After imperatives, we can use the question tags (see 273) *will you? won't you? would you? can you? can't you?* and *could you?*

> *Come and help me,* ***will you****?*
> *Give me a cigarette,* ***could you****?*
> *Be quiet,* ***can't you****?*

▷   For the 'first-person plural imperative' *let's*, see 191.

171 in and into (prepositions)

1   To talk about the position of something (with no movement), we use *in*.

> *'Where's Susie?' '****In*** *the bedroom.'*
> *My mother's the woman* ***in*** *the chair by the window.*

2   When we talk about a movement, we usually use *into*.

> *She came* ***into*** *my room holding a paper.*
> *I walked out* ***into*** *the garden to think.*

After some words, both are possible. (For example *throw, jump, cut, push*.) We prefer *into* when we think of the movement, and *in* when we think of the end of the movement—the place where something will be. Compare:

> *She threw her ring* ***into*** *the air.*
> *She threw her ring* ***in****(to) the river.*

We use *in* after *sit down*, and very often after *put*.

> *He* ***sat down in*** *his favourite armchair.* (NOT *He sat down into* ...)
> *I* ***put*** *my hand* ***in*** *my pocket.*

172 in case

1   We use *in case* to talk about things we do because something else might happen.

> *Take an umbrella* ***in case*** *it rains.* (= ... *because it might rain*.)
> *I've bought a chicken* ***in case*** *your mother stays to lunch.*
> *I wrote down her address* ***in case*** *I forgot it.*

After *in case*, we use a present tense with a future meaning.

... *in case it **rains**.* (NOT ... ~~*in case it **will rain**.*~~)

We can also use *should* + infinitive. In this stucture, *should* means 'might'.

*I've bought a chicken **in case** your mother **should stay** to lunch.*
*I wrote down her address **in case I should forget** it.*

The structure with *should* is more common in the past.

2 Don't confuse *in case* and *if*.
'I do A in case B happens' =
'I do A first because B might happen later.' A is first.
'I do A if B happens' =
'I do A if B has happened first.' B is first.
Compare:

*Let's get a bottle of wine **in case** Roger comes.*
(= *We'll buy some wine now because Roger might come later.*)

*Let's buy a bottle of wine **if** Roger comes.*
(= *We'll wait and see. If Roger comes, then we'll buy the wine. If he doesn't we won't.*)

173 in spite of

In spite of is a preposition.

| *In spite of* + noun | = | *although* + cause | .

*We went out **in spite of** the rain.*
(= *We went out **although** it was raining.*)
*We understood him **in spite of** his accent.*
(= *We understood him **although** he had a strong accent.*)

In spite of is the opposite of *because of*. Compare:

*He passed the exam **because of** his good teachers.*
*He passed the exam **in spite of** his bad teachers.*

174 indeed

We use *indeed* to strengthen *very*.

*Thank you **very** much **indeed**.*
*I was **very** pleased **indeed** to hear from you.*
*He was driving **very** fast **indeed**.*

We do not usually use *indeed* after an adjective or adverb without *very*.
(NOT ~~*He was driving fast **indeed**.*~~)

175 infinitive: negative, progressive, perfect, passive

1 **Negative infinitive:** $\boxed{\textit{not} + \textbf{infinitive}}$

> *Try **not to be** late.* (NOT ... ~~to not be late.~~)
> *I decided **not to study** medicine.* (NOT ... ~~to not study~~ ...)
> *You'd better **not say** that again.*
> *Why **not tell** me about your problems?*

For the difference between the infinitive with and without *to*, see 179.

2 **Progressive infinitive:** $\boxed{\textit{(to) be} ... \textbf{-ing}}$

> *It's nice **to be sitting** here with you.*
> *This time tomorrow I'll **be lying** on the beach.*

3 **Perfect infinitive:** $\boxed{\textit{(to) have} + \textbf{past participle}}$

> *It's nice **to have finished** work.*
> *Ann said she was sorry **to have missed** you.*
> *You should **have told** me you were coming.*

For perfect infinitives after modal verbs (*should*, *might* etc), see 202.3.

4 **Passive infinitive:** $\boxed{\textit{(to) be} + \textbf{past participle}}$

> *There's a lot of work **to be done**.*
> *She ought **to be told** about it.*
> *That window must **be repaired** before tonight.*

For the meaning of passive forms, see 237.

176 infinitive: use

1 **Subject**

An infinitive can be the subject of a sentence.

> ***To learn** Chinese is not easy.*

But we more often use a structure with *it* as a 'preparatory subject' (see 187), or with an *-ing* form as subject (see 180).

> *It is not easy **to learn** Chinese.*
> ***Learning** Chinese isn't easy.*

2 **After verb**

We often use an infinitive after another verb.

> *It's **beginning to rain**.*
> *I **expect to be free** tomorrow evening.*
> *I don't **want to see** you again.*

Some common verbs that can have an infinitive after them:

afford	happen	prefer
appear	hate	prepare
arrange	help	pretend
ask	hope	promise
(can't) bear	intend	refuse
begin	learn	remember
dare (see 94)	like	seem
decide	love	start
expect	manage	try
fail	mean	want
forget	offer	wish

Some of these verbs can be used with object + infinitive (for
example *I **want her to be** happy*). For details, see 3 below.
After some of these verbs, we can also use an *-ing* form. The meaning is
not always the same (for example, *try running/try to run*). For details, see
182.

3 Verb + object + infinitive

After some verbs, we can use   object + infinitive   .

> *She didn't **want me to go**.*
> (NOT ~~She didn't want that I go.~~)
> *I didn't **ask you to pay** for the meal.*

Some common verbs that are used in this structure:

advise	hate	prefer
allow	help (see 158)	remind
ask	invite	teach
(can't) bear	like	tell
cause	mean	want
encourage	need	warn
expect	order	wish
get (see 143)	persuade	

For   verb + infinitive without *to* , see 179.

4 After adjective

Infinitives are used after some adjectives.

> *I'm **pleased to see** you.*
> *John was **surprised to get** Ann's letter.*
> *His accent is not **easy to understand**.* (NOT *... ~~to understand it~~.*)
> *She's very **nice to talk to**.* (NOT *... ~~to talk to her~~.*)

For structures like *I'm **anxious for the meeting to finish** early*, see 132.

For *enough* and *too* with   adjective + infinitive , see 113; 348.

5 After noun

We can use infinitives after some nouns.

> *I have no **wish to change**.*
> *I told her about my **decision to leave**.*

The infinitive often explains the purpose of something: what it will do, or what somebody will do with it.

> *Have you got a key **to open this door**?*
> *I need some more work **to do**.*

▷ For information about the structures that are possible with any verb,
   adjective or noun, look in a good dictionary.
   For the 'infinitive of purpose', see 178.
   For infinitives after *who, what, how* etc, see 177.
   For *to* used instead of the whole infinitive, see 108.5.
   For the use of the infinitive without *to*, see 179.

177 infinitive after **who, what, how** etc

1 In reported speech (see 282; 284), we can use an infinitive after the
question-words *who, what, where* etc (but not *why*) to talk about
questions and the answers to questions.

> verb + question-word + infinitive

> *I wonder **who to invite**.*
> *Show me **what to do**.*
> *Can you tell me **how to get** to the station?*
> *I don't know **where to put** the car.*
> *Tell me **when to pay**.*
> *I can't decide **whether to answer** her letter.*

2 We cannot begin a direct question with *How to ... ?, What to ... ?* etc.
We often use *shall* or *should*.

> *How **shall** I tell her?* (NOT ~~How to tell her?~~)
> *What **shall** we do?* (NOT ~~What to do?~~)
> *Who **should** I pay?* (NOT ~~Who to pay?~~)

For questions beginning   *Why (not)* + infinitive   , see 179.3.

178 infinitive of purpose

We often use an infinitive to talk about a person's purpose—why he or
she does something.

> *I sat down for a minute **to rest**.*
> *He went abroad **to forget**.*
> *I'm going to Austria **to learn German**.*

In a more formal style, we often use *in order to* or *so as to*.

>*He got up early **in order to have time** to pack.*
>*I moved to a new flat **so as to be near** my work.*

In negative sentences, we nearly always use the structure with *so as not to* or *in order not to*.

>*I'm going to leave now, **so as not to be late**.*
>(NOT ~~I'm going to leave now, **not to be late**.~~)

179 infinitive without **to**

We usually put *to* before the infinitive (for example *I want **to** go; It's nice **to** see you*). But we use the infinitive without *to* in the following cases:

1 Modal auxiliary verbs

After the modal auxiliary verbs *will, shall, would, should, can, could, may, might* and *must*, and after *had better*, we use the infinitive without *to*.

>*I **must go** now.*
>***Will** you **help** me?*
>*It **might rain**.*
>*You **had better stop**.*

2 *let, make, hear* etc

After some verbs, we use an object and the infinitive without *to*. The most common of these verbs are *let, make, see, hear, feel, watch*, and *notice*.

> verb + object + infinitive without *to*

>*She **lets her children do** what they want to.*
>*I **made them give** me the money back.*
>*I didn't **see you come in**.*
>*I **heard her say** that she was tired.*

In an informal style, we often use *help* with this structure.

>*Could you **help me push** the car?*

3 *why (not)*

We can use an infinitive without *to* after *why*. This usually means that it is unnecessary or stupid to do something.

>***Why pay** more at other shops? Our prices are the lowest.*

Why not . . . ? is used to make suggestions.

>***Why not** ask Susan to help you?*

4 *and, or, except, but, than*

We can join two infinitives with *and, or, except, but,* or *than*. The second infinitive is usually without *to.*

> *I'd like **to lie down and go** to sleep.*
> *Do you want **to eat** now **or wait** till later?*
> *We had nothing **to do except look** at the garden.*
> *I'll **do** anything **but work** on a farm.*
> *It's easier **to do** it yourself **than explain** to somebody else how to do it.*

180 -ing form ('gerund')

1 Gerund or participle

Words like *smoking, walking* are verbs. But we can also use them as adjectives or nouns. Compare:

> *You're **smoking** too much these days.* (part of a verb)
> *There was a **smoking** cigarette end in the ashtray.* (adjective)
> ***Smoking** is bad for you.* (noun: subject of sentence)

When -*ing* forms are used as verbs or adjectives, they are called 'present participles'. For details, see 234–236. When they are more like nouns, grammars call them 'gerunds'.
For the use of gerunds, see this section and the next two.

2 Subject, object or complement of a sentence

An -*ing* form can be a subject, object or complement.

> ***Smoking** is bad for you.* (subject)
> *I hate **packing**.* (object)
> *My favourite activity is **reading**.* (complement)

The -*ing* form subject, object or complement is still a verb, and can have its own object.

> ***Smoking cigarettes** is bad for you.*
> *I hate **packing suitcases**.*
> *My favourite activity is **reading poetry**.*

We can use determiners (for example *the, my*) with -*ing* forms.

> ***the opening** of Parliament*
> *Do you mind **my smoking**?*
> (OR, not so formal: *Do you mind **me** smoking?*)

3 After verb

After some verbs we can use an -*ing* form, but not an infinitive.

> *I **enjoy travelling**.* (NOT ~~I enjoy to travel.~~)
> *He's **finished mending** the car.* (NOT ... ~~to mend~~ ...)

Common verbs which are followed by an *-ing* form are:

avoid	forgive	practise
consider	give up	put off
delay	go	risk
dislike	(can't) help	(can't) stand
enjoy	imagine	spend time/money
excuse	keep	suggest
feel like	mind	understand
finish	miss	

Examples:

> I ***dislike arguing*** about money.
> ***Forgive my interrupting*** you.
> Let's ***go swimming***.
> I can't ***understand his being*** so late.

After some verbs, we can use either an *-ing* form or an infinitive. For example: *like, start, try, remember, forget*.

> How old were you when you ***started to play/playing*** the piano?

With some verbs, the two structures have different meanings. For details, see 182.

4 After verb (passive meaning)

After *need* and *want*, an *-ing* form has a passive meaning.

> Your hair ***needs cutting***. (= ... needs ***to be cut***.)
> The car ***wants servicing***. (= ... needs ***to be serviced***.)

5 After preposition

After prepositions we use *-ing* forms, not infinitives.

> Check the oil ***before starting*** the car. (NOT ... ***before to start*** ...)
> You can't make an omelette ***without breaking*** eggs.
> You can get there faster ***by going*** on the motorway.

When *to* is a preposition, we use an *-ing* form after it. (See 181.)

> I look forward ***to hearing*** from you. (NOT ... ***to hear from you***.)

6 *it ... -ing*

We can use *it* as a 'preparatory subject' for an *-ing* form (see 187).

> ***It's*** nice ***being*** with you.

This is common in the structures *It's no good ... -ing* and *It's no use ... ing*.

> ***It's no good talking*** to him—he never listens.
> ***It's no use expecting*** her to say thank-you.

For *It's (not) worth ... -ing*, see 368.

181 -ing form after **to**

We sometimes use an -*ing* form after *to*.

> *I look forward **to seeing** you.* (NOT ... *to see you.*)
> *I'm not used **to getting up** early.*

These structures may seem strange.
In fact, *to* is two words:

a. a part of the infinitive

> *I want **to go** home.*
> *Help me **to understand**.*

b. a preposition

> *I look forward **to** your next letter.*
> *I prefer meat **to** fish.*
> *I'm not used **to** London traffic.*

After the preposition *to*, we can use an -*ing* form, but not usually an infinitive.

> *I look forward **to hearing** from you.*
> (NOT ... *to hear from you.*)
> *I prefer riding **to walking**.*
> *I'm not used **to driving** in London.*

If you want to know whether *to* is a preposition, try putting a noun after it. Compare:

a. *I want to your letter.* (Not possible: *to* is not a preposition. Use the infinitive after *I want*.)

b. *I'm looking forward **to** your letter.* (This is all right, so *to* is a preposition. Use the -*ing* form after *look forward to*.)

182 -ing form or infinitive?

Some verbs and adjectives can be followed by an infinitive or by an -*ing* form, often with a difference of meaning.

1 *remember* and *forget*

We *remember* or *forget* *doing* things in the past—things that we did.
Forget ... -*ing* is used especially in the structure *I'll never forget* ... -*ing*.

> *I still **remember buying** my first packet of cigarettes.*
> *I'll never **forget meeting** the Queen.*

We *remember* or *forget* *to do* things which we have to do.

> *Did you **remember to buy** my cigarettes?*
> *You mustn't **forget to go** and meet Mr Lewis at the station tomorrow.*

2 *stop*

If you *stop doing* something, you don't do it any more.

*I really must **stop smoking**.*

If you *stop to do* something, you pause (in the middle of something else) in order to do it.

*Every hour I **stop** work **to have** a little rest.*

3 *go on*

If you *go on doing* something, you continue—you do it more.

*She **went on talking** about her illnesses until everybody went to sleep.*

If you *go on to do* something, you do it next—you stop one thing and start another.

*She stopped talking about her illnesses and **went on to tell** us about all her other problems.*

4 *regret*

You *regret doing* something in the past—you are sorry that you did it.

*I don't **regret telling** her what I thought, even if it made her angry.*

The expression *I regret to say / tell you / announce* etc means 'I'm sorry that I have to say . . .'.

*British Rail **regret to announce** that the 13.15 train for Cardiff will leave approximately thirty-seven minutes late. This delay is due to the late running of the train.*

5 *allow*

After *allow*, we use . . . *-ing* in active clauses if there is no object. If there is an object, we use an infinitive.

*We don't **allow smoking** in the lecture room.*
*We don't **allow people to smoke** in the lecture room.*

6 *see, watch* and *hear*

If you *saw, watched* or *heard something happening*, it *was happening*: you saw or heard it while it was going on. If you *saw, watched* or *heard something happen*, it *happened*: you saw or heard a complete action. Note the infinitive without *to*: see 179.
(For the difference between *it was happening* and *it happened*, see 242.)

*I looked out of the window and **saw Mary crossing** the road.*
(= She was in the middle of crossing the road.)
*I **saw Mary** step off the pavement, **cross** the road and disappear into the post office.*

7 *try*

Try... -ing = 'make an experiment; do something to see what will happen'.

> I **tried sending** her flowers, **giving** her presents, **writing** her letters; but she still wouldn't speak to me.

Try to ... = 'make an effort'. It is used for things that are difficult.

> I **tried to write** a letter, but my hands were too cold to hold a pen.

8 *afraid*

We use *afraid of ... -ing* to talk about accidents.

> I don't like to drive fast because I'm **afraid of crashing**.
> (NOT ... I'm **afraid to crash**.)

In other cases, we can use *afraid of ... -ing* or *afraid to ...* with no difference of meaning.

> I'm not **afraid of telling/to tell** her the truth.

9 *sorry*

We use *sorry for ... -ing* or *sorry about ... -ing* to talk about past things that we regret.

> I'm **sorry for/about waking** you up. (= I'm sorry that I woke you up.)

We can use a perfect infinitive with the same meaning.

> I'm **sorry to have woken** you up.

Sorry + infinitive is used to apologize for something that we are doing or going to do.

> **Sorry to disturb** you—could I speak to you for a moment?
> I'm **sorry to tell** you that you failed the exam.

10 *certain* and *sure*

If I say that somebody is *certain/sure of doing* something, I am talking about his or her feelings—he or she feels sure.

> Before the game she felt **sure of winning**, but after five minutes she realized that it wasn't going to be so easy.

If I say that somebody is *certain/sure to do* something, I am talking about my own feelings—I am sure that he or she will succeed.

> 'Kroftova's **sure to win**—the other girl hasn't got a chance.' 'Don't be so sure.'

11 *like, love, hate, prefer, begin, start, attempt, intend, continue, can't bear*

After these verbs, we can use either the *-ing* form or the infinitive without much difference of meaning.

*I **hate working/to work** at weekends.*
*She **began playing/to play** the guitar when she was six.*
*I **intend telling her/to tell** her what I think.*

In British English, we usually use *like ... -ing* to talk about enjoyment, and *like to ...* to talk about choices and habits. Compare:

*I **like climbing** mountains.*
*I **like to start** work early in the morning.*

After the conditionals *would like, would prefer, would hate* and *would love*, we use the infinitive.

***I'd like to tell** you something.*
*'Can I give you a lift?' 'No, thanks. **I'd prefer to walk.***'
***I'd love to have** a coat like that.*

Compare:

Do you like dancing? (= *Do you enjoy dancing?*)
***Would** you like **to dance**?* (An invitation. = *Do you want to dance now?*)

▷ For the difference between ⎡ *used to* + infinitive ⎤ and

⎡ *be used to ... -ing* ⎤ , see 353; 354.

183 instead of ...-ing

After *instead of*, we can use a noun or an *-ing* form, but not an infinitive.

*Would you like to take a taxi **instead of a bus**?*
*Would you like to take a taxi **instead of going by bus**?*
(NOT ... ***instead to go** by bus.*)

184 inversion: auxiliary verb before subject

⎡ auxiliary verb + subject + main verb ⎤

We put an auxiliary verb before the subject of a clause in several different structures.

1   questions (see 270)

***Have your father and mother** arrived?*
(NOT *Have arrived your father and mother?*)
*Where **is the concert** taking place?*
(NOT *Where is taking place the concert?*)

Spoken questions do not always have this word order (see 271).

***You're coming** tomorrow?*

Reported questions do not usually have this order (see 284).

*I wondered what time **the film was starting**.*
(NOT ... *what time was the film starting.*)

2 *if*

In a formal style, *had I . . .* , *had he . . .* etc can be used instead of *if I had . . .* , *if he had . . .* etc.

> ***Had I known*** *what was going to happen, I would have warned you.* (= *If I had known . . .*)

3 *neither, nor, so* (see 217; 312)

These words are followed by   auxiliary verb + subject   .

> *'I'm hungry.' 'So* ***am I.****'*
> *'I don't like Mozart.' 'Neither/Nor* ***do I.****'*

4 **Negative adverbial expressions**

In a formal style, we may put a negative adverb or adverb phrase at the beginning of a clause. The order is

  negative adverb (phrase) + auxiliary + subject + verb

> ***Under no circumstances can we*** *accept cheques.*
> ***Hardly had I*** *arrived when trouble started.*

5 *only*

The same thing happens with expressions containing *only*.

> ***Only then did I*** *understand what she meant.*
> ***Not only did we*** *lose our money, but we were also in danger of losing our lives.*

6 **Exclamations**

Exclamations often have the same structure as negative questions (see 120.3).

> ***Isn't it*** *cold!*   ***Hasn't she*** *got lovely eyes!*

185 inversion: whole verb before subject

1 *here, there* etc

If we begin a sentence with *here* or *there*, we put the whole verb before the subject, if this is a noun.

> *Here* ***comes Mrs Foster.***   (NOT *Here ~~Mrs Foster comes~~.*)
> *There* ***goes your brother***.

If the subject is a pronoun, it comes before the verb.

> *Here* ***she comes***.   *There* ***he goes***.

This structure is possible with some other short adverbs like *down*, *up*.

> *So I stopped the car, and* ***up walked a policeman***.

2 Other adverbs (literary style)

In descriptive writing and story-telling, other adverbs of place can come at the beginning of a clause, followed by verb + subject.

> *Under a tree was sitting the biggest man I have ever seen.*
> *On the bed lay a beautiful young girl.*

3 Reporting (literary style)

In books, the subject often comes after verbs like *said*, *asked* in reporting direct speech.

> *'What do you mean?' asked Henry.*

If the subject is a pronoun, it comes before the verb.

> *'What do you mean?' he asked.*

186 irregular verbs

1 This is a list of common irregular verbs. You may like to learn them by heart.

Infinitive	Simple past	Past participle
arise	arose	arisen
awake	awoke	awoken
be	was, were	been
beat	beat	beaten
become	became	become
begin	began	begun
bend	bent	bent
bite	bit	bitten
bleed	bled	bled
blow	blew	blown
break	broke	broken
bring	brought	brought
build	built	built
burn	burnt/burned	burnt/burned
buy	bought	bought
can	could/was able	been able
catch	caught	caught
choose	chose	chosen
come	came	come
cost	cost	cost
cut	cut	cut
deal /diːl/	dealt /delt/	dealt /delt/
dig	dug	dug
do	did	done
draw	drew	drawn
dream /driːm/	dreamt /dremt/ dreamed /driːmd/	dreamt /dremt/ dreamed /driːmd/
drink	drank	drunk

Infinitive	Simple past	Past participle
drive	drove	driven
eat /iːt/	ate /et/	eaten /'iːtn/
fall	fell	fallen
feel	felt	felt
fight	fought	fought
find	found	found
fly	flew	flown
forget	forgot	forgotten
forgive	forgave	forgiven
freeze	froze	frozen
get	got	got
give	gave	given
go	went	gone/been
grow	grew	grown
hang	hung	hung
have	had	had
hear /hɪə(r)/	heard /hɜːd/	heard /hɜːd/
hide	hid	hidden
hit	hit	hit
hold	held	held
hurt	hurt	hurt
keep	kept	kept
know	knew	known
lay	laid	laid
lead	led	led
learn	learnt/learned	learnt/learned
leave	left	left
lend	lent	lent
let	let	let
lie	lay	lain
light	lit/lighted	lit/lighted
lose	lost	lost
make	made	made
mean /miːn/	meant /ment/	meant /ment/
meet	met	met
pay	paid	paid
put	put	put
read /riːd/	read /red/	read /red/
ride	rode	ridden
ring	rang	rung
rise	rose	risen
run	ran	run
say /seɪ/	said /sed/	said /sed/
see	saw	seen

Infinitive	Simple past	Past participle
sell	sold	sold
send	sent	sent
set	set	set
shake	shook	shaken
shine /ʃaɪn/	shone /ʃɒn/	shone /ʃɒn/
shoot	shot	shot
show	showed	shown
shut	shut	shut
sing	sang	sung
sit	sat	sat
sleep	slept	slept
smell	smelt/smelled	smelt/smelled
speak	spoke	spoken
spell	spelt/spelled	spelt/spelled
spend	spent	spent
stand	stood	stood
steal	stole	stolen
stick	stuck	stuck
strike	struck	struck
swim	swam	swum
take	took	taken
teach	taught	taught
tear	tore	torn
tell	told	told
think	thought	thought
throw	threw	thrown
understand	understood	understood
wake	woke	woken
wear	wore	worn
win	won	won
write	wrote	written

2 Verbs that are easy to confuse

Infinitive	Simple past	Past participle
fall	fell	fallen
feel	felt	felt
fill	filled	filled
lay (= 'put down flat')	laid	laid
lie (= 'be down')	lay	lain
lie (= 'say things that are not true')	lied	lied
leave (= 'go away')	left	left
live (= 'be alive', 'be at home')	lived	lived
raise (= 'put up')	raised	raised
rise (= 'go up')	rose	risen

187 **it**: preparatory subject

When the subject of a sentence is an infinitive or a clause, this does not usually come at the beginning. We prefer to start the sentences with the 'preparatory subject' *it*.

*It's nice **to be** with you.*
(*To be with you is nice* is possible, but unusual.)
*It's probable **that** we'll be a little late.*

1 We often use this structure in sentences with *be* + adjective.

> *It* + *be* + adjective + infinitive

*It's hard **to live** on my salary.*
*It is possible **to go** by road or rail.*
*It is important **to book** in advance.*

> *It* + *be* + adjective + clause

*It's possible **that** I'll be here again next week.*
*It's surprising **how many** unhappy people there are.*
*It wasn't clear **what** she meant.*
*Is **it** true your father's ill?*

2 We also use the structure to talk about the time that things take. (See 338.)

*It took me months **to get to know** her.*
*How long does **it** take **to get to London** from here?*

3 *It* can be a preparatory subject for an *-ing* form. This happens especially with *it's worth* (see 368) and *it's no good/use*. In other cases it is rather informal.

*It's **worth going** to Wales if you have the time.*
*It's **no use trying** to explain—I'm not interested.*
*It was nice **seeing** you.*

▷ For the use of *it* as a subject in emphatic structures, see 111.
For 'impersonal' *it* in sentences like *It's raining*, see 247.5.
For *it* as 'preparatory object', see 188.

188 **it**: preparatory object

We sometimes use *it* as a preparatory object. This happens most often in the structures *make it clear that* ... and *find/make it easy/difficult to* ...

*George **made it clear that** he wasn't interested.*
*I **found it easy to talk** to her.*
*You **make it difficult to refuse**.*

189 it's time

1 We can use an infinitive after *it's time*.

>*It's time to buy a new car.*   *It's time for you to go to bed.*

2 *It's time* may also be followed by a special structure with a past tense verb.

> *it's time* + subject + past verb ...

>*It's time you went to bed.*
>*It's time she washed that dress.*
>*I'm getting tired. It's time we went home.*

▷ For other structures in which a past verb has a present or future meaning, see 239.

190 last and the last

Last week, *last month* etc is the week or month just before this one. If I am speaking in July, *last month* was June; if I am speaking in 1985, *last year* was 1984. (Note that prepositions are not used before these time-expressions.)

>*I had a cold last week.*   *Were you at the meeting last Tuesday?*
>*We bought this house last year.*

The last week, *the last month* etc is the period of seven days, thirty days etc up to the moment of speaking. On July 15th, 1995, *the last month* is the period from June 15th to July 15th; *the last year* is the period from July 1994 to July 1995.

>*I've had a cold for the last week.* (= for the seven days up to today)
>*We've lived here for the last year.* (= since twelve months ago)

Note the use of the present perfect tense (see 243) when talking about a period of time that continues up to the present, like *the last week*.

▷ For the difference between *next* and *the next*, see 220.

191 let's

Let's + infinitive without *to* is often used to make suggestions. It is rather like a first-person plural imperative (see 170).

> ***Let's** have a drink.* (= *I think we should have a drink.*)
> ***Let's** go home, shall we?*

There are two possible negatives, with *Let's not* ... and *Don't let's* ...

> ***Let's** not get angry.*   ***Don't let's** get angry.*

Let's not is considered more 'correct'.

192 letters

The most important rules for writing letters are:

1 Write your address in the top right-hand corner (house-number first, then street-name, then town, etc). Do not put your name above the address.

2 Put the date under the address. One way to write the date is: number—month—year (for example *17 May 1992*). For other ways, see 95.

3 In a business letter, put the name and address of the person you are writing to on the left-hand side of the page (beginning on the same level as the date).

4 Begin the letter (*Dear X*) on the left-hand side of the page.

5 Leave a line, and begin your first paragraph on the left-hand side. Leave another line after each paragraph, and begin each new paragraph on the left.

6 If you begin *Dear Sir(s)* or *Dear Madam*, finish *Yours faithfully* . . . . If you begin with the person's name (*Dear Mrs Hawkins*), finish *Yours sincerely* or *Yours* (more informal). Friendly letters may begin with a first name (*Dear Keith*) and finish with an expression like *Yours* or *Love*.

7 On the envelope, put the first name before the surname. You can write the first name in full (*Mr Keith Parker*), or you can write one or more initials (*Mr K Parker; Mr K S Parker*). Titles like *Mr, Ms, Dr* are usually written without a full stop in British English.

Examples of letters and envelopes

a formal

14 Plowden Road
Torquay
Devon
TQ6 1RS

The Secretary   16 June 1985
Hall School of Design
39 Beaumont Street
London
W4 4LJ

Dear Sir

I should be grateful if you would send me
information about the regulations for admission
to the Hall School of Design. Could you also tell
me whether the School arranges accommodation for
students?

Yours faithfully

Keith Parker

Keith Parker

The Secretary

Hall School of Design

39 Beaumont Street

London

W4 4LJ

b informal

22 Green Street
London
W1B 6DH
19 March 1984

Dear Keith and Ann

Thanks a lot for a great weekend. Can I come again soon?

Bill and I were talking about the holidays. We thought it might be nice to go camping in Scotland for a couple of weeks. Are you interested? Let me know if you are, and we can talk about dates etc.

See you soon, I hope. Thanks again.

Yours
  Alan

Keith and Ann Parker
19 West Way House
Botley Road
Oxford
OX6 5JP

193 likely

Likely means the same as 'probable', but we use it in different structures.

1 | *be* + *likely* + infinitive |

> *I'm **likely to be** busy tomorrow.*
> *Are you **likely to be** at home this evening?*
> *Do you think **it's likely to rain**?*
> *He's **unlikely** to agree.*

2 | *it is likely* + *that*-clause |

> *It's **likely that** the meeting will go on late.*

194 long and for a long time

Long is most common in questions and negative sentences, and after *too* and *so*.

> *How **long** did you wait?   I didn't play for **long**.*
> *The concert was **too long**.*

In affirmative sentences, we usually use *a long time*.

> *I waited (for) **a long time**. (I waited **long** is possible, but not usual.)*
> *It takes **a long time** to get to her house.*

Much, *many* and *far* are also more common in questions and negative sentences. (See 205 and 125.)

195 look

1 *Look* can mean 'seem' or 'appear'. This is a 'copula verb' (see 91); it is followed by adjectives.

> *You look **angry**—what's the matter?*
> (NOT ~~You look **angrily** ...~~)
> *The garden looks **nice**.*

We can also use *like* or *as if* after *look*.

| *look like* + noun |

> *She **looks like her mother**.*
> *'What's that bird?' 'It **looks like a buzzard**.'*

| *look as if* + clause |

> *You **look as if you've** had a bad day.*
> *It **looks as if it's going** to rain.*

Look like + clause is also possible—see 49.3.

2 *Look* can also mean 'turn your eyes towards something'. It can be used with adverbs.

> *The boss looked at me **angrily**.*
> *She looked **excitedly** round the room.*

▷ For the difference between *look*, *watch*, and *see*, see 196.

196 look (at), watch and see

1 *See* is the ordinary word to say that something 'comes to our eyes'.

> *Suddenly I **saw** something strange.   Can you **see** me?*
> *Did you **see** the article about the strike in today's paper?*

See is not used in progressive tenses with this meaning (see 225). When we want to say that we see something at the moment of speaking, we often use *can see*. (See 81.)

> *I **can see** an aeroplane.* (NOT *I am seeing* ...)

2 We use *look (at)* to talk about concentrating, paying attention, trying to see as well as possible. Compare:

> *I **looked at** the photo, but I didn't **see** anybody I knew.*
> *'Do you **see** the man in the raincoat?' 'Yes.' '**Look** again.' 'Good heavens! It's Moriarty!'*

We use *look* when there is no object, and *look at* before an object. Compare:

> ***Look!*** (NOT *Look at!*)   ***Look at me!*** (NOT *Look me!*)

3 *Watch* is like *look (at)*, but suggests that something is happening, or going to happen. We *watch* things that change, move or develop.

> ***Watch** that man—I want to know everything he does.*
> *I usually **watch** a football match on Saturday afternoon.*

4 We *watch* TV, but we *see* plays and films. Compare:

> *Did you **watch** 'Top of the Pops' last night? (TV)*
> *'Have you **seen** any of the Chaplin films?' 'Where are they on?' 'At the cinema in High Street.'*

▷ The difference between *see* and *look (at)* is similar to the difference between *hear* and *listen (to)*. See 157.
For structures with the infinitive and the *-ing* form after these verbs, see 182.6.

197 marry and divorce

1 *Marry* and *divorce* are used without a preposition.

> *She **married** a builder.* (NOT *She married with a builder.*)
> *Will you **marry** me?   Andrew's going to **divorce** Carola.*

2   When there is no direct object, we usually prefer the expressions *get married* and *get divorced*, especially in an informal style.

> *Lulu and Joe **got married** last week.*
> (*Lulu and Joe **married**...* is not so natural.)
> *When are you going to **get married**?*
> *The Robinsons are **getting divorced**.*

3   We can use *get / be married* with | *to* + object | .

> *She **got married to** her childhood sweetheart.*
> *I've **been married to** you for sixteen years and I still don't know what goes on inside your head.*

198   may and might: forms

1   *May* is a 'modal auxiliary verb' (see 202).
There is no *-s* in the third person singular.

> *She **may** be here tomorrow.* (NOT ~~She mays~~...)

Questions and negatives are made without *do*.

> ***May** I help you?* (NOT ~~Do I may~~...?)

After *may*, we use the infinitive without *to*.

> *You **may** be right.* (NOT ~~You may to be right.~~)

2   *May* has no infinitive or participles. When necessary, we use other words.

> *She wants **to be allowed** to open a bank account.*
> (NOT ... ~~to may open~~ ...)

3   *Might* is a 'less definite' form of *may*—it does not have a past meaning. We use both *may* and *might* to talk about the present and the future (see 199; 200).

4   There is a contracted negative *mightn't*. (*Mayn't* is very unusual.)

▷   *May* and *might* are used mostly to talk about probability and to ask for and give permission. See 199; 200.

199   may and might: probability

1   Chances

We use *may* and *might* to say that there is a chance of something: perhaps it is true, or perhaps it will happen.

> *We **may** go climbing in the Alps next summer.* (= *Perhaps we'll go.*)
> *'Where's Emma?' 'I don't know. She **may** be shopping, I suppose.'*
> *Peter **might** phone. If he does, could you ask him to ring again later?*
> *'I **might** get a job soon.' 'Yes, and pigs might fly.'* (= *'It's very unlikely.'*)

2 Questions

We do not use *may* in questions about probability.

> *Do you think you'll go camping this summer?*
> (NOT ~~May you go camping this summer?~~)

3 *might*

Might is not the past of *may*. It is used to talk about a smaller chance than *may*. Compare:

> *I **may** go to London tomorrow.* (Perhaps a 50 per cent chance.)
> *Joe **might** come with me.* (Perhaps a 30 per cent chance.)

4 Conditional

Might (but not *may*) can have a conditional use.

> *If you went to bed for an hour you **might** feel better.*
> (= ... *perhaps you would feel better.*)

5 *may/might have ...*

We use a special structure to talk about the chance that something happened in the past.

> *may/might have* + past participle

> *'Polly's very late.' 'She **may have missed** her train.'*
> *'What was that noise?' 'It **might have been** a cat.'*

We can use the same structure (with *might* only) to say that something was possible, but did not happen.

> *That was a bad place to go skiing. You **might have broken** your leg.*

(*Could have* ... is used in the same way. See 79.3.)

200 *may* and *might*: permission

1 Asking for permission

May and *might* can be used to ask for permission. They are more formal than *can* and *could*. *Might* is very polite and formal, and is not common.

> ***May** I put the TV on?*   *I wonder if I **might** have a little more cheese?*

2 Giving and refusing permission

May is used to give permission. *May not* is used to refuse permission, and to forbid.

> *'May I put the TV on?' 'Yes, of course you **may**.'*
> *Students **may not** use the staff car park.*

These are rather formal. In informal language, we prefer *can* and *can't*. (See 80.)

3 Talking about permission

We do not usually use *may* and *might* to talk about permission which has already been given or refused. Instead, we use *can*, *could* or *be allowed to*.

> *These days, children **can** do what they like.*
> (NOT ... ~~may do~~ ...)
> *I **could** read what I liked when I was a child.*
> (NOT ~~I might~~ ...)

201 mind

Mind can mean 'dislike', 'be annoyed by', 'object to'. We use *mind* mostly in questions and negative sentences.

> *I **don't mind** you coming in late if you don't wake me up.*
> *'**Do you mind** the smell of tobacco?' 'Not at all.'*

Do you mind ...? and *Would you mind ...?* are often used to ask for permission, or to ask people to do things. We can use *-ing* forms or *if-*clauses.

> | *Do you mind / Would you mind ... -ing ...?* |
> | --- |

> *Would you mind **opening** the window?* (= *Please open the window.*)
> *Would you mind **my opening** the window?* (= *Can I open the window?*)
> *Do you mind **people smoking** in the kitchen?*

> | *Do you mind / Would you mind if ...?* |
> | --- |

> *Would you mind **if** I opened the window?*
> *Do you mind **if** people smoke in the kitchen?*
> *'**Do you mind if** I smoke?' 'No, please do.'*

Note that the answer 'No' is used to *give* permission after *Do you mind ...?* (*I don't mind* means 'I have nothing against it; it's all right'.)

202 modal auxiliary verbs

1 Forms

Modal auxiliary verbs are *can, could, may, might, must, will, would, shall, should, ought, dare* and *need*.
Modal verbs have no *-s* in the third person singular.

> *She **might** know his address.* (NOT ~~She mights~~ ...)

Questions and negatives are made without *do*.

> ***Can** you swim?* NOT ~~Do you can swim?~~)
> *You **shouldn't do** that.* (NOT ~~You don't should do that.~~)

After modal auxiliary verbs, we use the infinitive without *to*. (*Ought* is an exception: see 232.)

> *I **must remember** to write to Leslie.*
> (NOT ~~I must to remember~~ ...)

2 Meanings

We do not use modal verbs for situations that definitely exist, or for things that have definitely happened. We use them, for example, to talk about things which we expect, which are possible, which we think are necessary, which we are not sure about, or which did not happen.

> *She **will** be here tomorrow.*
> *I **may** come tomorrow if I have time.*
> *She **could** be in London or Paris or Tokyo—nobody knows.*
> *You **must** come and have dinner with us some time.*
> *What **would** you do if you had a free year?*
> *She **should** have seen a doctor when she first felt ill.*

3 Modal verb + perfect infinitive

We use the structure | modal verb + perfect infinitive | (for example *must have seen*, *should have said*) to talk about the past. This structure is used for speculating (thinking about what possibly happened) or imagining (thinking about how things could have been different).

> | modal verb + *have* + past participle |

> *She's two hours late. What **can have happened**?*
> *You **could have told** me you were coming.*
> *The potatoes **would have been** better with more salt.*
> *The plant's dead. You **should have given** it more water.*

▷ For more information, see the entries for *can*, *may* etc.
Dare and need can be used in two ways: as modal auxiliary verbs and as ordinary verbs. See 94 and 213.
For information about weak and strong pronunciations of modal auxiliary verbs, see 358.
For contracted forms, see 90.

203 more (of): determiner

1 We can use *more* before uncountable or plural nouns.

> | *more* + noun |

> *We need **more time**. (NOT ... ~~more of time.~~)*
> ***More people** are drinking wine these days.*

2 Before another determiner (for example *the*, *my*, *this*), we use *more of*.
We also use *more of* before a pronoun.

> | *more of* + determiner + noun |
> | *more of* + pronoun |

*Can I have some **more of the** red wine, please?*
*Have you got any **more of that** smoked fish?*
*I don't think any **more of them** want to come.*

3 We can use *more* alone, without a noun.

*I'd like some **more**, please.*

▷ For the use of *more* with comparative adjectives and adverbs, see 84; 87.
For *far more*, *much more* and *many more*, see 86.

204 most (of): determiner

1 We use *most* before uncountable or plural nouns.

> | *most* + noun |

*I hate **most** pop music.* (NOT ... ~~most of pop music.~~)
***Most** people disagree with me.*
(NOT ~~Most of people~~ ... NOT ~~The most people~~ ...)

2 Before another determiner (for example *the*, *my*, *this*), we use *most of*.
We also use *most of* before a pronoun.

> | *most of* + determiner + noun |
> | *most of* + pronoun |

*I've eaten **most of the** salad.*   *You've read **most of my** books.*
***Most of us** feel the same way.*

▷ For the use of *most* with superlative adjectives and adverbs, see 84; 87.

205 much, many, a lot etc

1 In an informal style, we use *much* and *many* mostly in negative sentences
and questions, and after *so*, *as* and *too*. In affirmative sentences (except
after *so*, *as* and *too*), we use other words and expressions. Compare:

*How **much** money have you got?*
*I've got **plenty**.* (NOT ~~I've got much.~~)

*I haven't got **many** pop records.*
*I've got **a lot of** jazz records.* (NOT USUALLY ~~I've got many jazz records.~~)

*You make **too many** mistakes.*
*You make **lots of** mistakes.* (NOT USUALLY *You make ~~many mistakes.~~*)

2 We use *a lot of* and *lots of* mostly in an informal style. They are both used before uncountable (singular) and plural nouns, and before pronouns. When *a lot of* is used with a plural subject, the verb is plural; when *lots of* is used with a singular subject, the verb is singular.

> *a lot of* / *lots of* + singular subject and verb

> *A lot of time **is** needed to learn a language.*
> ***There's** lots of coffee in the pot.* (NOT ~~*There are lots of coffee* ...~~)

> *a lot of* / *lots of* + plural subject and verb

> ***A lot of my friends think** there's going to be a war.*
> (NOT ~~*A lot of my friends **thinks*** ...~~)
> ***Lots of people live** in the country and work in London.*
> ***A lot of us would like** to change our jobs.*

We use *a lot of* and *lots of* before a noun or pronoun; we use *a lot* / *lots* without *of* alone, when there is no noun or pronoun. Compare:

> *She's lost **a lot of weight**.* (NOT ... ~~*a lot weight*.~~)

3 *A lot (of)* and *lots (of)* are rather informal. In a more formal style we use other expressions, like *a great deal (of)* (+ singular), *a large number (of)* (+ plural), or *plenty (of)* (+ singular or plural).

> *Mr Lucas has spent **a great deal of time** in the Far East.*
> *We have **a large number of problems** to solve.*
> *Thirty years ago there were **plenty of jobs**; now there are very few.*

In a formal style, we can also use *much* and *many* in affirmative sentences.

> *There has been **much** research into the causes of cancer.*
> ***Many** scientists believe ...*

▷ See also 125 (*far* and *a long way*) and 194 (*long* and *a long time*).

206 much (of), many (of): determiners

1 *Much* is used before uncountable (singular) nouns; *many* is used before plural nouns.

> *I haven't got **much time**.* (NOT ... ~~*much of time*.~~)
> *I haven't got **many friends**.* (NOT ... ~~*much friends*.~~)

2 We use *much of* and *many of* before other determiners (for example *the*, *my*, *this*, *these*), and before pronouns.

> *much* / *many* + *of* + determiner + noun

> *How **much of the** house do you want to paint this year?*
> *I don't think I'll pass the exam; I've missed too **many of my** lessons.*
> *You didn't eat **much of it**.*
> *How **many of you** are there?*

3 We can use *much* and *many* alone, without a following noun.

> *You haven't eaten **much**.*
> *'Did you find any mushrooms?' 'Not **many**.'*

▷ *Much* and *many* are used mostly in questions and negative sentences. See 205.

207 must: forms

1 *Must* is a 'modal auxiliary verb' (see 202). There is no -*s* in the third person singular.

> *He **must** start coming on time.* (NOT *He **musts**...*)

Questions and negatives are made without *do*.

> ***Must** you go?* (NOT *Do you must go?*)
> *You **mustn't** worry.* (NOT *You don't must worry.*)

After *must*, we use the infinitive without *to*.

> *I **must** write to my mother.* (NOT *I must to write...*)

2 *Must* has no infinitive or participles. When necessary, we use other expressions, such as *have to*.

> *He**'ll have** to start coming on time.* (NOT *He'll must...*)
> *I don't want **to have to** tell you again.* (NOT *I don't want to must...*)

3 *Must* has no past tense. We can talk about past obligation with *had to*.

> *I **had to** push the car to start it this morning.* (NOT *I must push...*)

Must can have a past meaning in reported speech (see 282; 283).

> *I told her she **must** be home by midnight.*

4 There is a contracted negative *mustn't*.
For 'weak' and 'strong' pronunciations of *must*, see 358.

208 must: obligation

1 We use *must* to give strong advice or orders, to ourselves or other people.

> *I really **must** stop smoking.*
> *You **must** be here before eight o'clock.*

In questions, we use *must* to ask what the hearer thinks is necessary.

> ***Must** I clean all the rooms?*
> *Why **must** you always leave the door open?*

Must not or *mustn't* is used to tell people not to do things.

> *You **mustn't** open this parcel before Christmas Day.*

2 We can also use *have (got) to* to talk about obligation. (See 156.) For the difference between *must* and *have (got) to*, see 209.

3 *Must* is not used to talk about past obligation (*must* is used mainly for giving orders, and you cannot give orders in the past). For the use of *had to*, see 156.

▷ For the difference between *must not* and *don't have to*, *haven't got to*, *don't need to* and *needn't*, see 209.

209 must and have to; mustn't, haven't got to, don't have to, don't need to and needn't

1 *Must* and *have (got) to* are not exactly the same. We usually use *must* to give or ask for orders—the obligation comes from the person who is speaking or listening.

We use *have (got) to* to talk about an obligation that comes from 'outside'—perhaps because of a law, or a rule, or an agreement, or because some other person has given orders. Compare:

> *I **must** stop smoking. (I want to.)*
> *I**'ve got to** stop smoking. Doctor's orders.*

> *This is a terrible party. We really **must** go home.*
> *This is a lovely party, but we**'ve got to** go home because of the babysitter.*

> *I've got bad toothache. I **must** make an appointment with the dentist.*
> *I can't come to work tomorrow morning because I**'ve got to** see the dentist. (I have an appointment.)*

> ***Must** you wear dirty old jeans all the time? (= Is it personally important for you?)*
> ***Do you have to** wear a tie at work? (= Is it a rule?)*

2 *Mustn't* is used to tell people not to do things: it expresses 'negative obligation'.

Haven't got to, *don't have to*, *don't need to* and *needn't* are all used to say that something is unnecessary. They express absence of obligation: no obligation. Compare:

> *You **mustn't** tell George. (= Don't tell George.)*
> *You **don't have to** tell Alice. (= You can if you like, but it's not necessary.)*

> *You **don't have** to wear a tie to work, but you **mustn't** wear jeans. (= Wear a tie or not, as you like. But no jeans.)*

Haven't got to, *don't have to*, *needn't* and *don't need to* all mean more or less the same.

210 **must**: deduction

1 We can use *must* to say that we are sure about something (because it is logically necessary).

> *If A is bigger than B, and B is bigger than C, then A **must** be bigger than C.*
> *Mary keeps crying. She **must** have some problem.*
> *There's the doorbell. It **must** be Roger.*
> *'I'm in love.' 'That **must** be nice.'*

2 In questions and negatives, we use *can* and *can't* with this meaning, not *must* and *mustn't*.

> *'There's somebody at the door. Who **can** it be?*
> *'It **can't** be the postman. It's only seven o'clock.'*
> *What do you think this letter **can** mean?*

3 We use   `must have + past participle`   for deductions about the past (*can have* in questions and negatives).

> `must / can't / can't have + past participle`

> *'We went to Rome last month.' 'That **must have been** nice.'*
> *I don't think he **can have heard** you. Call again.*
> *Where **can** John **have put** the matches? He can't have thrown them away.*

211 names and titles

We can use names and titles when we talk about people, and when we talk to them. There are differences.

1 Talking about people

When we talk about people, we can name them in four ways.

a **First name.**
This is informal. We use first names mostly to talk about friends and children.

> *Where's **Peter**? He said he'd be here at three.*
> *How's **Maud** getting on at school?*

b **First name + surname.**
This can be formal or informal.

> *Isn't that **Peter Conolly**, the actor?*
> *We're going on holiday with **Mary and Daniel Sinclair**.*

c **Title (*Mr, Mrs* etc) + surname.**
This is more formal. We talk like this about people we do not know, or when we want to show respect or be polite.

> *Can I speak to **Mr Lewis**, please?*
> *We've got a new teacher called **Mrs Campbell**.*
> *Ask **Miss Andrews** to come in, please.*
> *Dear **Ms Sanders**, ...*

d **Surname only.**
We often use just the surname to talk about public figures—politicians, sportsmen and sportswomen, writers and so on.

> *I don't think **Eliot** is a very good dramatist.*
> *The women's marathon was won by **Waltz**.*

We sometimes use surnames alone for employees (especially male employees), and for members of all-male groups (for example footballers, soldiers, schoolboys).

> *Tell **Patterson** to come and see me at once.*
> *Let's put **Billows** in goal and move **Carter** up.*

2 Talking to people

When we talk to people, we can name them in two ways.

a **First name.**
This is usually friendly and informal.

> *Hello, **Pamela**. How are you?*

b **Title + surname.**

This is more formal or respectful.

> *Good morning, **Mr Williamson**.*

Note that we do not usually use both the first name and the surname of people we are talking to. It would be unusual to say '*Hello, **Peter Matthews**'*, for example.

Note also that we do not normally use *Mr, Mrs, Miss* or *Ms* alone. If you want to speak to a stranger, for example, just say *Excuse me*, not *Excuse me, Mr* or *Excuse me, Mrs* (see 3 below).

3 Titles

Note the pronunciations of the titles:

> *Mr* /'mɪstə(r)/   *Mrs* /'mɪsɪz/   *Miss* /mɪs/   *Ms* /mɪz, məz/

Mr (= *Mister*) is not usually written in full, and the others cannot be.

Ms is used to refer to women who do not wish to have to say whether they are married or not.

Dr (/'dɒktə(r)/) is used as a title for doctors (medical and other).

Professor (abbreviated *Prof*) is used only for certain high-ranking university teachers.

Note that the wives and husbands of doctors and professors do not share their partners' titles. We do not say, for example, *Mrs Dr Smith*.

Sir and *madam* are used mostly by shop assistants. Some employees call their male employer *sir*, and some schoolchildren call their male teachers *sir*. (Female teachers are often called *miss*.)

Dear Sir and *Dear Madam* are ways of beginning letters (see 192). In other situations *sir* and *madam* are unusual.

> *Excuse me. Could you tell me the time?* (NOT ~~Excuse me, sir, ...~~)

212 nationality words

For each country, you need to know four words:

a.   the adjective

> ***American** civilization*   ***French** perfume*   ***Danish** bacon*

b.   the singular noun (used for a person from the country)

> *an **American***   *a **Frenchman***   *a **Dane***

c.   the plural expression *the ...* (used for the nation)

> ***the Americans***   ***the French***   ***the Danes***

d.   the name of the country

> ***America** OR **The United States***   ***France***   ***Denmark***

The name of the language is often the same as the adjective.

> *Do you speak **French**?*   ***Danish** is difficult to pronounce.*

Usually, the singular noun is the same as the adjective (for example *American*, *Greek*), and the plural expression is the same as the adjective + *-s* (*the Greeks*, *the Americans*). There are some exceptions, mostly with adjectives which end in *-sh* or *-ch*.

All nationality words—adjectives and nouns—have capital letters. Here are some examples of nationality words. For others, see a good dictionary.

Group 1 (regular)

Adjective	Person	Nation	Country
American	an American	the Americans	America
Belgian	a Belgian	the Belgians	Belgium
German	a German	the Germans	Germany
Italian	an Italian	the Italians	Italy
Mexican	a Mexican	the Mexicans	Mexico
Moroccan	a Moroccan	the Moroccans	Morocco
Norwegian	a Norwegian	the Norwegians	Norway
Russian	a Russian	the Russians	Russia
Czech	a Czech	the Czechs	Czechoslovakia
Greek	a Greek	the Greeks	Greece
Thai	a Thai	the Thais	Thailand
Chinese	a Chinese	the Chinese	China
Japanese	a Japanese	the Japanese	Japan
Portuguese	a Portuguese	the Portuguese	Portugal
Swiss	a Swiss	the Swiss	Switzerland

(For words ending in *-ese*, and *Swiss*, the plural expression is exactly the same as the adjective—we do not add *-s*.)

Group 2 (exceptions)

Adjective	Person	Nation	Country
British	a Briton / Britisher	the British	Britain
Dutch	a Dutchman / Dutchwoman	the Dutch	Holland / the Netherlands
English	an Englishman / Englishwoman	the English	England
French	a Frenchman / Frenchwoman	the French	France
Irish	an Irishman / Irishwoman	the Irish	Ireland
Spanish	a Spaniard	the Spanish	Spain
Welsh	a Welshman / Welshwoman	the Welsh	Wales

Adjective	Person	Nation	Country
Danish	a Dane	the Danes	Denmark
Finnish	a Finn	the Finns	Finland
Polish	a Pole	the Poles	Poland
Scottish	a Scot	the Scots	Scotland
Swedish	a Swede	the Swedes	Sweden
Turkish	a Turk	the Turks	Turkey

(The Scots prefer the adjective *Scottish*, but other people often use the word *Scotch*. *Scotch* is used for whisky. British people do not usually use the words *Briton* or *Britisher* themselves. *Briton* appears mostly in newspaper headlines—for example TWO BRITONS KILLED IN AIR CRASH. *Britisher* is used mainly by Americans, Australians etc.)

213 need

1 Ordinary verb

Need usually has the forms of an ordinary verb. The third person singular has -*s*; questions and negatives are made with *do*; *need* is followed by an infinitive with *to*.

> *Everybody **needs to** rest sometimes.*
> ***Do we need to** reserve seats on the train?*

2 Modal auxiliary verb

Need can also have the forms of a modal auxiliary verb (third person singular without -*s*; *do* not used; following infinitive without *to*). We do not use these forms so often, except for *needn't*, which is common.

> *We **needn't** reserve seats—there'll be plenty of room on the train.*
> *You **needn't** explain—I quite understand.*

3 needn't + perfect infinitive

If we say that somebody *needn't have done* something, we mean that the person did it, but that it was unnecessary—a waste of time.

> *You **needn't have woken** me up. I don't have to go to work today.*
> *I **needn't have cooked** so much food. Nobody was hungry.*

Compare:

> *I **needn't have watered** the flowers. Just after I finished it started raining.*
> *It started raining, so I **didn't need to** water the flowers.*
> (*I didn't water them.*)

▷ For the difference between *needn't* and *mustn't*, see 209.

214 negative questions

1 Structure

> | auxiliary verb + *n't* + subject ... |

> **Doesn't she** *understand?*
> **Haven't you** *booked your holiday yet?*

> | auxiliary verb + subject + *not* ... |

> **Does she not** *understand?*
> **Have you not** *booked your holiday yet?*

The forms with *not* are formal.

2 Meaning

When we ask a negative question, we often expect the answer *yes*.

> **Didn't you go** *and see Helen yesterday? How is she?*

Negative questions are common in exclamations and invitations.

> **Isn't it** *a lovely day!*
> **Won't you** *come in for a minute?*

We can use negative questions to show that we are surprised that
something has not happened, or is not happening.

> **Hasn't the postman come** *yet?*
> **Aren't you** *supposed to be working?*

3 Polite requests

We do not usually use negative questions to ask people to do things for
us. Compare:

> **Can you** *help me?* (ordinary question: used for a request)
> **You can't** *help me,* **can you?** (negative statement + question tag:
> common in spoken requests)
> **Can't you** *help me?* (negative question: has a critical meaning—like
> *Why can't you help me?*)

See 286 for more information about polite requests.

4 *yes* and *no*

We answer negative questions like this.

> '**Haven't you** *written to Mary?*'
> '**Yes.**' (= *I have written to her.*)
> '**No.**' (= *I haven't written to her.*)

> '**Didn't** *the postman come?*'
> '**Yes.**' (= *He came.*) '**No.**' (= *He didn't come.*)

215 negative structures

1 Negative verbs

We make negative verbs with auxiliary verb + *not*.

> *We **have not** forgotten you.*
> *It **was not** raining.*

In an informal style, we use contracted negatives with *n't* (see 90).

> *We **haven't** forgotten you.*
> *It **wasn't** raining.*

If there is no auxiliary verb, we use *do* with *not*.

> *I like the salad, but I **don't** like the soup.*

2 Imperatives

We make negative imperatives with *do not* or *don't* + infinitive (see 170).

> ***Don't worry**—I'll look after you.* (NOT ~~Worry not~~ ...)
> ***Don't believe** a word he says.*
> ***Don't be** rude.* (See 57.)

3 Infinitives and *-ing* forms

We put *not* before infinitives and *-ing* forms. *Do* is not used.

> *It's important **not to worry**.* (NOT ... ~~to don't worry.~~)
> *The best thing on holiday is **not working**.*

4 Other parts of a sentence

We can put *not* with other parts of a sentence, not only a verb.

> *Ask the vicar, **not his wife**.*
> *Come early, but **not before six**.*
> *It's working, but **not properly**.*

We do not usually put *not* with the subject. Instead, we use a structure with *it* (see 111).

> ***It was not George** that came, but his brother.*
> (NOT ~~**Not George** came, but his brother.~~)

For the difference between *not* and *no* with nouns, see 222.

5 Other negative words

Other words besides *not* can give a clause a negative meaning. Compare:

> *He's **not** at home.*
> *He's **never** at home.*
> *He's **seldom / rarely / hardly ever** at home.*

We do not use the auxiliary *do* with these other words.
Compare:

> He **doesn't work**.
> He never **works**.
> (NOT *He does never work.*)
> He seldom/rarely/hardly ever **works**.

6 *some* and *any*, etc

We do not usually use *some*, *somebody*, *someone*, *something* or
somewhere in questions and negative sentences. Instead, we use *any*,
anybody etc. (See 314.)
Compare:

> I've found **some** mushrooms.
> I **haven't** found **any** mushrooms.

7 *think, believe, suppose, imagine* and *hope*

When we introduce negative ideas with *think, believe, suppose* and
imagine, we usually make the first verb (*think* etc) negative, not the
second.

> I **don't think** you've met my wife.
> (NOT *I think you haven't met my wife.*)
> I **don't believe** she's at home.

Hope is an exception (see 162).

> I **hope** it **doesn't** rain.
> (NOT *I don't hope it rains.*)

Short answers are possible with *not* after the verb.

> 'Will it rain?' '**I hope not**.'

With *believe, imagine* and *think*, we prefer the structure with *not . . . so*
(see 311).

> 'Will it rain?' '**I don't think so**.'

▷ For negative questions, see 214.

216 neither (of): determiner

1 We use *neither* before a singular noun to mean 'not one and not the
other'.

> | *neither* + singular noun |

> '*Can you come on Monday or Tuesday?*' '*I'm afraid* **neither day** *is
> possible.*'

2 We use *neither of* before another determiner (for example *the*, *my*, *these*), and before a pronoun. The noun or pronoun is plural.

> *neither of* + determiner + plural noun
> *neither of* + pronoun

> **Neither of my brothers** can sing.
> **Neither of us** saw it happen.

After *neither of* + noun/pronoun, we use a singular verb in a formal style.

> *Neither of my sisters **is** married.*

In an informal style, a plural verb is possible.

> *Neither of my sisters **are** married.*

217 neither, nor and not ... either

1 We use *neither* and *nor* to mean 'also not'. They mean the same.
Neither and *nor* come at the beginning of a clause, and are followed by auxiliary verb + subject.

> *neither/nor* + auxiliary verb + subject

> *'I can't swim.' '**Neither** can I.'* (NOT ~~I also can't.~~)
> *'I don't like opera.' '**Nor** do I.'* (NOT ~~I don't too.~~)

2 We can use *not ... either* with the same meaning.

> *'I can't swim.' 'I **can't either**.'*
> *'I don't like opera.' 'I **don't either**.'*

▷ For other uses of *either*, see 106; 107.
   For *so am I, so do I* etc, see 312.

218 neither ... nor ...

We use this structure to join two negative ideas. (It is the opposite of *both ... and ...*)

> **Neither** James **nor** Virginia was at home.
> *I **neither** smoke **nor** drink.*
> *The film was **neither** well made **nor** well acted.*

In an informal style, we can use a plural verb after two subjects joined by *neither ... nor ...*

> *Neither James nor Virginia **were** at home.*

219 next and nearest

1 *Nearest* is used for place—it means 'most near in space'.

> *Excuse me. Where's the **nearest** tube station?*
> (NOT ... *the **next** tube station?*)
> *If you want to find Alan, just look in the **nearest** pub.*

Next is usually used for time—it means 'nearest in the future'.

> *We get off at the **next** station.* (= *the station that we will reach first*)
> *I'm looking forward to her **next** visit.*

2 We use *next* in a few expressions to mean 'nearest in space'.
The most common are *next door* and *next to*.

> *My girl-friend lives **next door**.*
> *Come and sit **next to** me.*

220 next and the next

Next week, next month etc is the week or month just after this one. If I am speaking in July, *next month* is August; if I am speaking in 1995, *next year* is 1996. (Note that prepositions are not used before these time-expressions.)

> *Goodbye! See you **next week**!*
> *I'm spending **next Christmas** with my family.*
> *Next year will be difficult.* (= *the year starting next January*)

The next week, the next month etc can mean the period of seven days, thirty days etc starting at the moment of speaking. On July 15th, 1995, *the next month* is the period from July 15th to August 15th; *the next year* is the period from July 1995 to July 1996.

> *I'm going to be very busy for **the next week**.* (= the seven days starting today)
> ***The next year** will be difficult.* (= the twelve months starting now)

▷ For the difference between *last* and *the last*, see 190.

221 no and none

1 We use *no* (= 'not a', 'not any') immediately before a noun.

> no + noun

> ***No aeroplane** is 100% safe.*
> *There's **no time** to talk about it now.*

Before another determiner (for example *the*, *my*, *this*), we use *none of*. We also use *none of* before a pronoun.

> *none of* + determiner + noun
> *none of* + pronoun

> ***None of the** keys would open the door.*
> ***None of my** brothers remembered my birthday.*
> ***None of us** speaks French.*

When we use *none of* with a plural noun, the verb can be singular (more formal) or plural (more informal).

> *None of my **friends is/are** interested.*

2 We can use *none* alone, without a noun.

> 'How many of the books have you read?' '**None**.'

3 When we are talking about two people or things, we use *neither*, not *none* (see 216).

> **Neither of** my parents could be there.
> (NOT ~~None of~~ ...)

▷ For *no* and *not a/not any*, see 223.

222 no and not

If we want to make a word, expression or clause negative, we use *not*.

> **Not surprisingly**, we missed the train.
> (NOT ~~No surprisingly,~~ ...)
> The students went on strike, but **not the teachers**.
> (NOT ... ~~but no the teachers.~~)
> I can see you tomorrow, but **not on Thursday**.
> I **have not** received his answer.

We can use *no* with a noun to mean 'not a' or 'not any' (see 223).

> **No teachers** went on strike. (= There were **not any** teachers on strike.)
> I've got **no Thursdays** free this term. (= ... **not any** Thursdays ...)
> I telephoned, but there was **no answer**. (= ... **not an** answer.)

Sometimes *verb + not* and *no + noun* can give a similar meaning.

> There **wasn't an answer**./There **was no answer**.

We can use *no* with an *-ing* form.

> *NO SMOKING*

223 no and not a/not any

1 *No* is a determiner (see 96). We use *no* before singular (countable and uncountable) nouns and plural nouns.
No means the same as *not a* or *not any*, but we use *no*:
(a) at the beginning of a sentence
(b) when we want to make the negative idea emphatic.

a **No cigarette** is completely harmless.
  (NOT ~~Not any cigarette~~ ...)
  No beer? How do you expect me to sing without beer?
  No tourists ever come to our village.

b I can't get there. There's **no bus**.
  (More emphatic than *There isn't a bus*.)
  Sorry I can't stop. I've got **no time**.
  There were **no letters** for you this morning, I'm afraid.

2   *Nobody, nothing, no-one* and *nowhere* are used in similar ways to *no*. Compare:

> **Nobody** came. (NOT ~~*Not anybody came.*~~)
> *I saw **nobody**.* (More emphatic than *I didn't see **anybody**.*)

3   We only use *no* immediately before a noun. In other cases we use *none (of)*. See 221.

224 no more, not any more, no longer, not any longer

We use *no more* to talk about quantity or degree—to say 'how much'.

> *There's **no more** bread.*   *She's **no more** a great singer that I am.*

We do not use *no more* to talk about time. Instead, we use *no longer* (usually before the verb), *not ... any longer*, or *not ... any more*.

> *I **no longer** support the Conservative Party.* (NOT ~~*I no more ...*~~)
> *This **can't** go on **any longer**.*   *Annie **doesn't** live here **any more**.*

(*Not ... any more* is informal.)

225 non-progressive verbs

1   Some verbs are never used in progressive forms.

> *I **like** this music.* (NOT ~~*I'm liking this music.*~~).

Other verbs are not used in progressive forms when they have certain meanings. Compare:

> *I **see** what you mean.* (NOT ~~*I'm seeing what you mean.*~~)
> *I'm **seeing** the doctor at ten o'clock.*

Many of these 'non-progressive' verbs refer to mental activities (for example *know, think, believe*). Some others refer to the senses (for example *smell, taste*).

2   The most important 'non-progressive' verbs are:

> *like   dislike   love   hate   prefer   want   wish*
> *surprise   impress   please*
> *believe   feel (see 128)   imagine   know   mean   realize*
> *recognize   remember   suppose   think (see 346)   understand*
> *hear   see (see 290)   smell (see 310)   sound (see 318)*
> *taste (see 340)*
> *weigh (= 'have weight')   belong to   contain   depend on*
> *include   matter   need   owe   own   possess*
> *appear   seem   be (see 59)*

3   We often use *can* with *see, hear, feel, taste* and *smell* to give a 'progressive' meaning. See 81.

226 noun + noun

1 Structure

It is very common in English to put two nouns together without a preposition.

tennis shoes   *a sheepdog*   *the car door*   *orange juice*

The first noun is like an adjective in some ways. Compare:

a race horse   (= a sort of horse)
a horse-race   (= a sort of race)

a flower garden   (= a sort of garden)
a garden flower   (= a sort of flower)

milk chocolate   (= something to eat)
chocolate milk   (= something to drink)

The first noun is usually singular in form, even if the meaning is plural.

*a **shoe**-shop*   (NOT *a **shoes** shop*)
*a **bus**-stop*   (NOT *a **buses** stop*)

Some common short | noun + noun | expressions are written as one word (for example *sheepdog*). Others are written with a hyphen (for example *horse-race*) or separately (for example *milk chocolate*). There are no very clear rules, and we can often write an expression in more than one way. To find out what is correct in a particular case, look in a good dictionary.

2 Meaning

The first noun can modify the second in many different ways.
It can say what the second is made of or from:

***milk** chocolate*   *a **glass** bowl*

or where it is:

*a **table** lamp*   ***Oxford** University*

or when it happens:

*a **day**dream*   ***afternoon** tea*

or what it is for:

***car** keys*   *a **conference** room*

3 Noun + noun + noun + noun ...

We can put three, four or more nouns in a group.

road accident researcch centre (= a centre for research into accidents on roads)

Newspaper headlines often have this structure.

HELICOPTER CRASH PILOT DEATH FEAR

4 Other structures

It is not always easy to know whether to use the noun + noun structure
(for example *the chair back*), the *of*-structure (for example *the back of his
head*) or the possessive structure (for example *John's back*). The rules are
very complicated; experience will tell you which is the correct structure in
a particular case.

227 numbers

1 Fractions

We say fractions like this:

$\frac{1}{8}$ *one eighth* $\frac{3}{7}$ *three sevenths*

$\frac{2}{5}$ *two fifths* $\frac{11}{16}$ *eleven sixteenths*

We normally use a singular verb after fractions below 1.

*Three quarters of a ton **is** too much.*

We use a plural noun with fractions and decimals over 1.

*one and a half **hours*** (NOT ~~one and a half hour~~)
*1·3 **millimetres*** (NOT ~~1·3 millimetre~~)

2 Decimals

We say decimal fractions like this:

0·125   nought point one two five
(NOT ~~0,125   nought comma one two five~~)
3·7   three point seven

3 *nought, zero, nil* etc

The figure 0 is usually called *nought* in British English, and *zero* in
American English.
When we say numbers one figure at a time, 0 is often called *oh* (like the
letter 0).

*My account number is four one three **oh** six.*

In measurements of temperature, 0 is called *zero*.

***Zero** degrees Centigrade is thirty-two degrees Fahrenheit.*

Zero scores in team games are called *nil* (American *zero*).
Zero in tennis and similar games is called *love*.

4 Telephone numbers

We say each figure separately. When the same figure comes twice, we
usually say *double* (British English only).

307 4922   three oh seven four nine double two

5 Kings and Queens

We say the numbers like this:

Henry VIII   *Henry **the Eighth*** (NOT ~~*Henry Eight*~~)
Louis XIV   *Louis **the Fourteenth***

6 Floors

The ground floor of a British house is the first floor of an American house; the British first floor is the American second floor, etc.

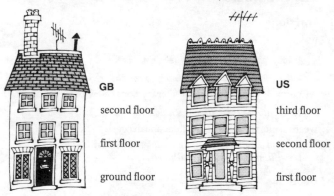

GB	US
second floor	third floor
first floor	second floor
ground floor	first floor

7 and

In British English, we use *and* between the hundreds and the tens in a number.

310   *three hundred **and** ten* (US *three hundred ten*)
5,642   *five thousand, six hundred **and** forty-two*

Note that in writing we use commas (,) to separate thousands.

8 a and one

We can say *a hundred* or *one hundred*, *a thousand* or *one thousand*. *One* is more formal.

*I want to live for **a** hundred years.*
(NOT ... *for hundred years.*)
*Pay Mr J Baron **one** thousand pounds.* (on a cheque)

We only use *a* at the beginning of a number. Compare:

***a** hundred*   *three thousand **one** hundred*

We can use *a* with other measurement words.

***a** pint*   ***a** foot*   ***a** mile*

9 Plurals without -s

After a number or determiner, *hundred*, *thousand*, *million* and *dozen* have no final -s. Compare:

> *five **hundred** pounds*
> ***hundreds** of pounds*
>
> *several **thousand** times*
> *It cost **thousands**.*

Other number expressions have no -s when they are used as adjectives.

> *a five-**pound** note*   *a three-**mile** walk*

10 Measurements

We use *be* in measurements.

> *She's five feet eight (inches tall).*
> *I'm sixty-eight kilos.*
> *What shoe size **are** you?*

In an informal style, we often use *foot* instead of *feet* when we talk about people's heights.

> *My father's six **foot** two.*

11 Money

> *1p*   *one penny* (informal: *one p* /piː/) or *a penny*
> *5p*   *five pence* (informal: *five p*)
> *£3.75*   *three pounds seventy-five*

When we use sums of money as adjectives, we use singular forms.

> *a five-**pound** note* (NOT *a five-**pounds** note*)

12 Adjectives

When expressions of measurement, amount and quantity are used as adjectives, they are normally singular.

> *a ten-**mile** walk* (NOT *a ten-**miles** walk*)
> *six two-**hour** lessons*
> *a three-**month**-old baby*

We can use possessives in expressions of time.

> *a **week's** holiday*   *four **days'** journey*

13 *there are ...*

When we count the number of people in a group, we often use the structure *there are* + number + *of* + pronoun.

> ***There are** only **seven of us** here today.*
> ***There were twelve of us** in my family.*
> (NOT *We were twelve ...*)

14 Spoken calculations

Common ways of calculating are:

$2 + 2 = 4$	*two and two is/are four* (informal)
	two plus two equals four (formal)
$7 - 4 = 3$	*four from seven is three* (informal)
	seven minus four equals three (formal)
$3 \times 4 = 12$	*three fours are twelve* (informal)
	three multiplied by four equals twelve (formal)
$9 \div 3 = 3$	*nine divided by three equals three*

▷ For ways of saying and writing dates, see 95.

228 once

When *once* has the indefinite meaning 'at some time', we use it to talk about the past, but not the future. Compare:

*I met her **once** in Venezuela.*
***Once** upon a time there were three baby rabbits . . .*
*Come up and see me **some time**. (NOT . . . once.)*
*We must have a drink together **one day**. (NOT . . . once.)*

229 one and you: indefinite personal pronouns

1 We can use *one* or *you* to talk about people in general.

***You** can't learn a language in six weeks.*
***One** can't learn a language in six weeks.*

One is more formal.

2 *One* and *you* mean 'anybody (including the speaker)'. They are only used to talk about people in general. We do not say *you* or *one* when we are talking about one person, or a group which could not include the speaker. Compare:

***One** usually knocks at a door before going into somebody's house.*
***Somebody's** knocking at the door. (NOT **One is knocking** . . .)*

***One** can usually find people who speak English in Sweden.*
*English **is spoken** in this shop. (NOT **One speaks English**. The meaning is not 'people in general'.)*

***One** has to believe in something.*
*In the sixteenth century **people** believed in witches.*
*(NOT . . . **one believed** . . . The group could not include the speaker.)*

3 *One* can be a subject or object; there is a possessive *one's*, and a reflexive pronoun *oneself*.

*He talks to **one** like a teacher.*   ***One's** family can be very difficult.*
*One should always give **oneself** plenty of time to pack.*

230 one: substitute word

1 We often use *one* instead of repeating a noun.

> *I'm looking for a flat. I'd like **one** with a garden.*
> (= ... *a flat with a garden.*)
> *'Can you lend me a pen?' 'Sorry, I haven't got **one**.'*
> *'Which is your child?' 'The **one** in the blue coat.'*

2 We only use *a/an* before *one* if there is an adjective. Compare:

> *I'd like **a big one** with cream on.*
> *I'd like **one** with cream on.* (NOT ... ~~a one~~ ...)

3 There is a plural *ones*, used after *the* or an adjective.

> *'Which shoes do you want?' 'The **ones** at the front of the window.'*
> *How much are the red **ones**?*

Compare:

> *I've got five green **ones**.*
> *I've got five.* (NOT ... ~~five ones~~.)

4 We only use *one* for countable nouns. Compare:

> *If you haven't got a fresh chicken, I'll take a frozen **one**.*
> *If you haven't got fresh milk, I'll take tinned.* (NOT ... ~~tinned one~~.)

231 other and others

When *other* is an adjective, it has no plural.

> *Where are the **other** photos?* (NOT ... ~~the others photos?~~)
> *Have you got any **other** colours?*

When *other* is used alone, without a noun, it can have a plural.

> *Some grammars are easier to understand than **others**.*
> *I'll be late. Can you tell the **others**?*

▷ For *another*, see 33.

232 ought

1 Forms

Ought is a 'modal auxiliary verb' (see 202). The third person singular has no *-s*.

> *She **ought** to understand.*

We usually make questions and negatives without *do*.

> ***Ought** we to go now?* (NOT ~~Do we ought~~ ... ?)
> *It **oughtn't** to rain today.*

After **ought**, we use the infinitive with *to*. (This makes *ought* different from other modal auxiliary verbs.)

> *You **ought to see** a dentist.*

2 Obligation

We can use *ought* to advise people (including ourselves) to do things; to tell people that they have a duty to do things; to ask about our duty. The meaning is similar to the meaning of *should* (see 294); not so strong as *must* (see 208).

> *What time **ought** I to arrive?*
> *I really **ought** to phone Mother.*
> *People **ought** not to drive like that.*

3 Deduction

We can use *ought* to say that something is probable (because it is logical or normal).

> *Henry **ought** to be here soon—he left home at six.*
> *'We're spending the winter in Miami.' 'That **ought** to be nice.'*

4 *ought to have ...*

We can use *ought* + perfect infinitive to talk about the past. This structure is used to talk about things which did not happen, or which may or may not have happened (see 202.3).

> | *ought to* + *have* + past participle |

> *I **ought to have phoned** Ed this morning, but I forgot.*
> *Ten o'clock: she **ought to have arrived** at her office by now.*

▷ For the differences between *ought*, *should* and *must*, see 295.

233 own

1 We only use *own* after a possessive word.

> *It's nice if a child can have **his own** room.*
> (NOT ... ~~an own room.~~)
> *I'm **my own** boss.*

2 Note the structure *a ... of one's own*.

> *It's nice if a child can have **a room of his own**.*
> *I'd like to have **a car of my own**.*

3 We can use *own* without a following noun.

> *'Would you like one of my cigarettes?' 'No thanks. I prefer **my own**.'*

234 participles: 'present' and 'past' participles (-**ing** and -**ed**)

1 'Present' participles:

>   *breaking   going   drinking   making   beginning*
>   *opening   working   stopping*

For rules of spelling, see 321; 322.
When -*ing* forms are used like nouns, they are often called *gerunds*. For
details, see 180.1.

2 'Past' participles:

>   *broken   gone   drunk   made   begun   opened*
>   *worked   stopped*

3 The names 'present' and 'past' participle are not very good (although they
are used in most grammars). Both kinds of participle can be used to talk
about the past, present or future.

>   *She was **crying** when I saw her.* (past)
>   *Who's the man **talking** to Elizabeth?* (present)
>   *This time tomorrow I'll be **lying** on the beach.* (future)
>
>   *He was **arrested** in 1972.* (past)
>   *You're **fired**.* (present)
>   *The new school is going to be **opened** next week.* (future)

4 We use participles with auxiliary verbs to make some tenses.

>   *What are you **doing**?*
>   *I've **broken** my watch.*

▷   For other ways of using participles, see the next two sections.

235 participles used as adjectives

1 We can often use participles as adjectives.

>   *It was a very **tiring** meeting.*
>   *There are **broken** toys all over the floor.*
>   *I thought the film was pretty **boring**.*
>   *You look terribly **frightened**.*

2 Don't confuse pairs of words like *tiring* and *tired*, *interesting* and
interested, *boring* and *bored*, *exciting* and *excited*.
The present participle (. . . -*ing*) has an active meaning: if something is
interesting it ***interests*** you.
The past participle (. . . -*ed*) has a passive meaning: an ***interested*** person ***is
interested by*** (or ***in***) something.

Compare:

> *I thought the lesson was **interesting**.*
> *I was **interested** in the lesson.*
> (NOT ~~I was **interesting** in the lesson.~~)

> *Sheila's party was pretty **boring**.*
> *I went home early because I felt **bored**.*
> (NOT ... ~~because I felt **boring**.~~)

> *It was an **exciting** story.*
> *When I read it I felt **excited**.*

> *The explanation was **confusing**. I got **confused**.*
> *It was a **tiring** day. It made me **tired**.*

3 There are a few exceptional past participles which can have active
meanings. The most important:

> ***fallen** rocks*   *a **retired** army officer*
> *a **grown-up** daughter*   *an **escaped** prisoner*

236 participle clauses

1 We can use a participle rather like a conjunction, to introduce a
'participle clause'.

> *Who's the fat man **sitting in the corner**?*
> *Do you know the number of people **employed by the government**?*
> ***Jumping into a small red sports car**, she drove off.*

2 Participle clauses can have different uses. Some of them are 'adjectival':
they modify nouns, rather like adjectives or relative clauses (see 280).
Compare:

> *What's the name of the **noisy** child?* (adjective)
> *What the name of the child **making the noise**?* (participle clause)
> *What's the name of the child **who is making the noise**?* (relative
> clause)

Other participle clauses are 'adverbial'. They may express ideas of time,
cause, consequence or condition, for example.

> ***Putting down my newspaper**, I walked over to the window.*
> (time: one thing happened before another)
> *I sat **reading some old letters**.*
> (time: two things happened at the same time)
> ***Not knowing what to do**, I telephoned the police.*
> (reason: *Because I did not know ...*)
> *It rained all the time, **completely ruining our holiday**.*
> (consequence: *... so that it ruined our holiday.*)
> ***Driven carefully**, the car will do fifteen kilometres to the litre of
> petrol.*
> (condition: *If it is driven carefully ...*)

3 The subject of a participle clause is usually the same as the object of the rest of the sentence.

> ***Hoping** to surprise her, **I** opened the door very quietly.*
> (***I** hoped to surprise her; **I** opened the door.*)
> ***Wanting** some excitement, **Mary** became a pilot.*
> (***Mary** wanted excitement; **Mary** became a pilot.*)

We do not usually make sentences where the subjects are different. For example, we would probably not say:

> ***Looking** out of the window, the mountains were beautiful.*
> (This sounds as if the mountains were looking out of the window.)

4 Sometimes a participle clause has its own subject.

> *A little girl walked past, **her hair blowing** in the wind.*

We often use *with* to introduce clauses like this.

> *A car drove past **with smoke pouring** out of the back.*
> ***With all the family travelling** in America, the house seems very empty.*

5 We can use conjunctions and prepositions to introduce participle clauses.

> ***After talking** to you I always feel better.*
> ***Before driving** off, always check your mirror.*
> ***When telephoning** London from abroad, dial 1 before the number.*
> ***On being introduced** to somebody, a British person may shake hands.*
> *I got there **by taking** a new route through Worcester.*

▷ For *-ing* clauses after | *see, hear* + object | (for example *I saw her crossing the road*), see 182.6.

237 passive structures: introduction

> *They **built** | *this house* | in 1486.* (active)
> | *This house* | ***was built** in 1486.* (passive)

> *Channel Islanders **speak** | *French* | and English.* (active)
> | *French* | ***is spoken** in France, Belgium, Switzerland, the Channel Islands, ...* (passive)

> *A friend of ours **is repairing** | *the roof* | .* (active)
> | *The roof* | ***is being repaired** by a friend of ours.* (passive)

> *This book **will change** | *your life* | .* (active)
> | *Your life* | ***will be changed** by this book.* (passive)

When we say what people or things *do*, we use active verbs. (For example *built, speak, is repairing, will change*.)

When we say what *happens* to people or things—what *is done* to them—we use passive verbs. (For example *was built, is spoken, is being repaired, will be changed*.)

The object of an active verb corresponds to the subject of a passive verb.

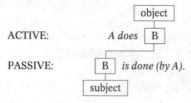

ACTIVE: *A does* [B] ← object

PASSIVE: [B] *is done (by A).* → subject

2 Active or passive?

We often prefer to begin a sentence with something that is already known, and to put the 'news' at the end. Compare.

Your little boy broke my kitchen window this morning.

That window was broken by your little boy.

In the first sentence, the hearer does not know about the broken window. So the speaker starts with the little boy, and puts the 'news'—the window—at the end. In the second sentence, the hearer knows about the window, but does not know who broke it. By using a passive structure, we can again put the 'news' at the end.
Another example:

'John's writing a play.' 'I didn't know that.'
'This play was written by Marlowe.' 'Was it? I didn't know that.'

3 To make passive verb forms, we use the auxiliary *be*.
  For details, see next section.

▷ For information about the use of *get* as a passive auxiliary, see 143.3.
  For verbs with two objects (for example *give*) in passive structures, see 356.4.
  For prepositions at the end of passive clauses (for example *He's been
  written to*), see 257.1c.

238 passive verb forms

We make passive verb forms with the different tenses of *be*, followed by
the past participle (= pp).

TENSE	STRUCTURE	EXAMPLE
simple present	*am / are / is* + pp	English **is spoken** here.
present progressive	*am / are / is being* + pp	Excuse the mess: the house **is being painted**.
simple past	*was / were* + pp	I **wasn't invited**, but I went anyway.
past progressive	*was / were being* + pp	I felt as if I **was being watched**.
present perfect	*have / has been* + pp	**Has** Mary **been told**?
past perfect	*had been* + pp	I knew why I **had been chosen**.
future	*will be* + pp	You**'ll be told** when the time comes.
future perfect	*will have been* + pp	Everything **will have been done** by Tuesday.
'going to'	*going to be* + pp	Who's **going to be invited**?

Future progressive passives and perfect progressive passives (*will be
being* + pp and *has been being* + pp) are very unusual. Passive tenses follow
the same rules as active tenses. Look in the index to see where to find
information about the use of the present progressive, present perfect, etc.

239 past tense with present or future meaning

A past tense does not always have a past meaning. In some kinds of
sentence we use verbs like *I had, you went* or *I was wondering* to talk
about the present or future.

1 After *if* (see 165).

> *If I **had** the money now I'd buy a car.*
> *If you **caught** the ten o'clock train tomorrow you could be in Edinburgh by supper-time.*

2 After *it's time* (see 189), *would rather* (see 370) and *I wish* (see 367).

> *Ten o'clock—**it's time** you **went** home.*
> *Don't come and see me today—**I'd rather** you **came** tomorrow.*
> *I **wish** I **had** a better memory.*

3 We can express politeness or respect, when we ask for something, by beginning *I wondered, I thought, I hoped, I was wondering, I was thinking* or *I was hoping.*

> *I **wondered** if you were free this evening.*
> *I **thought** you might like some flowers.*
> *I **was hoping** we could have dinner together.*

4 If we are talking about the past, we usually use past tenses even for things which are still true, and situations which still exist.

> *Are you deaf? I asked how old you **were**.*
> *I'm sorry we left Liverpool. It **was** such a nice place.*
> *Do you remember that nice couple we met on holiday? They **were** German, **weren't** they?*

240 past time: the past and perfect tenses (introduction)

We can use six different tenses to talk about the past:
☐ the simple past (*I worked*)
☐ the past progressive (*I was working*)
☐ the present perfect simple (*I have worked*)
☐ the present perfect progressive (*I have been working*)
☐ the past perfect simple (*I had worked*)
☐ the past perfect progressive (*I had been working*)

The two past tenses (simple past and past progressive) are used to talk about past actions and events.

> *I **worked** all day yesterday.*
> *The boss came in while I **was working**.*

The two present perfect tenses are used to show that a past action or event has some connection with the present.

> *I've **worked** with children before, so I know what to expect in my new job.*
> *I've **been working** all day—I've only just finished.*

The past perfect tenses are used for a 'before past'—for things that had already happened before the past time that we are talking about.

> *I looked carefully, and realized that **I had seen** her somewhere before.*
> *I was tired, because **I had been working** all day.*

241 past time: simple past

1 Forms

Affirmative	Question	Negative
I worked	did I work?	I did not work
you worked	did you work?	you did not work
he/she/it worked, etc	did he/she/it work? etc	he/she/it did not work, etc

2 Meanings

We use the simple past tense to talk about many kinds of past events: short, quickly finished actions and happenings, longer situations, and repeated events.

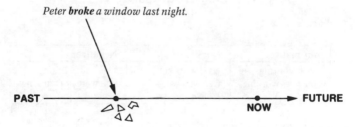

*Peter **broke** a window last night.*

PAST   NOW   FUTURE

*I **spent** all my childhood in Scotland.*

PAST   SCOTLAND   NOW   FUTURE

*Regularly every summer, Janet **fell** in love.*

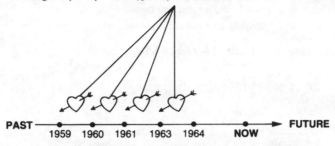

We use the simple past in 'narrative'—when we tell stories, and when we tell people about past events.

> *Once upon a time there **was** a beautiful princess who **lived** with her father. One day the king **decided** ...*
> *I **saw** John this morning. He **told** me ...*
> (NOT ~~I **have seen** John this morning. He **has told** me~~ ...)

A simple rule: use the simple past tense if you do not have a good reason for using one of the other past or perfect tenses.

242 past time: past progressive

1 Forms

Affirmative	Question	Negative

I was working
you were working,
    etc
	was I working?
	were you working?
	    etc
		I was not working
		you were not working,
		    etc

2 Meaning

We use the past progressive to say that something was going on around a particular past time.

*What **were you doing** at eight o'clock yesterday evening?*

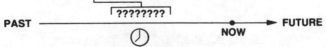

We often use the past progressive together with a simple past tense.
The past progressive refers to a longer 'background' action or situation;
the simple past refers to a shorter action or situation that happened in the middle, or interrupted it.

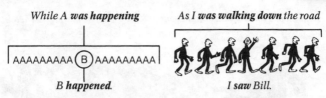

*While A **was happening***

*As I **was walking down** the road*

AAAAAAAAA ⓑ AAAAAAAAA

*B **happened**.*

*I **saw** Bill.*

*The phone **rang** while I **was having** dinner.*

Some verbs are not used in progressive tenses. (See 225.)

> *I tried a bit of the cake to see how it **tasted**.*
> (NOT ... ~~how it was tasting~~.)

▷ For *I **was wondering** if you could help me*, and similar structures, see 239.3.

243 past time: present perfect simple

1 Forms

Affirmative	Question	Negative
I have worked you have worked, etc	have I worked? have you worked? etc	I have not worked you have not worked, etc

2 Meaning

We use the present perfect simple to say that something in the past is connected with the present in some way.

If we say that something *has happened*, we are thinking about the past and the present at the same time.

We could often change a present perfect sentence into a present sentence with the same meaning.

> *I've **broken** my leg. = My leg **is** broken now.*
> ***Have** you **read** the Bible? = **Do** you **know** the Bible?*

We do not use the present perfect simple if we are not thinking about the present.

> *I **saw** Lucy yesterday.*
> (NOT ~~I have seen Lucy yesterday.~~)

3 Finished actions: result now

We often use the present perfect to talk about finished actions, when we are thinking of their present consequences: the results that they have now.

*Somebody **has shot** the manager.*   *The manager is dead.*

| FINISHED ACTION | ──────────────► | RESULT NOW |

Other examples:

> ***Have** you **read** the Bible?* ──────► ***Do** you **know** the Bible?*
> *Mary **has had** a baby.* ──────► *Baby.*
> *I've **broken** my leg.* ──────► *I can't walk.*
> *Utopia **has invaded** Fantasia.* ──────► *War.*

| FINISHED ACTION | ──────────────► | RESULT NOW |

We often use the present perfect to give news.

> *And here are the main points of the news again. The pound **has fallen** against the dollar. The Prime Minister **has said** that the government's economic policies are working. The number of unemployed **has reached** five million. There **has been** a fire...*

4 Finished actions: time up to now

We often use the present perfect to ask if something has *ever* happened; to say that it has happened *before*; or that it has *never* happened; or *not since* a certain date; or *not for* a certain period; to ask if it has happened *yet*; or to say that it has happened *already*.

> ***Have** you **ever seen** a ghost?*

> *I'm sure **we've met before**.*   *We **haven't had** a holiday **for** ages.*
> *I **haven't seen** Peter **since** Christmas.*
> *'**Has** Ann **come yet**?' 'Yes, she **has already arrived**.'*

5 Repeated actions up to now

We use the present perfect to say that something has happened several times up to the present.

*I've **written** six letters since lunchtime.*

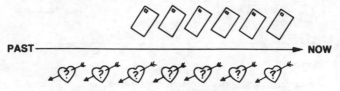

*How often **have you been** in love in your life?*

6 Actions and states continuing up to now

We use the present perfect to talk about actions, states and situations which started in the past and still continue.

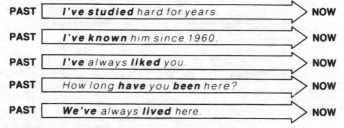

We also use the present perfect progressive in this way.
For the difference, see 244.4.
Do not use the simple present to say how long something has gone on.

*I've **known** him since 1960.* (NOT ~~I know him~~ ...)

7 Present perfect not used

We do not use the present perfect with adverbs of finished time (like *yesterday, last week, then, three years ago, in 1960*).

*I **saw** Lucy **yesterday**.* (NOT ~~I have seen Lucy yesterday.~~)
*Tom **was** ill **last week**.* (NOT ~~Tom has been ill last week.~~)
*What **did** you **do then**?* (NOT ~~What have you done then?~~)
*She **died three years ago**.* (NOT ~~She has died three years ago.~~)
*He **was born in 1960**.* (NOT ~~He has been born in 1960.~~)

We do not use the present perfect in 'narrative'—when we tell stories, or give details of past events. (See 241.)

▷ For the structure *This is the first time I have* ..., see 246.

244 past time: present perfect progressive

1 Forms

Affirmative	Question	Negative
I have been working you have been working, etc	have I been working? have you been working? etc	I have not been working, etc

2 Meaning

We use the present perfect progressive to talk about actions, states and situations which started in the past and still continue, or which have just stopped.

Have you been waiting long?

3 *since* and *for*

We often use the present perfect progressive with *since* or *for*, to say how long something has been going on.

> *It's been raining* non-stop *since* Monday.
> *It's been raining* non-stop *for* three days.

> *We've been living* here *since* July.
> *We've been living* here *for* two months.

We use *since* when we mention the *beginning* of the period (for example *Monday, July*).
We use *for* when we mention the *length* of the period (for example *three days; two months*).
For the differences between *since, for, from* and *ago*, see 133.

4 Present perfect simple and progressive

We can use both the present perfect simple and the present perfect progressive to talk about actions and situations which started in the past and which still continue.
We prefer the present perfect progressive for more temporary actions and situations; when we talk about more permanent (long-lasting) situations, we prefer the present perfect simple. Compare:

> *That man's **been standing** on the corner all day.*
> *For 900 years, the castle **has stood** on the hill above the village.*

> *I **haven't been working** very well recently.*
> *He **hasn't worked** for years.*

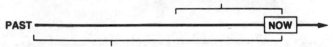

> *I've been living in Sally's flat for the last month.*

> *My parents **have lived** in Bristol all their lives.*

Some verbs are not used in progressive forms (see 225).

> *I've only known* her for two days.
> (NOT ~~I've only been knowing her~~ ...)
> *I've had* a cold since Monday. (NOT ~~I've been having~~ ...)

5 Present perfect progressive and present

To say how long something has been going on, we can use the present perfect progressive, but not the present.

> *I've been working* since six this morning. (NOT ~~I am working~~ ...)
> *She's been learning* English for six years.
> (NOT ~~She learns English for~~ ...)

245 past time: past perfect simple and progressive

1 Forms

Past perfect simple

Affirmative	Question	Negative
I had worked you had worked he had worked, etc	had I worked? had you worked? had he worked? etc	I had not worked you had not worked, etc

Past perfect progressive

Affirmative	Question	Negative

I had been working
you had been
  working, etc
	had I been working?
	had you been
	  working? etc
		I had not been
		  working, etc

2 Meaning

We use the past perfect simple to 'go back' to a 'second past'. If we are already talking about the past, we use the past perfect simple to talk about things that had *already happened* at the time we are talking about.

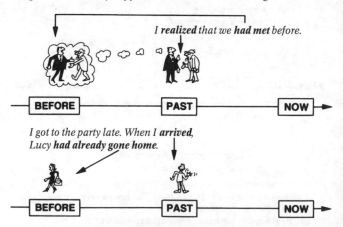

I realized that we had met before.

BEFORE — PAST — NOW

I got to the party late. When I arrived,
Lucy had already gone home.

BEFORE — PAST — NOW

We often use the past perfect simple in reported speech, to talk about things that *had already happened* at the time when we were talking or thinking.

> *I told her that I had finished.*
> *I wondered who had left the door open.*
> *I thought I had sent the cheque a week before.*

3 Past perfect progressive

We use the past perfect progressive to talk about longer actions or situations, which had continued up to the past moment that we are thinking about.

*When I found Mary, she **had been crying** for several hours.*

4 *if* etc

After *if, if only, wish* and *would rather*, the past perfect is used to talk about things that did not happen. (See 165, 167, 367 and 370.)

*If I **had gone** to university I would have studied medicine.*
*I **wish** you **had told** me the truth.*

246 perfect tenses with
this is the first time ..., etc

1 We use a present perfect tense after the following expressions:

This/that/it is the first/second/third/fourth/etc
This/that/it is the only ...
This/that/it is the best/worst/finest/most interesting/etc

Examples:

*This is **the first time** (that) **I've heard** her sing.*
(NOT ... that I hear her sing.)
*That's **the third time** you've asked me that question.*
(NOT ... the third time you ask me ...)
*It's one of **the most interesting** books **I've ever read**.*

2 When we talk about the past, we use a past perfect tense after the same expressions.

*It was **the third time** he **had been** in love that year.*
(NOT ... the third time he was ...)

247 personal pronouns (*I, me, it* etc)

1 The words *I, me, you, he, him, she, her, it, we, us, they* and *them* are called 'personal pronouns'. This is not a very good name: these words are used for both persons and things.

2   *Me, you, him, her, us* and *them* are not only used as objects. We can use
   them in other ways (see 331).

   'Who's there?' 'Me.'   *I'm older than her.*

3   We can use *it* to refer to a person when we are identifying somebody
   (saying who somebody is). Compare:

   'Who's that?' 'It's John Cook. He's a friend of my father's.'
   (NOT *He's John Cook.*   NOT *It's a friend* ...)

4   We use *it* to refer to *nothing, everything* and *all.*

   Nothing happened, did it?
   Everything's all right, isn't it?
   I did all I could, but it wasn't enough.

5   We use *it* as an 'empty' subject (with no meaning) to talk about time,
   weather, temperature and distances.

   It's ten o'clock.
   It's Monday again.
   It rained for three days.
   It's thirty degrees.
   It's ten miles to the nearest petrol station.

6   *It* can mean 'the present situation'.

   *It's terrible—everybody's got colds, and the central heating isn't
   working.*
   Isn't it lovely here!

7   We cannot leave out personal pronouns.

   It's raining. (NOT *Is raining.*)
   She loved the picture because it was beautiful.
   (NOT ... *because was beautiful.*)
   They arrested him and put him in prison.
   (NOT ... *put in prison.*)
   'Have some chocolate.' 'No, I don't like it.'
   (NOT ... *I don't like.*)

   Note that we do not always put *it* after *I know.*

   'It's getting late.' 'I know.' (NOT *I know it.*)

8   One subject is enough. We do not normally need a personal pronoun if
   there is already a subject in the clause.

   My car is parked outside. (NOT *My car it is parked* ...)
   The boss really makes me angry. (NOT *The boss he really* ...)
   The situation is terrible. (NOT *It is terrible the situation.*)

   For the use of *it* as a 'preparatory subject' for an infinitive or a clause,
   see 187.

9 We do not use personal pronouns together with relative pronouns. (See 277.1.)

> *That's the girl **who** lives in the flat upstairs.*
> (NOT *That's the girl **who she** lives …*)
> *Here's the money (**that**) you lent me.*
> (NOT *Here's the money (**that**) you lent **it** me.*)

▷ For the use of *they*, *them* and *their* to refer to *somebody*, *anybody* etc, see 307.
For the use of *he* and *she* to refer to animals etc, see 141.
For the 'indefinite' personal pronoun *one*, see 229.

248 play and game

A *play* is a piece of literature written for the theatre or television.

> *Julius Caesar is one of Shakespeare's early **plays**.*

A *game* is, for example, chess, football, or bridge.

> *Chess is a very slow **game**.* (NOT *… a very slow **play**.*)

Verbs: people *act* in plays or films, and *play* games.

> *My daughter is **acting** in her school play.*
> *Have you ever **played** rugby football?*

249 please and thank you

1 We use *please* to make a request more polite.

> *Could I have some more, **please**?*
> *'Would you like some wine?' 'Yes, **please**.'*

Note that *please* does not change an order into a request.

> *Stand over there.* (order)　　*Please stand over there.* (polite order)

For details of how to make requests, see 286.

2 We do not use *please* to ask people what they said. (See 121.)

> *'I've got a bit of a headache.' 'I beg your pardon?'* (NOT *… '**Please?**'*)

We do not use *please* when we give things to people.

> *'Have you got a light?' 'Yes, here you are.'* (NOT *… '**Please.**'*)

We do not use *please* as an answer to *Thank you*. (See 4 below.)

> *'Thanks a lot.' 'That's OK.'* (NOT *… '**Please.**'*)

3 *Thanks* is more informal than *thank you*. We use them as follows:

> *Thank you.* (NOT *Thanks you.*)
> *Thank you very much.*　　*Thanks very much.*　　*Thanks a lot.*

We can use an *-ing* form after *thank you / thanks*.

> *'Thank you **for coming**.' 'Not at all. Thank you **for having** me.'*

We often use *Thank you* to accept things (like *Yes please*).

> *'Would you like some potatoes?' '**Thank you**.' 'How many?'*

To make it clear that you are refusing something, say *No thank you*.
Note the expression *Thank God*.

> ***Thank God** it's Friday!* (NOT ~~*Thanks God*~~ ...)

4   We do not automatically answer when people say *Thank you*. If we want
to answer, we can say *Not at all*, *You're welcome* (especially in American
English), *That's all right* or *That's OK* (informal). Compare:

> *'Here's your coat.' 'Thanks.'* (No answer.)
> *'Thanks so much for looking after the children.' '**That's all right**. Any
> time.'*

250 possessive **'s**: forms

1 Spelling

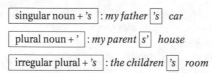

We sometimes just add an apostrophe (') to a singular noun ending in -*s*:
Socrates' ideas. But *'s* is more common: *Charles's wife*.
We can add *'s* to a whole phrase: *the man next door's wife*.

2 Pronunciation

The ending *'s* is pronounced just like a plural ending (see 302). The
apostrophe (') in a form like *parents'* does not change the pronunciation
at all.

3   Possessives are not usually used together with other determiners.
*The car that is John's is **John's** car*, not *the John's car*.

> *Have you met **Jack's** new girl-friend?*
> (NOT ... ~~*the Jack's new girl-friend?*~~)

For the structure *a friend of John's* etc, see 252.

4   We can use the possessive without a following noun.

> *'Whose is that?' '**Peter's**.'*

We often talk about shops and people's houses in this way.

> *Alice is at **the hairdresser's**.*
> *We had a nice time at **John and Susan's** last night.*

▷   For the meanings and use of the possessive, see 251.

251 possessive **'s**: use

1 Meanings

We can use the possessive *'s* to talk about several different sorts of ideas.
The meaning is often similar to the meaning of *have*.

> That's **my father's** house. (*My father has* that house.)
> **Mary's** brother is a lawyer. (*Mary has* a brother who is a lawyer.)
> the **plan's** importance (*the importance that the **plan has**)

Other meanings are possible.

> I didn't believe **the girl's** story. (The girl **told** a story.)
> Have you read **John's** letter? (John **wrote** a letter.)
> **the government's** decision (The government **made** a decision.)
> **the train's** arrival (The train **arrived**.)

2 *'s* and *of*

We use the possessive structure (*A's B*) most often when the first noun
(A) is the name of something living. In other cases, we often use a
structure with *of* (*the B of A*). Compare:

> my **father's** house (NOT *the house of my father*)
> the **plan's** importance OR the importance **of** the plan

3 Time expressions

We often use the possessive to refer to particular times, days, weeks etc.

> **this evening's** performance
> **last Sunday's** paper
> **next week's** TV programmes
> **this year's** profits

But we do not use the possessive when the expression of time has a
'general' meaning.

> the **nine o'clock** news
> (NOT *the nine o' clock's news*)
> a **Sunday** newspaper
> (NOT *a Sunday's newspaper*)

We also use the possessive in 'measuring' expressions of time which begin
with a number.

> **ten minutes'** walk   **two weeks'** holiday

4 | noun + noun |

We can also put two nouns together in the structure | noun + noun |
(for example a **table leg**; a **Sunday newspaper**). For details of this
structure, see 226.

252 possessives with determiners (**a friend of mine**, etc)

We cannot put a possessive together with another determiner before a noun. We can say *my friend*, *Ann's friend*, *a friend* or *that friend*, but not *a my friend* or *that Ann's friend*.

> determiner + noun + *of* + possessive

*That policeman is **a friend of mine**.*
*Here's **that friend of yours**.*
*I met **another boyfriend of Lucy's** yesterday.*
*He's **a cousin of the Queen's**.*
*Have you heard **this new idea of the boss's**?*

253 possessives: **my** and **mine** etc

1 *My, your, his, her, its, one's, our* and *their* are determiners (see 96). In grammars and dictionaries they are often called 'possessive adjectives'.

> *That's **my** watch.*

We cannot use *my, your* etc together with other determiners (for example *a, the, this*). You cannot say *a my friend* or *the my car* or *this my house*. (For the structure *a friend of mine*, see 252.)
Don't confuse *its* (possessive) and *it's* (= *it is/has*).

> *'We've got a new cat.' 'What's **its** name?' 'It's called Polly.'*

2 *Mine, yours, his, hers, ours* and *theirs* are pronouns.

> *That watch is **mine**.   Which car is **yours**?*

We do not use articles with *mine* etc.

> *Can I borrow your keys? I can't find **mine**.*
> (NOT *I can't find the mine.*)

3 We can use *whose* as a determiner (like *my*) or as a pronoun (like *mine*).

> ***Whose** bag is that?   **Whose** is that bag?*

4 After a plural possessive, we do not usually use a singular word to express a plural meaning.

> *The teacher told the children to open their **books**.*
> (NOT *... to open their **book**.*)

254 prepositions after particular words and expressions

(This is a list of expressions which often cause problems.
For the use of *of* with determiners, see 96.)

ability at (NOT ~~in~~)
*She shows great **ability at** mathematics.*

afraid of (NOT ~~by~~)
*Are you **afraid of** spiders?*

agree with a person
*I entirely **agree with** you.*

agree about a subject of discussion
*We **agree about** most things.*

agree on a matter for decision
*Let's try to **agree on** a date.*

agree to a suggestion
*I'll **agree to** your suggestion if you lower the price.*

angry with (sometimes **at**) a person **for** doing something
*I'm **angry with** her **for** not telling me.*

angry about (sometimes **at**) something
*What are you so **angry about**?*

apologize for
*I must **apologize for** disturbing you.*

arrive at or **in** (NOT ~~to~~)
*What time do we **arrive at** Cardiff?*
*When did you **arrive in** England?*

ask: see 53

bad at (NOT ~~in~~)
*I'm not **bad at** tennis.*

believe in God, Father Christmas etc (= believe that … exists)
*I half **believe in** life after death.*

believe a person or something that is said (= accept as true)
*Don't **believe** her. I don't **believe** a word she says.*

blue with cold, **red with** anger
*My hands were **blue with** cold when I got home.*

borrow: see 67

call after
*We **called** him Thomas, **after** his grandfather.*

clever at (NOT ~~in~~)
*I'm not very **clever at** cooking.*

congratulate/congratulations on (NOT ~~for~~)
*I must **congratulate** you **on** your exam results.*
***Congratulations on** you new job!*

crash into (NOT ~~against~~)
*I wasn't looking where I was going, and **crashed into** the car in front.*

depend/dependent on (NOT ~~from~~ or ~~of~~)
*We may play football—it **depends on** the weather.*
*He doesn't want to be **dependent on** his parents.*

But: **independent of**

different from (sometimes **to**; American **from** or **than**)
*You're very **different from** your brother.*

difficulty with something, **(in) doing** something
(NOT ~~difficulty to~~ ...)
*I'm having **difficulty with** my travel arrangements.*
*You won't have much **difficulty (in) getting** to know people in Italy.*

disappointed with somebody
*My father never showed it if he was **disappointed with** me.*

disappointed with/at/about something
*You must be pretty **disappointed with/at/about** your exam results.*

a **discussion about** something
*We had a long **discussion about** politics.*

to **discuss** something (no preposition)
*We'd better **discuss** your travel plans.*

divide into (NOT ~~in~~)
*The book is **divided into** three parts.*

dream of (= think of, imagine)
*I often **dreamed of** being famous when I was younger.*

dream about
*What does it mean if you **dream about** mountains?*

dress in (NOT ~~with~~)
*Who's the woman **dressed in** green?*

drive into
*Granny **drove into** a tree again yesterday.*

example of (NOT ~~for~~)
*Sherry is an **example of** a fortified wine.*

explain something **to** somebody (NOT ~~explain somebody something~~)
*Could you **explain** this rule **to** me?*

get in(to) and **out of** a car, taxi or small boat
*When I **got into** my car, I found the radio had been stolen.*

get on(to) and **off** a bus, train, plane or ship
*We'll be **getting off** the train in ten minutes.*

good at (NOT ~~in~~)
*Are you any **good at** tennis?*

the idea of ... **-ing** (NOT ~~the idea to~~ ...)
*I don't like the **idea of getting** married yet.*

ill with
> *The boss has been **ill with** flu this week.*

impressed with/by
> *I'm very **impressed with/by** your work.*

independent of; independence of/from
> *She got a job so that she could be **independent of** her parents.*
> *When did India get her **independence from** Britain?*

insist on (NOT ~~to~~ ...)
> *George's father **insisted on** paying.*

interest/interested in (NOT ~~for~~)
> *When did your **interest in** social work begin?*
> *Not many people are **interested in** grammar.*

kind to (NOT ~~with~~)
> *People have always been very **kind to** me.*

laugh at
> *I hate being **laughed at**.*

listen to
> *If you don't **listen to** people, they won't **listen to** you.*

look at (= 'point one's eyes at')
> *Stop **looking at** me like that.*

look after (= take care of)
> *Thanks for **looking after** me when I was ill.*

look for (= try to find)
> *Can you help me **look for** my keys?*

marriage to; get married to (NOT ~~with~~)
> *Her **marriage to** Philip didn't last very long.*
> *How long have you been **married to** Sheila?*

nice to (NOT ~~with~~)
> *You weren't very **nice to** me last night.*

pay for something (NOT ~~pay something~~)
> *Excuse me, sir. You haven't **paid for** your drink.*

pleased with somebody
> *The boss is very **pleased with** you.*

pleased with/about/at something
> *I wasn't very **pleased with/about/at** my exam results.*

polite to (NOT ~~with~~)
> *Try to be **polite to** Uncle Richard for once.*

prevent ... from ... -ing (NOT ~~to~~ ...)
> *The noise of your party **prevented** me **from sleeping***

proof of (NOT ~~for~~)
> *I want **proof of** your love. Lend me some money.*

reason for (NOT ~~of~~)
> *Nobody knows the **reason for** the accident.*

remind of
*She **reminds** me **of** a girl I was at school with.*

responsible/responsibility for
*Who's **responsible for** the shopping this week?*

rude to (NOT ~~with~~)
*Peggy was pretty **rude to** my family last weekend.*

run into (= meet)
*I **ran into** Philip at Victoria Station this morning.*

search for (= look for)
*The customs were **searching for** drugs at the airport.*

search without preposition (= look through; look everywhere in/on)
*They **searched** everybody's luggage.*
*They **searched** the man in front of me from head to foot.*

shocked by/at
*I was terribly **shocked at/by** the news of Peter's accident.*

shout at (aggressive)
*If you don't stop **shouting at** me I'll come and hit you.*

shout to = call to
*Mary **shouted to** us to come in and swim.*

smile at
*If you **smile at** me like that I'll give you anything you want.*

sorry about something that has happened
*I'm **sorry about** your exam results.*

sorry for/about something that one has done
*I'm **sorry for/about** breaking your window.*

sorry for a person
*I feel really **sorry for** her children.*

suffer from
*My wife **is suffering from** hepatitis.*

surprised at/by
*Everybody was **surprised at/by** the weather.*

take part in (NOT ~~at~~)
*I don't want to **take part in** any more conferences.*

think of/about (NOT USUALLY ~~think to~~ ...)
*I'm **thinking of** studying medicine.*
*I've also **thought about** studying dentistry.*

the thought of ... (NOT ~~the thought to~~ ...)
*I hate **the thought of** going back to work.*

throw ... at (aggressive)
*Stop **throwing** stones **at** the cars.*

throw ... to (in a game etc)
*If you get the ball, **throw** it **to** me.*

typical of (NOT ~~for~~)
> *The wine's **typical of** the region.*

write: see 356.6

wrong with
> *What's **wrong with** Rachel today?*

255 prepositions before particular words and expressions

(This is a list of a few expressions which often cause problems. For information about other preposition + noun combinations, see a good dictionary.)

at the cinema; **at** the theatre; **at** a party; **at** university

a book **by** Joyce; a concerto **by** Mozart; a film **by** Fassbinder (NOT ~~of~~)

for ... reason
> *My sister decided to go to America **for** several reasons.*

in pen, pencil, ink etc
> *Please fill in the form **in** ink.*

in the rain, snow etc
> *I like walking **in** the rain.*

in a ... voice
> *Stop talking to me **in** that stupid voice.*

in a suit, raincoat, shirt, skirt, hat etc
> *Who's the man **in** the funny hat over there?*

in the end = finally, after a long time
> *In the end, I got a visa for the Soviet Union.*

at the end = at the point where something stops
> *I think the film's a bit weak **at** the end.*

in time = with enough time to spare; not late
> *I didn't get an interview because I didn't send in the form **in** time*

on time = at exactly the right time
> *Concerts never start **on** time.*

on the radio; **on** TV

256 prepositions: expressions without prepositions

(This is a list of important expressions in which we do not use prepositions, or can leave them out.)

1 We do not use prepositions after *discuss*, *marry* and *lack*.
> *We must **discuss** your plans.*   *She **married** a friend of her sister's.*
> *He's clever, but he **lacks** experience.*

2 No preposition before expressions of time beginning *next*, *last*, *this*, *one*, *every*, *each*, *some*, *any*, *all*.

> See you **next Monday**.   The meeting's **this Thursday**.
> Come **any day** you like.   The party lasted **all night**.

Note also *tomorrow morning*, *yesterday afternoon*, etc.
(NOT ~~on tomorrow morning~~ etc)

3 In an informal style, we sometimes leave out *on* before the names of the days of the week. This is very common in American English.

> Why don't you come round **(on) Monday evening**?

4 We use *a* instead of a preposition in *three times a day*, *sixty miles an hour*, *eighty pence a pound*, and similar expressions.

5 We usually leave out *at* in *(At) what time ... ?*

> **What time** does Granny's train arrive?

6 Expressions containing words like *height*, *length*, *size*, *shape*, *age*, *colour*, *volume*, *area* are usually connected to the subject of the sentence by the verb *be*, without a preposition.

> **What colour** are her eyes?
> He's just **the right height** to be a policeman.
> She's **the same age** as me.
> You're **a very nice shape**.
> I'm **the same weight** as I was twenty year ago.
> **What shoe size** are you?

7 We often leave out *in* (especially in spoken English) in the expressions *(in) the same way*, *(in) this way*, *(in) another way* etc.

> They plant corn **the same way** their ancestors used to, 500 years ago.

8 We do not use *to* before *home*.

> I'm going **home**.

In American English, *at* can be left out before *home*.

> Is anybody **home**?

257 prepositions at the end of clauses

1 Prepositions often come at the ends of clauses in English. This happens in several kinds of structure:

a   questions beginning *what*, *who*, *where* etc.

> **What** are you looking **at** ?
> **Who** did you go **with**?
> **Where** did you buy it **from**?

b relative clauses

> *There's the house (that) I told you **about**.*
> *You remember the boy I was going out **with**?*

c passive structures

> *I hate **being laughed at**.*
> *They took him to hospital yesterday and **he's** already*
> ***been operated on**.*

d infinitive structures

> *It's a boring place **to live in**.*
> *I need something **to write with**.*

2 In a more formal style, we can put a preposition before a question-word or a relative pronoun.

> ***To whom** is that letter addressed?*
> *She met a man **with whom** she had been friendly years before.*
> ***On which** flight is the general travelling?*

258 prepositions and adverb particles

Words like *down*, *in* are not always prepositions. Compare:

> *I ran **down** the road.*   *He's **in** his office.*
> *Please sit **down**.*   *You can go **in**.*

In the expressions ***down** the road* and ***in** his office*, *down* and *in* are prepositions: they have objects (*the road, his office*).
In *Please sit **down*** and *You can go **in***, *down* and *in* have no objects. They are not prepositions, but adverbs of place, which modify the verbs *sit* and *go*.
Small adverbs like this are usually called 'adverb particles' or 'adverbial particles'. They include *in, out, up, down, on, off, through, past, away, back, across, over, under*. Adverb particles often join together with verbs to make two-word verbs, sometimes with completely new meanings.
Examples: *break down* = 'stop working'; *put off* = 'delay', 'postpone'; *work out* = 'calculate'; *give up* = 'stop trying'. For information about these verbs, see the next section.

259 prepositionl verbs and phrasal verbs

Many English verbs have two parts: a 'base' verb like *bring, come, sit, break* and another small word like *in, down, up*.

> *Could you **bring in** the coffee?*
> *Come in and **sit down**.*
> *He **broke up** a piece of bread and threw the bits to the birds.*

The second part of the verb is sometimes a preposition, and sometimes an adverb particle (see 258). When these verbs are used with objects, the sentence structure is not the same for the two kinds of verb.

Prepositional verbs

Phrasal verbs
(verbs with adverb particles)

verb + preposition + noun

*She **ran down** the road.*

*He **sat on** the table.*

verb + particle + noun
verb + noun + particle

*She **threw down** the paper.*
*She **threw** the paper **down**.*
*He **put on** his coat.*
*He **put** his coat **on**.*

verb + preposition + pronoun

*She **ran down** it.*
*He **sat on** it.*

verb + pronoun + particle

*She **threw** it **down**.*
*He **put** it **on**.*

For detailed information about phrasal and prepositional verbs, see the *Oxford Dictionary of Current Idiomatic English, Volume 1*, or the *Longman Dictionary of English Idioms*.

260 present tenses: introduction

'Present tenses' are used to talk about several different kinds of time.

1   Now, at this exact moment

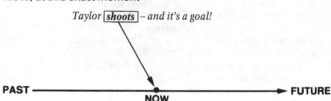

Taylor ⟨shoots⟩ – *and it's a goal!*

PAST ─────────────────── NOW ───────────→ FUTURE

2   Around now

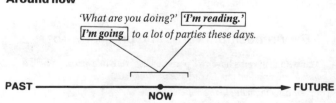

'*What are you doing?*' '*I'm reading.*'
I'm going *to a lot of parties these days.*

PAST ─────────────────── NOW ───────────→ FUTURE

3 **'General time'**—at any time, all the time, not just around now

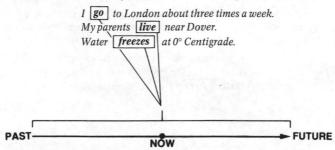

I [*go*] *to London about three times a week.*
My parents [*live*] *near Dover.*
Water [*freezes*] *at 0° Centigrade.*

PAST————————————————→ FUTURE
               NOW

When we talk about time 'around now', we usually use the 'present progressive tense' (for example, *I'm going, I'm reading*). In other cases, we usually use the 'simple present' tense (for example *I go, I read*). For details, see the next two sections.
We use a present perfect tense, not a present tense, to say how long something has been going on.

> *I've **known** her since 1960.* (NOT ~~I know her~~ . . .)
> *I've **been learning** English for three years.* (NOT ~~I'm learning~~ . . .)

For details, see 243 and 244.

261 present tenses: simple present

1 **Forms**

Affirmative	Question	Negative
I work	do I work?	I do not work
you work	do you work?	you do not work
he/she/it works	does he/she/it work?	he/she/it does not work
we work	do we work?	we do not work
they work	do they work?	they do not work

Verbs ending in *-s, -z, -x, -ch,* and *-sh* have *-es* in the third person singular (for example *misses, buzzes, fixes, watches, pushes*).
Other verbs have *-s*. Exceptions: *goes, does*.
Verbs ending in consonant + *y* have *-ies* in the third person singular (for example *hurries, worries*).
The pronunciation of *-(e)s* in the third person follows exactly the same rules as the pronunciation of plural *-(e)s*. See 302 for details.

2 'General time'

We can use the simple present to talk about actions and situations in 'general time'—things which happen at any time, or repeatedly, or all the time.

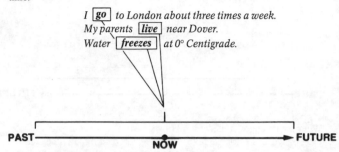

I go to London about three times a week.
My parents live near Dover.
Water freezes at 0° Centigrade.

PAST————————————————→ FUTURE
NOW

3 'Momentary' actions

We can also use the simple present to talk about 'momentary' present actions—things which take a very short time to happen. This tense is often used in sports commentaries.

*Lydiard **passes** to Taylor, Taylor to Morrison, Morrison back to Taylor . . . and Taylor **shoots**—and it's a goal!!!*

4 Actions 'around now' (present progressive)

We do not usually use the simple present to talk about longer actions and situations which are going on *around now*. In this case, we prefer the present progressive. (See 262.)

*'What **are you doing**?' 'I'm **reading**.'* (NOT . . . *'I read.'*)

There are a few exceptions: verbs which are not used in progressive forms (see 225).

*I **like** this wine.* (NOT *I'm liking this wine.*)

5 Future

We can use the simple present to talk about the future. We do this:

a. after conjunctions (see 343):

*I'll phone you **when I come** back.*
*She won't come **if you don't ask** her.*
*I'll always love you **whatever you do**.*

b. when we talk about programmes and timetables.

*The train **arrives** at 7.46.   I **start** work tomorrow.*

In other cases, we do not use the simple present to talk about the future. We prefer the present progressive (see 262).

***Are you going** out tonight?* (NOT *Do you go out tonight?*)

262 present tenses: present progressive

1 Forms

Affirmative	Question	Negative
I am working you are working he/she/it is working, etc	am I working? are you working? is he/she/it working? etc	I am not working you are not working he/she/it is not working, etc

2 'Around now'

We use the present progressive to talk about actions and situations that are going on 'around now': before, during and after the moment of speaking.

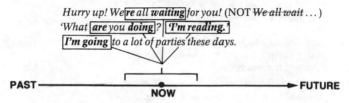

Hurry up! We're all waiting for you! (NOT *We all wait ...*)
'*What are you doing?*' '*I'm reading.*'
I'm going to a lot of parties these days.

PAST ——————————————— FUTURE
            NOW

3 Changes

We also use the present progressive to talk about developing and changing situations.

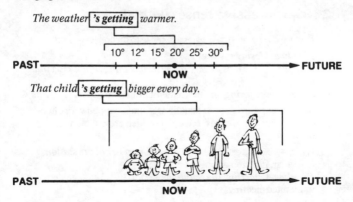

The weather 's getting warmer.

10° 12° 15° 20° 25° 30°
PAST ——————————————— FUTURE
            NOW

That child 's getting bigger every day.

PAST ——————————————— FUTURE
            NOW

4 Present progressive and simple present

We do not use the present progressive to talk about 'general time'.
For this, we use the simple present. (See 261.) Compare:

> *My sister's **living** at home for the moment.* (around now)
> *You **live** in North London, don't you?* (general time)

> *Why **is** that girl **standing** on the table?*
> *Chetford Castle **stands** on a hill outside the town.*

> *The leaves **are going** brown.*
> *I **go** to the mountains about twice a year.*

5
We often use the present progressive to talk about the future. (For details, see 135.)

> *What **are you doing** tomorrow evening?*

6
Some verbs are not used in progressive forms. (See 225.)

> *I **like** this wine.* (NOT *I'm liking ...*)

7
Verbs that refer to physical feelings (for example *feel, hurt, ache*) can be used in the simple present or present progressive without much difference of meaning.

> *How **do you feel**?* OR *How **are you feeling**?*
> *My head **aches**.* OR *My head **is aching**.*

8
For the use of *always* with progressive forms (for example *She's always losing her keys*), see 263.

263 progressive tenses with **always**

We can use *always* with a progressive tense to mean 'very often'.

> *I'm **always losing** my keys.*
> *Granny's nice. **She's always giving** people things and doing things for people.*
> *I'm **always running** into* (= 'accidentally meeting') *Paul these days.*

We use this structure to talk about things which happen very often (perhaps more often than expected), but which are not planned.
Compare:

> *When Alice comes to see me, **I always meet her** at the station.*
> (a regular, planned arrangement)
> *I'm **always meeting** Mrs Bailiff in the supermarket.* (accidental, unplanned meetings)

> *When I was a child, **we always had** picnics on Saturdays in the summer.* (regular, planned)
> *Her mother **was always arranging** little surprise picnics and outings.* (unexpected, not regular)

264 punctuation: apostrophe

We use apostrophes (') in two important ways.

a. To show where we have left letters out of a contracted form. (See 90.)

can't (= *cannot*)   *she's* (= *she is*)   *I'd* (= *I would*)

b. In possessive forms of nouns. (See 250.)

the **girl's** father   **Charles's** wife   three **miles'** walk

We do not use apostrophes in plurals, possessive determiners (except *one's*) or possessive pronouns.

blue **jeans** (NOT ~~blue jean's~~)
The dog wagged **its** tail. (NOT ... ~~it's tail.~~)
This is **yours**. (NOT ... ~~your's.~~)

265 punctuation: colon

1 We often use colons (:) before explanations.

We decided not to go on holiday: we had too little money.
Mother may have to go into hospital: she's got kidney trouble.

2 We also use colons before quotations.

In the words of Murphy's Law: 'Anything that can go wrong will go wrong'.

266 punctuation: comma

Some ways of using commas:

1 We use commas (,) to separate things in a series or list. We do not use them between the last two words or expressions (except when these are long).

I went to Spain, Italy, Switzerland, Austria and Germany.
You had a holiday at Christmas, at New Year and at Easter.
I spent yesterday playing cricket, listening to jazz records, and talking about the meaning of life.

We separate adjectives by commas after a noun, but not always before. Compare:

a tall(,) dark(,) handsome cowboy
The cowboy was tall, dark and handsome.

We put commas in a series of colour adjectives.

a green, red and gold carpet

2 If we put adverbs in unusual places in a clause, we often put commas before and after them.

> *My father, **however**, did not agree.*
> *Jane had, **surprisingly**, paid for everything.*
> *We were, **believe it or not**, in love with each other.*

3 In sentences that begin with conjunctions, we usually put a comma after the first clause.

> ***If** you're ever in London, come and see me.*
> ***As soon as** we stop, get out of the car.*

4 We do not put commas before 'reported speech' clauses.

> *Everybody realized that I was a foreigner.*
> (NOT *Everybody realized, that* ...)
> *I didn't know where I should go.*
> (NOT *I didn't know, where* ...)
> *Fred wondered if lunch was ready.*
> (NOT *Fred wondered, if* ...)

5 We do not usually use commas between grammatically separate sentences (in places where a full stop would be possible).

> *The blue dress was warmer. On the other hand, the purple one was prettier.*
> (OR *The blue dress was warmer; on the other hand* ...)
> (NOT *The blue dress was warmer, on the other hand* ...)

6 In numbers, we often use a comma after the thousands.

> *3,164 = three thousand, one hundred and sixty-four*

We do not use commas in decimals.

> *3·5 = three point five or three and a half*
> (NOT *3,5 three comma five*)

▷ For the use of commas in relative clauses, see 280.

267 punctuation: dash

We often use a dash (—) in informal writing. A dash can come before an afterthought.

> *We'll be arriving on Monday morning—at least, I think so.*

Dashes are common in personal letters instead of colons or semi-colons, or instead of brackets.

> *There are three things I can never remember—names, faces, and I've forgotten the other.*
> *We had a great time in Greece—the kids really loved it.*
> *My mother—who rarely gets angry—really lost her temper.*

268 punctuation: quotation marks

Quotation marks ('...' "...") can also be called 'inverted commas'.

1 We can use quotation marks when we say what name something has.

> *... can be called 'inverted commas'.*

And quotation marks are often used when we mention titles.

> *His next book was 'Heart of Darkness'.*

2 We can use quotation marks when we mention a word, or when we use it in an unusual way.

> *The word 'disinterested' does not mean 'uninterested'.*
> *A textbook can be a 'wall' between a teacher and a class.*

3 We use quotation marks (single '...' or double "...") when we quote direct speech.

> *'Hello,' she said.* OR *"Hello," she said.*

269 punctuation: semi-colons and full stops

We can use semi-colons (;) or full stops (.) between grammatically separate sentences.

> *Some people like Picasso. Others dislike him.*
> *Some people like Picasso; others dislike him.*

We often prefer semi-colons when the ideas are very closely connected.

> *It is a good idea; whether it will work or not is another question.*

270 questions: basic rules

(Some spoken questions do not follow these rules. See 271.)

1 Put an auxiliary verb before the subject.

> auxiliary verb + subject + main verb

> ***Have you** received my letter of June 17?*
> (NOT ~~*You have received* ...~~)
> *Why **are you** laughing?* (NOT *Why **you are** laughing?*)
> *How much **does the room** cost?* (NOT ~~*How much **the room costs**?*~~)

2 If there is no other auxiliary verb, use *do* or *did*.

> *do* + subject + main verb

> ***Do you** like Mozart?* (NOT ~~***Like you** Mozart?*~~)
> *What **does** 'periphrastic' mean?* (NOT ~~*What **means** ...?*~~)
> ***Did you** like the concert?*

3 Do not use *do* together with another auxiliary verb, or with *be*.

> ***Can you*** tell me the time? (NOT ~~Do you can tell me~~ ...?)
> ***Have you*** seen John? (NOT ~~Do you have seen John?~~)
> ***Are you*** ready?

4 After *do*, use the infinitive without *to*.

> ***Did you go*** camping last weekend?
> (NOT ~~Did you went~~ ...? NOT ~~Did you to go~~ ...?)

5 Put *only* the auxiliary verb before the subject.

> ***Is your mother*** coming tomorrow?
> (NOT ~~Is coming your mother~~ ...?)
> *When* ***was your reservation*** *made?*
> (NOT ~~When was made your reservation?~~)

6 When *who, which, what* or *how many* is the subject of a sentence, do not use *do*.

> ***Who left*** the door open? (NOT ~~Who did leave the door open?~~)
> ***Which costs*** more—the blue one or the grey one?
> (NOT ~~Which does cost more~~ ...?)
> ***What happened?*** (NOT ~~What did happen?~~)
> ***How many people work*** in your office?
> (NOT ~~How many people do work~~ ...?)

When *who, which, what* or *how many* is the object, use *do*.

> ***Who do*** you want to speak to?
> ***What do*** you think?

7 In *reported* questions, do not put the verb before the subject (see 284). Do not use a question mark.

> *Tell me when* ***you are going*** *on holiday.*
> (NOT ~~Tell me when are you going~~ ...?)

271 questions: word order in spoken questions

In spoken questions, we do not always use 'interrogative' word order.

> ***You're*** working late tonight?

We ask questions in this way:

a. when we think we know something, but we want to make sure

> ***That's*** the boss? (= I suppose that's the boss, isn't it?)

b. to express surprise

> ***THAT's*** the boss? I thought he was the cleaner.

This order is not possible after a question-word (*what, how* etc).

> *Where* ***are you*** *going?* (NOT ~~Where you are going?~~)

272 questions: reply questions

1 We often answer people with short 'questions'. Their structure is

> auxiliary verb + personal pronoun

> *'It was a terrible party.' **'Was it**?' 'Yes, ...'*

These 'reply questions' do not ask for information. They just show that we are listening and interested. More examples:

> *'We had a lovely holiday.' **'Did you**?' 'Yes. We went ...'*
> *'I've got a headache.' **'Have you, dear**? I'll get you an aspirin.'*
> *'John likes that girl next door.' 'Oh, **does he**?'*
> *'I don't understand.' **'Don't you**? I'm sorry.'*

We can answer an affirmative sentence with a negative reply question. This is like a negative-question exclamation (see 120.3)—it expresses emphatic agreement.

> *'It was a lovely concert.' 'Yes, **wasn't it**? I did enjoy it.'*
> *'She's put on a lot of weight.' 'Yes, **hasn't she**?'*

▷ Question tags have a similar structure. See 273.
See also 293 (short answers).

273 question tags

We often put small questions at the ends of sentences in speech.

> *That's the postroom, **isn't it**?*   *You take sugar in tea, **don't you**?*
> *Not a very good film, **was it**?*

We use these 'question tags' to ask if something is true, or to ask somebody to agree with us.

1 Structure

We do not put question tags after questions.

> ***You're** the new secretary, **aren't you**?*
> (NOT ~~Are you the new secretary, aren't you?~~)

We put negative tags after affirmative sentences, and non-negative tags after negative sentences.

+	−

*It's cold, is**n't** it?*

−	+

*It's **not** warm, is it?*

If the main sentence has an auxiliary verb (or *be*), the question tag has the same auxiliary verb (or *be*).

> *Sally **can** speak French, **can't** she?*
> *You **haven't** seen my keys, **have** you?*
> *The meeting**'s** at ten, **isn't** it?*

If the main sentence has no auxiliary verb, the question tag has *do*.

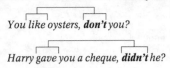

*You like oysters, **don't** you?*

*Harry gave you a cheque, **didn't** he?*

2 Meaning and intonation

We show the meaning of a question tag by the intonation. If the tag is a real question—if we really want to know something, and are not sure of the answer—we use a rising intonation: the voice goes up.

The meeting's at four o'clock, isn't it?

If the tag is not a real question—if we are sure of the answer—we use a falling intonation: the voice goes down.

It's a beautiful day, isn't it?

3 Requests

We often ask for help or information by using the structure

negative question + question-tag

*You **couldn't** lend me a pound, **could you**?*
*You **haven't** seen my watch anywhere, **have you**?*

4 Note

a The question tag for *I am* is *aren't I*?

   *I'm late, **aren't I**?*

b After imperatives, we use *won't you?* (to invite people to do things) and *will you? would you? can you? can't you?* and *could you?* (to tell people to do things).

   *Do sit down, **won't you**?*   *Open a window, **would you**?*
   *Give me a hand, **will you**?*   *Shut up, **can't you**?*

After a negative imperative, we use *will you?*

   *Don't forget, **will you**?*

After *Let's . . .*, we use *shall we?*

   *Let's have a party, **shall we**?*

c *There* can be a subject in question tags.

   *There's something wrong, isn't **there**?*
   *There weren't any problems, were **there**?*

d We use *it* in question tags to refer to *nothing*, and *they* to refer to *nobody*.

   *Nothing can happen, can **it**?*   *Nobody phoned, did **they**?*

We also use *they* to refer to *somebody, everybody* (see 307).

   *Somebody wanted a drink, didn't **they**? Who was it?*

274 quite

1 *Quite* has two meanings. Compare:

> It's **quite** good.   It's **quite** impossible.

Good is a 'gradable' adjective: things can be more or less good.
Impossible is not 'gradable'. Things cannot be more or less impossible;
they are impossible or they are not.
With gradable adjectives, *quite* means something like 'fairly' or 'rather'.
(See 124.)

> 'How's your steak?' '**Quite** nice.'
> She's **quite** pretty. She'd look better if she dressed differently, though.

With non-gradable adjectives, *quite* means 'completely'.

> His French is **quite perfect**.   The bird was **quite dead**.

2 We put *quite* before *a / an*.

> **quite a** nice day   **quite an** interesting film

3 We can use *quite* with verbs.

> I **quite like** her.   Have you **quite finished**?

275 real(ly)

In informal English (especially American English), *real* is often used as an
adverb instead of *really* before adverbs and adjectives.

> That was **real** nice.   She cooks **real** well.

Some people consider this 'incorrect'.

276 reflexive pronouns

Reflexive pronouns are *myself, yourself, himself, herself, itself, oneself,
ourselves, yourselves, themselves*.

1 We use reflexive pronouns to talk about actions where the subject and the
object are the same person.

> I cut **myself** shaving this morning. (NOT *I cut me* ...)
> We got out of the river and dried **ourselves**. (NOT ... *dried us*.)
> Why's she talking to **herself**?

We do not usually use reflexive pronouns with *wash, dress* or *shave*.

> Do you **shave** on Sundays? (NOT ... *shave yourself* ...)

After prepositions, we use personal pronouns instead of reflexives when
it is clear which person we are talking about.

> She took her dog **with her**. (NOT ... *with herself*.)

2 We can use reflexive pronouns to mean 'that person/thing and nobody/nothing else'.

> *It's quicker if you do it **yourself**.*
> *The manager spoke to me **himself**.*
> *The house **itself** is nice, but the garden's very small.*

3 *By myself, by yourself* etc has two meanings.

a 'alone'

> *I often like to spend time **by myself**.*

b 'without help'

> *'Can I help you?' 'No, thanks. I can do it **by myself**.'*

4 Don't confuse *-selves* and *each other* (see 105).

***They** are thinking about **themselves**.*

***They** are thinking about **each other**.*

277 relative pronouns

1 Relative pronouns are *who, whom, whose, which, that* and *what*.
Relative pronouns do two things:
a. they join clauses together, like conjunctions
b. they are the subjects or objects of clauses (except *whose*).
Compare:

> *What's the name of the tall man? **He** just came in.*
> *What's the name of the tall man **who** just came in?*
> (*Who* joins the two clauses together. It is the subject of the second clause: we use *who* in the same way as *he*.)

> *This is Ms Rogers. You met **her** last year.*
> *This is Ms Rogers, **whom** you met last year.*
> (*Whom* joins the two clauses together. It is the object of the second clause: we use *whom* in the same way as *her*.)

*I've got a book. **It** might interest you.*
*I've got a book **which** might interest you.*
(*Which* joins the two clauses together. It is the subject of the second
clause: we use *which* in the same way as *it*.)

*I've found the paper. You were looking for **it**.*
*I've found the paper **which** you were looking for.*
(*Which* is the object of the second clause.)

One subject or object is enough.

*Here's the book **which** you asked for.*
(NOT ~~Here's the book **which** you asked for **it**.~~)

We use *who/whom* for people and *which* for things.

*She's a person **who** can do anything.* (NOT *... a person **which** ...*)
*It's a machine **which** can do anything.* (NOT *... a machine **who** ...*)

2 We often use *that* instead of *which* in 'identifying' relative clauses (see
280).

*I've got a book **that** might interest you.*
*Have you got a map **that** shows all the motorways?*

In an informal style, we also use *that* instead of *who(m)*.

*There's the woman **that** works in the photographer's.*
*You remember the boy **that** I was talking about?*

3 In 'identifying' relative clauses (see 280), we often leave out object
pronouns.

You remember the boy (that) I was talking about?
I've found the paper (that) you were looking for.

4 We can use *when* and *where* in a similar way to relative pronouns.

*Can you tell me **a time when** you'll be free?*
*(= ... **a time at which** ...)*
*I know **a place where** you can find wild strawberries.*

5 Do not use *what* instead of *that* or *which*.

*Everything **that** happened was my fault.* (NOT *... **what** happened ...*)
*She got married again, **which** surprised everybody.*
(NOT *... **what** surprised everybody.*)

6 Some relative clauses 'identify' nouns—they tell us which person or thing
is meant.

*What's the name of the tall man **who just came in**?*

Other relative clauses tell us more about a noun which is already
identified.

*This is Ms Rogers, **whom you met last year**.*

The grammar is not quite the same in the two kinds of clause. We use *that* in identifying clauses, and we can leave out object pronouns. But in non-identifying clauses, we cannot use *that*, and we cannot leave out object pronouns. For details, see 280.

▷ For *whose*, see 279. for *what*, see 278.

278 relative pronouns: **what**

1 *What* is different from other relative pronouns.
Other relative pronouns usually refer to a noun that comes before.

> I gave her **the money that** she needed.

> **The thing that** I'd like most is a home computer.

(*That* refers to—repeats the meaning of—*the money* and the *thing*.)

We use *what* as | noun + relative pronoun | together.

> I gave her **what** she needed. (*What* = *the money that*.)
> **What** I'd like most is a home computer. (*What* = *the thing that*.)

2 Do not use *what* with the same meaning as *that*.

> You can have everything (**that**) you like.
> (NOT ... *everything **what** you like.*)
> The only thing **that** makes me feel better is coffee.
> (NOT *The only thing **what*** ...)

We use *which*, not *what*, to refer to a whole sentence that comes before.

> Sally married George, **which** made Paul very unhappy.
> (NOT ... ***what** made Paul very unhappy.*)

279 relative pronouns: **whose**

Whose is a possessive relative word. It does two things:

a. it joins clauses together

b. it is a 'determiner' (see 96), like *his, her, its* or *their*. Compare:

> I saw a girl. **Her hair** came down to her waist.
> I saw a girl **whose hair** came down to her waist.

> This is Felicity. You met **her sister** last week.
> This is Felicity, **whose sister** you met last week.

> Our friends the Robbins—we spent the summer **at their farmhouse**—are moving to Scotland.
> Our friends the Robbins, **at whose farmhouse** we spent the summer, are moving to Scotland.

▷ For the interrogative pronoun *whose*, see 253.3.

280 relatives: identifying and non-identifying clauses

1   Some relative clauses 'identify' nouns. They tell us which person or thing is meant.

> *What's the name of the tall man **who just came in**?*
> (*who just came in* tells the hearer *which* tall man is meant: it *identifies* the man.)
> *Whose is the car **that's parked outside**?*
> (*that's parked outside* tells the hearer *which* car is meant: it *identifies* the car.)

Other relative clauses do not identify. They tell us more about a person or thing that is already identified.

> *This is Ms Rogers, **whom you met last year**.*
> (*whom you met last year* does not tell us *which woman* is meant: we already know that it is Ms Rogers.)
> *Have you seen my new car, **which I bought last week**?*
> (*which I bought last week* does not tell us *which car* is meant: we already know that it is 'my new car'.)

2   Non-identifying clauses are separated from the rest of the sentence by commas (,,). Identifying clauses do not have commas. Compare:

> *The woman **who does my hair** has moved to another hairdresser's.*
> *Dorothy, **who does my hair**, has moved to another hairdresser's.*

3   We only use *that* in identifying clauses. And we can only leave out the object in identifying clauses. Compare:

> *The whisky (**that**) you drank last night cost £15 a bottle.*
> *I gave him a large glass of whisky, **which** he drank at once.*
> (NOT ... *whisky, that he drank* ...) (NOT ... *whisky, he drank* ...)

4   *Whom* is unusual in identifying clauses. Compare:

> *The man (**that**) my daughter wants to marry has been divorced twice.*
> *Max Harrison, **whom** my daughter wants to marry, has been divorced twice.*

5   Non-identifying clauses are unusual in an informal style.

281 remind

1   You *remind* somebody to do something that he might forget.
We do not use *remember* with this meaning.

> remind + object + infinitive

> *Please **remind me to post** these letters.* (NOT *Please remember me* ...)
> *I **reminded her to send** her sister a birthday card.*

2 We use *remind . . . of* to say that something makes us remember the past.

> remind + object + *of . . .*

> *The smell of hay always **reminds me of** our old house in the country.*
> *She **reminds me of** her mother.* (= *She looks like her mother, or she behaves like her mother.*)

282 reported speech and direct speech

1 There are two ways of telling a person what somebody else said.

a. direct speech

> SUE: *What did Bill say?*
> PETER: *He said '**I want to go home**'.*

b. reported speech

> SUE: *What did Bill say?*
> PETER: *He said **that he wanted to go home**.*

When we use 'direct speech', we give the exact words (more or less) that were said. When we use 'reported speech', we change the words that were said to make them fit into our own sentence. (For example, when Peter is talking about Bill he says *he wanted*, not *I want*.) For details, see 283.

2 We use a conjunction to join a reported speech clause to the rest of the sentence.

a. reported statements: *that*

> *He said **that** he wanted to go home.*

In an informal style we can leave out *that*.

> *He said he wanted to go home.*

b. reported questions: *if, whether, what, where, how*, etc

> *She asked me **if** I wanted anything to drink.*
> *She asked me **what** my name was.*

When we report orders, requests, advice etc, we usually use an infinitive structure.

> *Who told you **to put** the lights off?*
> *I advised Lucy **to go** to the police.*

For more details of these structures, see 284; 285.

3 'Reported speech' is not only used to report what people say. We use the same structure to report people's thoughts, beliefs, knowledge etc.

> *I thought **something was wrong**.*
> *She knew **what I wanted**.*
> *Ann wondered **if Mr Blackstone really understood her**.*

283 reported speech: pronouns, 'here and now' words; tenses

> BILL (*on Saturday evening*): *I don't* like *this* party. *I want to go home.*
> PETER (*on Sunday morning*): *Bill said* ***he didn't*** *like* ***the*** *party, and* ***he*** *wanted to go home.*

1 Pronouns

In reported speech, we use the same pronouns to talk about people that we use in other structures.

> *Bill said* ***he*** *didn't like the party.*
> (NOT ~~Bill said **I** didn't like the party.~~)

2 'Here and now' words

When somebody is speaking, he or she uses words like *this*, *here*, *now* to talk about the place where he or she is speaking, and the time when the words are said.
If we report the words in a different place at a different time, we will not use *this*, *here*, *now* etc.

> *Bill said he didn't like* ***the*** *party.*
> (NOT ~~Bill said he didn't like **this** party.~~)

3 Tenses

When we report things that people said in the past, we do not usually use the same tenses as they used. (This is because the times are different.)

> *Bill said he* ***didn't*** *like the party.*
> (NOT ~~Bill said he **doesn't** like the party.~~)

Compare:

Original words	Reported speech
Will *you marry me?*	*I asked him if he* ***would*** *marry me.* (NOT ... ~~if he **will** marry me.~~)
You ***look*** *nice.*	*I told her she* ***looked*** *nice.* (NOT ... ~~she **looks** nice.~~)
*I'****m*** *learning French.*	*She said she* ***was*** *learning French.* (NOT ... ~~she **is** learning ...~~)
*I'****ve*** *forgotten.*	*He said he* ***had*** *forgotten.* (NOT ... ~~he **has** forgotten.~~)
John ***phoned***.	*She told me that John* ***had*** *phoned.* (NOT ... ~~that John **phoned**.~~)

4 Exceptions

If somebody said something in the past that is still true, we sometimes report it with the same tense as the original speaker:

Original words	Reported speech
*The earth **goes** round the sun.*	*He proved that the earth **goes/went** round the sun.*
*How old **are** you?*	*I asked how old you **are/were**.*

▷   For *must* in reported speech, see 207.3.

284 reported speech: questions

1   In reported questions, the subject comes before the verb.

> *He asked where **I was** going.*
> (NOT ... ~~where was I going.~~)
> *I asked where **the President and his wife were** staying.*
> (NOT ~~I asked where were~~ ...)

Auxiliary *do* is not used.

> *I wondered how **they felt**.*
> (NOT ... ~~how did they feel.~~)

Question marks are not used.

> *We asked where the money was.*
> (NOT ... ~~where the money was?~~)

2   When there is no question word (*who, what, how* etc), we use *if* or *whether* to introduce indirect questions.

> *The driver asked **if/whether** I wanted the town centre.*
> *I don't know **if/whether** I can help you.*

▷   For the difference between *if* and *whether*, see 361.

285 reported speech: orders, requests, advice etc

We usually use an infinitive structure to report orders, requests, advice and suggestions.

> | verb + object + infinitive |
> |---|

> *I **told Andrew to be** careful.*
> *The lady downstairs **has asked us to be** quiet after nine o'clock.*
> *I **advise you to think** again before you decide which one to buy.*
> *The policeman **told me not to park** there.*

We do not use *say* in this structure.

> *She **told** me to be quiet.* (NOT ~~She said me to be quiet.~~)

▷   For the exact difference between *say* and *tell*, see 289.

286 requests

1 We usually ask people to do things for us by making yes/no questions.
(This is because a yes/no question leaves people free to say 'No' if they
want to.)
Common structures used in polite requests:

> *Could you possibly help me for a few minutes?* (very polite)
> *I wonder if you could help me for a few minutes?* (very polite)
> *Could you help me for a few minutes?*
> *You couldn't help me for a few minutes, could you?*

2 If we use other structures (for example imperatives), we are not *asking*
people to do things, but *telling* them to do things (giving orders). This
may seem rude, and make people angry.
Please changes an order into a polite order, but it does not change it into
a request.

> *Please help me for a few minutes.*
> *Carry this for me, please.*
> *Please answer by return of post. Please type your letter.*
> *You had better help me.*

(These are all orders. They are NOT polite ways of asking people to do
things for you.)

▷ For the use of imperatives to give advice, make suggestions etc, see 170.

3 In shops, restaurants etc, we generally ask for things like this:

> ***Can I*** *have one of those, please?*
> ***Could I*** *have a red one?*
> ***I'd like*** *another glass of wine, please.*
> ***I would prefer*** *a small one.*

Could is a little 'softer' than *can*.

4 We do not use negative questions in polite requests. But we often use
negative *statements* with question tags.

> ***You couldn't*** *give me a light,* ***could you?***
> (NOT ~~Couldn't you give me a light?~~)

▷ For the use of negative questions, see 214.
For question tags, see 273.
For other rules of 'social' language, see 313.

287 road and street

1 A *street* is a road with houses on either side. We use *street* for roads in
towns, but not for country roads.

> *Cars can park on both sides of our* ***street***.

Road is used for both town and country.

> *Cars can park on both sides of our **road**.*
> *There's a narrow winding **road** from our village to the next one.*
> (NOT ... *a narrow winding ~~street~~* ...)

2 Note that, in street names, we stress the word *Road*, but the word before *Street*.

> *Marylebone 'Road.*   *'Oxford Street.'*

288 the same

We always use *the* before *same*.

> *Give me **the same** again, please.*
> (NOT *Give me ~~same again, please.~~*)
> *I want **the same** shirt as my friend's.*
> (NOT *I want ~~a same shirt like my friend.~~*)

We use *the same as* before a noun or pronoun.

> *Her hair's **the same colour as** her mother's.*
> (NOT ... *~~the same colour like~~ her mother's.*)

We use *the same that* before a clause.

> *That's **the same man that** asked me for money yesterday.*

289 say and tell

1 *Tell* means 'inform' or 'order'. After *tell*, we usually say who is told: a personal object is necessary.

> | *tell* + person |

> *She **told me** that she would be late.* (NOT *She ~~told that she~~* ...)
> *I **told the children** to go away.*

Say is usually used without a personal object.

> *She **said** that she would be late.* (NOT *She ~~said me~~* ...)

If we want to put a personal object after *say*, we use *to*.

> *She said 'Go away' **to** the children.*

2 *Say* is often used before direct speech. *Tell* is not.

> *She **said** 'Go away'.* (NOT *She ~~told 'Go away'.~~*)

3 In a few expressions, we use *tell* without a personal object. The most common: *tell the truth, tell a lie, tell the time* (= *know how to read a clock*).

> *I don't think she's **telling the truth**.* (NOT ... *~~saying the truth.~~*)
> *He's seven years old and he still can't **tell the time**.*

290 see

1 When *see* means 'use one's eyes', it is not usually used in progressive tenses. We often use a structure with *can* instead (see 81).

> *I can see a rabbit over there.* (NOT ~~I'm seeing~~ ...)

2 *See* can also mean 'understand'. We do not use progressive tenses.

> *'We've got a problem.' 'I see.'* (NOT ~~I'm seeing.~~)

3 When *see* means *meet*, *interview*, *talk to*, progressive tenses are possible.

> *I'm seeing Miss Barnett at four o'clock.*

▷ For the difference between *look (at)*, *watch* and *see*, see 196.

291 seem

1 *Seem* is a 'copula verb' (see 91). After *seem*, we use adjectives, not adverbs.

> ┌─────────────────────┐
> │ *seem* + adjective │
> └─────────────────────┘

> *You seem angry about something.* (NOT ~~You seem angrily~~ ...)

2 We use *seem to be* before a noun.

> ┌─────────────────────────┐
> │ *seem to be* + noun   │
> └─────────────────────────┘

> *I spoke to a man who seemed to be the boss.*

3 Other structures: *seem* + infinitive; *seem like*.

> ┌─────────────────────────┐
> │ *seem* + infinitive   │
> └─────────────────────────┘

> *Ann seems to have a new boyfriend.*

> ┌─────────────┐
> │ *seem like* │
> └─────────────┘

> *North Wales seems like a good place for a holiday—let's go there.*
> (NOT ... ~~seems as a good place~~ ...)

292 shall

1 *Shall* is a 'modal auxiliary verb' (see 202). We can use *shall* instead of *will* after *I* and *we*.

> *I'm catching the 10.30 train. What time shall I be in London?*
> (OR ... *will I be in London?*)

Contractions are *I'll*, *we'll* and *shan't* (see 90).

> *I'll see you tomorrow.*   *I shan't be late.*

2 When we make offers, or suggestions, and when we ask for orders or advice, we can use *shall I/we*, but not *will I/we*.

> **Shall I** *carry your bag?*   **Shall we** *go out for lunch?*
> *What* **shall we** *do?*

293 short answers

1 When we answer yes/no questions, we often repeat the subject and auxiliary verb of the question.

> *'Can he swim?' 'Yes,* **he can.***'*
> *'Has it stopped raining?' 'No,* **it hasn't.***'*

Be and *have* can be used in short answers.

> *'Are you happy?' 'Yes, I* **am.***'*   *'Have you a light?' 'Yes, I* **have.***'*

2 We can also use 'short answers' in replies to statements, requests and orders.

> *'You'll be on holiday soon.' 'Yes, I* **will.***'*   *'You're late.' 'No,* **I'm not.***'*
> *'Don't forget to telephone.' 'I* **won't.***'*

3 We use *do* and *did* in short answers to sentences with no auxiliary verb.

> *'She* **likes** *cakes.' 'Yes, she* **does.***'*
> *'That surprised you.' 'It certainly* **did.***'*

294 should

1 Forms

Should is a 'modal auxiliary verb' (see 202). It has no *-s* in the third person singular.

> *He* **should** *be here soon.* (NOT *He* ~~shoulds~~ ...)

Questions and negatives are made without *do*.

> **Should** *we tell Judy?* (NOT ~~Do we should~~ ... ?)

Should is followed by an infinitive without *to*.

> *Should I* **go**? (NOT *Should I* ~~to go~~?)

2 Obligation

We often use *should* to talk about obligation, duty and similar ideas.

> *People* **should** *drive more carefully.*
> *You* **shouldn't** *say things like that to Granny.*

Should I ...? is used to ask for advice, offer help or ask for instructions. (Like *Shall I ...?* See 292.)

> **Should** *I go and see the police, do you think?*
> **Should** *I help you with the washing up?*   *What* **should** *I do?*

For the differences between *should, ought* and *must*, see 295.

3 Deduction

We can use *should* to say that something is possible (because it is logical or normal).

> *Henry **should** be here soon—he left home at six.*
> *'We're spending the winter in Miami.' 'That **should** be nice.'*

4 *should have* ...

We can use | *should* + perfect infinitive | to talk about the past. This structure is used to talk about things which did not happen, or which may or may not have happened (see 202.3).

| *should* + *have* + past participle |

> *I **should have phoned** Ed this morning, but I forgot.*
> *Ten o'clock: she **should have arrived** in her office by now.*

5 Conditional

Should/would is a conditional auxiliary (see 88).

> *I **should/would be** very happy if I had nothing to do.*

▷ For *should* after *in case*, see 172. For *should* in *that*-clauses, see 332.1. For *should* and *would*, see 296.

295 should, ought and must

1 *Should* and *ought* are very similar. They are both used to talk about obligation and duty, to give advice, and to say what we think it is right for people to do. (See 294 and 232.)

> *You **ought to/should** see 'Daughter of the Moon'—it's a great film.*

There is sometimes a small difference. We use *should* or *ought* when we are talking about our own feelings, but we prefer *ought* when we are talking about 'outside' rules, laws, moral duties etc.

> *Everybody **ought** to give five per cent of their income to the Third World.*

2 *Must* is much stronger than *should* and *ought*. For example, we can give advice with *should* and *ought*; we can give orders with *must*. Compare:

> *You **ought** to give up smoking.* (= It's a good idea.)
> *The doctor said I **must** give up smoking.* (= He told me to.)

We can use *should* and *ought* to say that something is probable; we can use *must* to say that it is certain. Compare:

> *Henry ought to be at home now.* (= There is a good reason to think he's at home.)
> *Henry **must** be at home now.* (= There are reasons to be certain that he's at home.)

296 **should** and **would**

There are really three different verbs.

1 *should*

This verb (*I should/you should/he should* etc) can be used to talk about past habits, and to make polite requests. For details, see 294.

2 *would*

This verb (*I would/you would/he would* etc) can be used to talk about past habits, and to make polite requests. For details, see 369.

3 *should/would*

This verb—the conditional auxiliary—has the following forms:

> *I should/would*
> *you would*
> *he/she/it would*
> *we should/would*
> *they would*

The conditional is used in sentences with *if*, and in some other ways. For details, see 88.

297 **should** after **why** and **how**

1 We can ask a question beginning *Why should ...?* to show that we do not understand something.

> ***Why should*** *it get colder when you go up a mountain? You're getting nearer the sun.*

2 *Why should I?* and *How should I know?* show that we are angry.

> *'Give me a cigarette.'* ***'Why should*** *I?'*
> *'What's Susan's phone number?'* ***'How should*** *I know?'*

298 **should: (If I were you) I should ...**

We often give advice by saying *If I were you ...*

> ***If I were you,*** *I should get that car serviced.*
> *I shouldn't worry* ***if I were you.***

Sometimes we leave out *If I were you.*

> *I should get that car serviced.*
> *I shouldn't worry.*

In sentences like these, *I should* has a similar meaning to *you should*.

299 similar words

In this list you will find some pairs of words which look or sound similar. Some others (for example *lay* and *lie*) are explained in other parts of the book. Look in the Index to find out where.

1 *beside* and *besides*

Beside = 'at the side of' or 'by'.

> *Come and sit **beside** me.*

Besides = (a) 'as well as' (preposition)
>   (b) 'also', 'as well' (adverb)

> a. ***Besides** German, she speaks French and Italian.*
> b. *I don't like those shoes. **Besides**, they're too expensive.*

2 *clothes* and *cloths*

Clothes are things you wear: skirts, trousers etc.
Pronunciation: /kləʊðz/.
Cloths are pieces of material for cleaning.
Pronunciation: /klɒθs/.
Clothes has no singular: we say *something to wear*, or *an article of clothing*, or *a skirt* etc, but not ~~*a clothe*~~.

3 *dead* and *died*

Dead is an adjective.

> *a **dead** man   Mrs McGinty is **dead**.*
> *That idea has been **dead** for years.*

Died is the past tense and past participle of the verb *die*.

> *Shakespeare **died** in 1616.* (NOT ~~*Shakespeare dead* ...~~)
> *She **died** in a car crash.* (NOT ~~*She is **dead** in* ...~~)

4 *economic* and *economical*

Economic refers to the science of economics, or to the economy of a country, state etc.

> ***economic** theory   **economic** problems*

Economical means 'not wasting money'.

> *an **economical** little car   an **economical** housekeeper*

5 *elder* and *eldest*; *older* and *oldest*

Elder and *eldest* are often used before the names of relations: *brother, sister, son, daughter, grandson, granddaughter. Older* and *oldest* are also possible.

> *My **elder/older** brother has just got married.*
> *His **eldest/oldest** daughter is a medical student.*

If I say *my elder brother/sister*, I only have one brother or sister older than me. If I have more, I say *eldest*.

We say *elder son/daughter* when there are only two; if there are more we say *eldest*.

Elder and *eldest* are only used before *brother*, *sister* etc. In other cases we use *older* and *oldest*.

> *She likes **older men**.*
> *I'm the **oldest person** in my office.*

6 experience and experiment

The tests which scientists do are called *experiments*.

> *Newton did several **experiments** on light and colour.*
> (NOT ... ~~several experiences~~ ...)

We also use *experiment* for anything that people do to see what the result will be.

> *Try some of this perfume as an **experiment**.*

Experiences are the things that you 'live through': the things that happen to you in life.

> *I had a lot of interesting **experiences** during my year in Africa.*

The uncountable noun *experience* means 'learning by doing things' or 'the knowledge you get from doing things'.

> *Salesgirl wanted—**experience** unnecessary.*

7 female and feminine; male and masculine

Female and *male* say what sex people, animals and plants belong to.

> *A **female** fox is called a vixen.*
> *He works as a **male** nurse.*

Feminine and *masculine* are used for qualities and behaviour that are supposed to be typical of men or women.

> *She has a very **masculine** laugh.*
> *It was a very **feminine** bathroom.*

Feminine and *masculine* are also used for grammatical forms in some languages.

> *The word for 'moon' is **feminine** in French and **masculine** in German.*

8 its and it's

Its is a possessive determiner, like *my*, *your*, *his* and *her*.

> *The cat's hurt **its** foot.* (NOT ... ~~it's foot.~~)

It's is a contraction for *it is* or *it has*.

> *It's late.* (NOT ~~Its late.~~)   *It's stopped raining.*

9 *last* and *latest*

We use *latest* for things which are new.

*What do you think of his **latest** film?*

Last can mean 'the one before this'.

*I like his new film better than his **last** one.*

Last can also mean 'the one at the end', 'final'.

*This is your **last** chance.*

10 *look after* and *look for*

Look after = 'take care of'.

*Will you **look after** the children while I'm out?*

Look for = 'try to find'.

*'What are you doing down there?' '**Looking for** my keys.'*

11 *lose* and *loose*

Lose is a verb—the opposite of *find*.

*I keep **losing** my keys.* (NOT ... ~~loosing~~ ...)

Loose is an adjective—the opposite of *tight*.

*My shoes are too **loose**.*

12 *presently* and *at present*

Presently most often means 'not now, later'.

*'Mummy, can I have an ice-cream?' '**Presently**, dear.'*
*He's having a rest now. He'll be down **presently**.*

Presently is sometimes used to mean 'now', especially in American English. This is the same as 'at present'.

*Professor Holloway is **presently** researching into plant diseases.*

13 *price* and *prize*

The *price* is what you pay if you buy something.

*What's the **price** of the green dress?*

A prize is what you are given if you win a competition, or if you have done something exceptional.

*She received the Nobel **Prize** for physics.*

14 *principal* and *principle*

Principal is usually an adjective. It means 'main', 'most important'.

*What is your **principal** reason for wanting to be a doctor?*

The noun *Principal* means 'headmaster' or 'headmistress' (of a school for adults).

*If you want to leave early you'll have to ask the **Principal**.*

A *principle* is a scientific law or a moral rule.

*Newton discovered the **principle** of universal gravitation.*
*She's a girl with very strong **principles**.*

15 *quite* and *quiet*

Quite is an adverb of degree—it can mean 'fairly' or 'completely'. For details, see 274.

*Our neighbours are **quite** noisy.*

Quiet is the opposite of *loud* or *noisy*.

*She's very **quiet**. You never hear her moving about.*

16 *sensible* and *sensitive*

If you are *sensible* you have 'common sense'. You do not make stupid decisions.

*'I want to buy that dress.' 'Be **sensible**, dear. You haven't got that much money.'*

If you are *sensitive* you feel things easily or deeply—perhaps you can easily be hurt.

*Don't shout at her—she's very **sensitive**. (NOT ... very sensible.)*

17 *shade* and *shadow*

Shade is protection from the sun.

*I'm hot. Let's sit in the **shade** of that tree.*

We say *shadow* when we are thinking of the 'picture' made by an unlighted area.

*In the evening your **shadow** is longer than you are.*

18 *some time* and *sometimes*

Some time means 'one day'. It refers to an indefinite time, usually in the future.

*Let's have dinner together **some time** next week.*

Sometimes is an adverb of frequency (see 14.2). It means 'on some occasions', 'more than once'.

*I **sometimes** went skiing when I lived in Germany.*

300 since (conjunction of time): tenses

Since can be a conjunction of time. The tense in the *since*-clause can be present perfect or past, depending on the meaning. Compare:

*I've known her since **we were** at school together.*
*I've known her since **I've lived** in this street.*

Note that the tense in the main clause is normally present perfect (see 243.4–6; 244.3).

***I've known** her since . . .* (NOT ~~I know her since . . .~~)

301 singular and plural: spelling of plural nouns

1 If the singular ends in consonant + -*y* (for example -*by*, -*dy*, -*ry*, -*ty*), change *y* to *i* and add -*es*.

Singular	Plural
. . . consonant + *y*	. . . consonant + *ies*
baby	*babies*
lady	*ladies*
ferry	*ferries*
party	*parties*

2 If the singular ends in *ch*, *sh*, *s*, *x* or *z*, add -*es*.

Singular	Plural
-*ch* / -*sh* / -*s* / -*x* / -*z*	-*ches* / -*shes* / -*ses* / -*xes* / -*zes*
church	*churches*
crash	*crashes*
bus	*buses*
box	*boxes*
buzz	*buzzes*

3 With other nouns, add -*s* to the singular.

Singular	Plural	Singular	Plural
chair	*chairs*	*boy*	*boys*
table	*tables*	*girl*	*girls*

4 Some nouns ending in -*o* have plurals in -*es*. The most common:

Singular	Plural
echo	*echoes*
hero	*heroes*
negro	*negroes*
potato	*potatoes*
tomato	*tomatoes*

302 singular and plural: pronunciation of plural nouns

The plural ending -(e)s has three different pronunciations.

1 After one of the 'sibilant' sounds /s/, /z/, /ʃ/, /ʒ/, /tʃ/ and /dʒ/, -es is pronounced /ɪz/.

> *buses* /'bʌsɪz/   *crashes* /'kræʃɪz/   *watches* /'wɒtʃɪz/
> *quizzes* /'kwɪzɪz/   *garages* /'gærɑːʒɪz/   *bridges* /'brɪdʒɪz/

2 After any other 'unvoiced' sound (/p/, /f/, /θ/, /t/ or /k/), -(e)s is pronounced /s/.

> *cups* /kʌps/   *baths* /bɑːθs/   *books* /bʊks/
> *coughs* /kɒfs/   *plates* /pleɪts/

3 After all other sounds (vowels and voiced consonants except /z/, /ʒ/ and /dʒ/), -(e)s is pronounced /z/.

> *days* /deɪz/   *knives* /naɪvz/   *hills* /hɪlz/   *dreams* /driːmz/
> *boys* /bɔɪz/   *clothes* /kləʊðz/   *legs* /legz/   *songs* /sɒŋz/
> *trees* /triːz/   *ends* /endz/

4 Exceptions:

> *house* /haʊs/, *houses* /haʊzɪz/   *mouth* /maʊθ/, *mouths* /maʊðz/

Third-person singular verbs (for example *watches*, *wants*, *runs*) and possessives (for example *George's*, *Mark's*, *Joe's*) follow the same pronunciation rules.

303 singular and plural: irregular plurals

1 The most common words with irregular plurals are:

Singular	Plural	Singular	Plural	Singular	Plural
calf	calves	series	series	child	children
half	halves	analysis	analyses		
knife	knives	basis	bases	sheep	sheep
leaf	leaves	crisis	crises	fish	fish
life	lives			aircraft	aircraft
loaf	loaves	cactus	cacti		
self	selves	fungus	fungi		
shelf	shelves	nucleus	nuclei		
thief	thieves	radius	radii		
wife	wives				
		bacterium	bacteria		
foot	feet				
tooth	teeth	vertebra	vertebrae		
goose	geese				
man	men	criterion	criteria		
woman	women	phenomenon	phenomena		
mouse	mice				

2   *Cattle, people* and *police* are plural words with no singular.

> ***Cattle are*** *selling for very high prices this year.*
> (NOT ~~Cattle is selling~~ ...)
> ***The police are*** *searching for a tall dark man with a beard.*
> (NOT ~~The police is searching~~ ...)
> ***People are*** *funny.* (NOT ~~People is funny.~~)

304 singular and plural: singular words ending in -s

Some words that end in *-s* are singular. Some important examples are:

a   *billiards, draughts* and other names of games ending in *-s*

> *Draughts **is** an easier game than chess.*

b   *measles, rabies* and other names of illnesses ending in *-s*

> *Rabies **is** widespread in Europe. We hope we can keep **it** out of Britain.*

c   *athletics, politics, mathematics* and other words ending in *-ics*

> *The mathematics that I did at school **has** not been very useful to me.*

d   *news*

> *Ten o'clock. Here **is** the news.*

305 singular and plural: singular words with plural verbs

1   We often use plural verbs with words like *family, team, government,* which refer to groups of people.

> ***My family have*** *decided to move to Nottingham.*

We also use plural pronouns, and we use *who,* not *which.*

> ***My family are*** *wonderful. **They** do all **they** can for me.*
> *'How **are** the team?' '**They** are very confident.' 'Not surprising. **They're** the only team **who have** ever won all **their** matches right through the season.'*

2   We prefer singular verbs and pronouns (and *which*) if we see the group as an 'impersonal' unit. (For example, in statistics.)

> *The average family (**which has** four members) ...*

3   *A number of* and *a group of* are used with plural nouns, pronouns and verbs.

> ***A number of my friends feel*** *that **they are** not properly paid for the work **they** do.* (NOT ~~A number of my friends feels~~ ...)

▷   For singular and plural with *a lot of,* see 205.2.

306 singular and plural: plural expressions with singular verbs

1 When we talk about amounts and quantities we usually use singular verbs, pronouns and determiners, even if the noun is plural.

> ***Where's that*** *five pounds I lent you?*
> (NOT ~~*Where are those five pounds ...?*~~)
> *Twenty miles **is** a long way to walk.*
> *'How much petrol have we got left?' 'About five litres.' **'That isn't** enough. We'll have to get some more.'*

For expressions like *another six weeks*, see 33.3.

2 The expression *more than one* is used with a singular noun and verb.

> *More than one **person is** going to lose his job.*

3 Expressions like *one of my* ... are followed by a plural noun and a singular verb.

> ***One of my friends is*** *going to Honolulu.*

4 Some expressions joined by *and* have singular verbs. This happens when we think of the two nouns as 'one thing'.

> ***Fish and chips is*** *getting very expensive.*
> (NOT ~~*Fish and chips are* ...~~)
> *'**War and Peace' is** the longest book I've ever read.*

307 singular and plural: **anybody** etc

Anybody, anyone, somebody, someone, nobody, no-one, everybody and *everyone* are used with singular verbs.

> ***Is*** *everybody ready?*
> (NOT ~~*Are everybody ready?*~~)

However, we often use *they, them* and *their* to refer to these words, especially in an informal style.

> *If anybody calls, tell **them** I'm out, but take **their** name and address.*
> *Nobody phoned, did **they**?*
> *Somebody left **their** umbrella behind yesterday. Would **they** please collect it from the office?*
> *Everybody thinks **they're** different from everybody else.*

They, them and *their* are not plural in sentences like these. They mean 'he or she', 'him or her' and 'his or her'. In a more formal style, we usually use *he, him* and *his* (meaning 'he or she', etc).

> *When somebody does not want to live, **he** can be very difficult to help.*

308 slow(ly)

In an informal style, we sometimes use *slow* as an adverb instead of *slowly*.

> *Drive **slow**—I think we're nearly there.*
> *Can you go **slow** for a minute?*

Slow is used in road signs.

> ***SLOW**—DANGEROUS BEND*

309 small and little

Small is used just to talk about size. It is the opposite of *big* or *large* (see 65).

> *Could I have a **small** brandy, please?*
> *You're too **small** to be a policeman.*

The adjective *little* is used to talk about | size + emotion | .

If we call something *little*, we usually have some sort of feeling about it—we like it, or we dislike it, or it makes us laugh, or we think it is sweet, for example.

> ***Poor little thing**—come here and let me look after you.*
> *'What's he like?' 'Oh, he's a **funny little man.**'*
> *What's that **nasty little boy** doing in our garden?*
> *They've bought a **pretty little house** in the country.*

Little is not usually used after a verb (see 10).

▷ For the determiners *little* and *few*, see 129.

310 smell

There are three ways to use *smell*.

1 As a 'copula verb' (see 91), to say what sort of smell something has. Progressive tenses are not used.

> | subject + *smell* + adjective |

> *That **smells** funny. What's in it?* (NOT *That is smelling* …)
> *Those roses **smell** beautiful.* (NOT … *beautifully.*)

> | subject + *smell of* + noun |

> *The railway carriage **smelt of** beer and old socks.*

2 To say what we perceive with our noses. Progressive tenses are not used. We often use *can smell* (see 81).

> ***Can you smell** burning?*   *I **can smell** supper.*

3 To say that we are using our noses to find something out. Progressive tenses can be used.

> *'What are you doing?' '**I'm smelling** my shirt to see if I can wear it for another day.'*

311 **so** and **not** with **hope, believe** etc

1 We use *so* after several verbs instead of repeating a *that*-clause.

> *'Do you think we'll have good weather?' 'I hope so.'*
> (= *'I hope that we'll have good weather.'*)

The most common expressions like this are: *hope so, expect so, believe so, imagine so, suppose so, guess so, reckon so, think so, be afraid so.*

> *'Is that Alex?' '**I think so.**'*
> *'Did you lose?' '**I'm afraid so.**'*

We do not use *so* before a *that*-clause.

> *I hope that we'll have good weather.*
> (NOT *I hope ~~so, that we'll have good weather.~~*)

2 We can make these expressions negative in two ways.

a. | subject + verb + *not* |

> *'Will it rain?' '**I hope not.**'*
> *'You won't be here tomorrow, will you.' '**I suppose not.**'*
> *'Did you win?' '**I'm afraid not.**'*

b. | subject + *do not* + verb + *so* |

> *'You won't be here tomorrow.' '**I don't suppose so.**'*
> *'Is he ready?' '**I don't think so.**'*
> *'Will it rain?' '**I don't expect so.**'*

Hope and *be afraid* are always used in the first structure.
(We don't say *I don't hope so* or *I'm not afraid so.*)
Think is usually used in the second structure.
(We don't often say *I think not.*)

312 **so am I, so do I** etc

We can use *so* to mean *also*, in a special structure with

| auxiliary verb + subject |.

> | *so* + auxiliary verb + subject |

> *Louise **can** dance beautifully, and **so can** her sister.*
> *'**I've** lost the address.' '**So have I.**'*

Be and *have* can be used in this structure, even when they are not auxiliary verbs.

> *I **was** tired, and **so were** the others.*
> *'I **have** a headache.' '**So have** I.'*

After a clause with no auxiliary verb, we use *do / did*.

> *'I **like** whisky.' '**So do** I.'*

▷   For the negative structure *neither / nor am I*, etc, see 217.

313   'social' language

Every language has fixed expressions which are used on particular social occasions—for example, when people meet, leave each other, go on a journey, sit down to meals, and so on. English does not have very many expressions of this kind: here are some of the most important.

1   Introductions

Common ways of introducing strangers to each other are:

> *John, do you know Helen?*
> *Helen, this is my friend John.*
> *Sally, I don't think you've met Elaine.*
> *I don't think you two know each other, do you?*
> *Can / May I introduce John Willis?* (more informal)

When people are introduced, they say *Hello* or *How do you do?* (more formal). Note that *How do you do?* is not a question, and there is no answer to it. (It does not mean the same as *How are you?*)

> *CELIA: I don't think you two know each other, do you?*
> *Alec Sinclair—Paul McGuire.*

> *ALEC:* ⎤
> *   ⎬ How do you do?*
> *PAUL:* ⎦

People who are introduced often shake hands.

2   Greetings

> *Hello.   Hi.* (very informal)

More formal greetings:

> *Good morning / afternoon / evening.*

When leaving people:

> *Goodbye.*
> *Bye.* (informal)
> *Bye-bye.* (often used to and by children)
> *See you.* (informal)
> *Cheers.* (informal)
> *Good morning / afternoon / evening / night.* (formal)

3 Asking about health etc

When we meet people, we often ask politely about their health or their general situation.

> *How are you?*   *How are things?* (informal)
> *How's it going?* (informal)

Answers:

> *Very well, thank you. And you?*   *Fine, thank you.*

Informal answers:

> *Not too bad.*
> *OK.*
> *So-so.*
> *All right.*
> *(It) could be worse.*

4 Special greetings

Greetings for special occasions are:

> *Happy birthday!* OR *Many happy returns!*
> *Happy New Year/Easter!*
> *Happy/Merry Christmas!*

5 Holidays

Before somebody starts a holiday, we may say:

> *Have a good holiday.*

When the holiday is over, we may say:

> *Did you have a good holiday?*

6 Journeys

We do not *always* wish people a good journey, but common expressions are:

> *Have a good trip.*   *Have a good journey.*
> *Safe journey home.*

After a journey (for example, when we meet people at the airport or station), we may say:

> *Did you have a good journey/flight?*
> *Did you have a good trip?*

7 Meals

We do not have fixed expressions for the beginning and end of meals. At family meals, people may say something nice about the food during the meal (for example *This is very nice*) and after (for example *That was lovely: thank you very much*). Some religious people say 'grace' (a short prayer) before and after meals.

8 Visits and invitations

There are no fixed expressions which have to be used when you visit people.
Invitations often begin:

> *Would you like to ...?*

Possible replies:

> *Thank you very much. That would be very nice.*
> *Sorry. I'm afraid I'm not free.*

It is normal to thank people for hospitality at the moment of leaving their houses.

> *Thank you very much. That was a wonderful evening.*

9 Sleep

When somebody goes to bed, people often say *Sleep well.*
In the morning, we may ask *Did you sleep well?*
Did you have a good night? or *How did you sleep?*

10 Giving things

We do not have an expressions which is always used when we give things.
We sometimes say *Here you are*, especially when we want to make it clear that we are giving something.

> *'Have you got a map of London?' 'I think so. Yes, **here you are**.'*
> *'Thanks.'*

11 Asking for things

We normally ask for things by using yes/no questions.

> ***Could you lend** me a pen?* (NOT *Please lend me a pen.*)

For details, see 286.

12 Thanks

Common ways of thanking people are:

> *Thank you very much.*   *Thank you.*
> *Thanks.* (informal)   *Thanks a lot.* (informal)

If we want to reply to thanks, we can say:

> *Not at all.*   *You're welcome.*
> *That's (quite) all right.*   *That's OK.* (informal)

▷ For more information about *please* and *thank you*, see 249.
For requests (asking for things), see 286.
For the use of *excuse me*, *pardon* and *sorry*, see 121.
For the use of names and titles, see 211.
For expressions used when telephoning, see 341.
For rules for letter-writing, see 192.

314 some and any

1 *Some* and *any* are determiners (see 96). We use them before uncountable and plural nouns. Before another determiner or a pronoun we use *some of* and *any of*. Compare:

> *Would you like **some** ice-cream?*
> *Would you like **some of this** ice-cream?*
>
> *I can't find **any** cigarettes.*
> *I can't find **any of my** cigarettes.*

2 *Some* and *any* have the same sort of meaning as the indefinite article *a/an* (see 39). They refer to an indefinite quantity or number. Compare:

> *Have you got **an** aspirin?* (singular countable noun)
> *Have you got **any** aspirins?* (plural countable noun)
> *I need **some** medicine.* (uncountable noun)

3 We usually use *some* in affirmative clauses, and *any* in questions and negatives. Compare:

> *I want **some** razor-blades.*
> *Have you got **any** razor-blades?*
> *Sorry, I have**n't** got **any** razor-blades.*

We use *some* in questions if we expect or want people to say 'yes'; for example, in offers and requests.

> *Would you like **some** more beer?*
> *Could I have **some** brown rice, please?*
> *Have you got **some** glasses that I could borrow?*

We use *any* after words that have a negative meaning: for example *never, hardly, without*. We often use *any* after *if*.

> *You **never** give me **any** help.*
> *We got there **without any** trouble.*
> *There's **hardly any** tea left.*
> *If you want **some/any** help, let me know.*

4 When *some* is used before a noun, it usually has the 'weak' pronunciation /səm/ (see 358).

▷ For other uses of *any*, see 34; 35.
For other uses of *some*, see 315.
For *somebody* and *anybody*, *something* and *anything* etc, see 317.
For the difference between *some/any* and no article, see 316.
For *not . . . any*, *no* and *none*, see 221; 223.

315 **some**: special uses

1 We can use *some* (with the strong pronunciation /sʌm/) to make a contrast with *others*, *all* or *enough*.

Some people like the sea; others prefer the mountains.
Some of us were late, but we were all there by ten o'clock.
I've got some money, but not enough.

2 We can use *some* (/sʌm/) with a singular countable noun, to talk about an unknown person or thing.

There must be some job I could do.
She's living in some village in Yorkshire.

We can use this structure to suggest that we are not interested in somebody or something, or that we do not think much of somebody or something.

Mary's gone to Australia to marry some sheep farmer or other.
I don't want to spend my life doing some boring little office job.

316 **some/any** and no article

1 We use *some* and *any* when we are talking about fairly small numbers or quantities. Compare:

Have you got any animals? (NOT *Have you got animals?*)
Do you like animals? (= all animals)

2 *Some* and *any* refer to uncertain, indefinite or unknown numbers or quantities. Compare:

You've got some great pop records.
You've got beautiful toes.
(NOT *You've got some beautiful toes.* This would mean an uncertain number—perhaps six or seven, perhaps more or less.)

Would you like some more beer?
(Not a definite amount—as much as the hearer wants.)
We need beer, sugar, eggs, butter, rice and toilet paper.
(The usual quantities—more definite.)

317 **somebody** and **anybody, something** and **anything**, etc

The difference between *somebody* and *anybody*, *someone* and *anyone*, *somewhere* and *anywhere*, *something* and *anything* is the same as the difference between *some* and *any*. (See 314.) Most important, we use *somebody* etc in affirmative clauses, and *anybody* etc usually in questions and negatives.

> *There's **somebody** at the door.*
> *Did **anyone** telephone?*
> *I **don't** think **anybody** telephoned.*

> *Let's go **somewhere** nice for dinner.*
> *Do you know **anywhere** nice?*
> *I **don't** want to go **anywhere** too expensive.*

Somebody, something, anybody and *anything* are singular. Compare:

> ***There is somebody** waiting to see you.*
> ***There are some people** waiting to see you.*

318 sound

1 *Sound* is a 'copula verb' (see 91). We use it with adjectives, not adverbs.

> *You **sound unhappy**. What's the matter?*
> (NOT *You sound **unhappily**...*)

2 We do not usually use *sound* in progressive tenses.

> *The car **sounds** a bit funny.* (NOT *The car **is sounding**...*)

3 Note the structure *sound like.*

> *That **sounds like** Arthur coming upstairs.*

319 spelling: capital letters

We use capital (big) letters at the beginning of the following words:

days, months and public holidays

> *Sunday   Tuesday   March   September   Easter   Christmas*

the names of people and places

> *John   Mary   Canada   The United States   Mars*
> *North Africa   The Ritz Hotel   The Super Cinema*

people's titles

> *Mr Smith   Professor Jones   Colonel Blake   Dr Webb*

'nationality' and regional words (nouns or adjectives)

> *He's Russian   I speak German   Japanese history*
> *Catalan cooking*

the first word (and often other important words) in the names of books, plays, films, pictures, magazines etc

> *Gone with the wind* OR *Gone with the Wind   New Scientist*

320 spelling: **ch** and **tch**, **k** and **ck**

1 After one vowel, at the end of a word, we usually write -*ck* and -*tch* for the sounds /k/ and /tʃ/.

  back   neck   sick   lock   stuck
  catch   fetch   stitch   botch   hutch

Exceptions:

  rich   which   such   much

2 After a consonant or two vowels, we write -*k* and -*ch*.

  bank   work   talk   march   bench
  break   book   week   peach   coach

321 spelling: doubling final consonants

When we add -*ed*, -*ing*, -*er* or -*est* to a word, we sometimes double the final consonant.

  big bigger   sit sitting   stop stopped

1 We double the following letters:

b:	*rub rubbing*	*n*:	*begin beginner*
d:	*sad sadder*	*p*:	*stop stopped*
g:	*big bigger*	*r*:	*prefer preferred*
l:	*travel travelling*	*t*:	*sit sitting*
m:	*slim slimmer*		

2 We only double these letters when they come at the end of a word. Compare:

  hop hopping   BUT   *hope hoping*
  fat fatter   BUT   *late later*
  plan planned   BUT   *phone phoned*

3 We only double when there is one consonant after *one* vowel letter. Compare:

  fat fatter   BUT   *fast faster* (NOT *fastter*)
  bet betting   BUT   *beat beating* (NOT *beatting*)

4 In longer words, we only double a consonant if the *last* syllable of the word is stressed. Compare:

  up'set up'setting   BUT   *'visit 'visiting*
  be'gin be'ginning   BUT   *'open 'opening*
  re'fer re'ferring   BUT   *'offer 'offering*

Note the spelling of these words:

'gallop 'galloping 'galloped (NOT ~~gallopping gallopped~~)
de'velop de'veloping de'veloped (NOT ~~developping developped~~)

5 In British English, we double *l* at the end of a word even in an unstressed syllable.

'travel 'travelling   'equal 'equalled

(In American English, *l* is not doubled in unstressed syllables: *'traveling.*)

6 The reason for doubling is to show that a vowel has a 'short' sound. This is because in the middle of a word, a stressed vowel before *one* consonant is usually pronounced long. Compare:

hoping /'həʊpɪŋ/   *hopping* /'hɒpɪŋ/
later /leɪtə(r)/   *latter* /lætə(r)/
dining /'daɪnɪŋ/   *dinner* /'dɪnə(r)/

322 spelling: final **-e**

1 When a word ends in *-e*, and we add something that begins with a vowel (*-ing*, *-able* or *-ous*), we usually leave out the *-e*.

hope hoping
make making
note notable
fame famous

This does not happen with words ending in *-ee*.

see seeing   agree agreeable

2 In words that end in *-ge* or *-ce*, we do not leave out *-e* before *a* or *o*.

courage courageous   replace replaceable

323 spelling: full stops with abbreviations

A full stop is the small dot (.) that comes at the end of a sentence.
In American English, full stops are often used after abbreviations (shortened words), and after letters that are used instead of full names.

Mr. Lewis   Ms. Johnson   Andrew J. McCann
etc.   e.g.   U.S.A.
S.E. Asia   T.S. Eliot

In British English, we now usually write abbreviations without full stops.

Mr Lewis   Ms Johnson   Andrew J McCann
etc   e g   USA
S E Asia   T S Eliot

324 spelling: hyphens

1 A hyphen is the short line (-) that we put between two words in an
   expression like *book-shop* or *ex-husband*.
   The rules about hyphens are complicated and not very clear. If you are
   not sure, look in the dictionary, or write an expression as two separate
   words. Note:

   a. We usually put a hyphen in a two-part adjective like *blue-eyed*,
   broken-hearted, *grey-green*, *nice-looking*.

   b. When we use a group of words as an adjective before a noun, we use
   hyphens. Compare:

   > He's **out of work.**   an **out-of-work** lorry driver
   > It cost **ten pounds**   a **ten-pound** note

   c. In groups of words where the first word is stressed, we usually put
   hyphens. Compare:

   > 'book-case   a paper 'bag
   > 'make-up   to make 'up

2 We use a hyphen to separate the parts of a long word at the end of a line.
   (To see where to divide words, look in a good dictionary.)

   > …is not in accordance with the policy of the present govern-
   > ment, which was…

325 spelling: **ie** and **ei**

The sound /iː/ (as in *believe*) is often written *ie*, but not usually *ei*.
However, we write *ei* after *c*. English children learn a rhyme:

'*i* before *e*
except after *c*.'

> believe   chief   field   grief
> ceiling   deceive   receive   receipt

326 spelling: **-ise** and **-ize**

Many English verbs can be spelt with either *-ise* or *-ize*. In American
English, *-ize* is preferred in these cases. Examples:

> mechan**ize**/mechan**ise** (GB)   mechan**ize** (US)
> computer**ize**/computer**ise** (GB)   computer**ize** (US)

Words of two syllables usually have *-ise* in both British and American
English.

> sur**prise** (NOT ~~surprize~~)   re**vise**   ad**vise**   com**prise**   des**pise**
> (but GB and US cap**size**, bap**tize**; GB also bap**tise**)

A number of longer words only have *-ise*, in both British and American English. These include:

> *compromise   exercise   improvise   supervise   televise*
> *advertise* (US also *advertize*)

Note also *analyse* (US *analyze*).
If in doubt, use *-ise*—it is almost always correct, at least in British English.

327 spelling: -ly

1   We often change an adjective into an adverb by adding **-ly**.

> *late lately   right rightly   hopeful hopefully*
> *real really* (NOT ~~realy~~)   *definite definitely*
> *complete completely* (NOT ~~completly~~)

2   *-y* changes to *-i-* (see 328).

> *happy happily   easy easily   dry drily*

3   If an adjective ends in *-le*, we change *-le* to *-ly*.

> *idle idly   noble nobly*

4   If an adjective ends in *-ic*, the adverb ends in *-ically*.

> *tragic tragically*

5   Exceptions: *truly, wholly, fully, shyly, publicly.*

328 spelling: y and i

1   When we add something to a word that ends in *-y*, we usually change *-y* to *-i-*.

> *hurry   hurried   marry   marriage*
> *happy   happily   fury   furious*
> *easy   easier   merry   merriment*
> *busy   business*

Generally, nouns and verbs that end in *-y* have plural or third person singular forms in *-ies*.

> *story stories   hurry hurries   spy spies*

2   We do not change *-y* to *-i-* before *-i-* (for example, when we add *-ing*, *-ish*, *-ism*, *ize*).

> *try trying   Tory Toryism   baby babyish*

3 We do not change -*y* to -*i*- after a vowel letter.

    buy buying   *play played*   *enjoy enjoyment*
    grey greyish

Exceptions: *say said*   *lay laid*   *pay paid*

4 We change -*ie* to -*y*- before -*ing*.

    die dying   *lie lying*

329 spelling and pronunciation

In many English words, the spelling is different from the pronunciation.
(This is because our pronunciation has changed over the last few
hundred years, while the spelling system has stayed more or less the
same.)
Here are some difficult common words:

1 two syllables, not three:

    asp(i)rin   *bus(i)ness*   *diff(e)rent*   *ev(e)ning*   *ev(e)ry*
    marri(a)ge   *med(i)cine*   *om(e)lette*   *rest(au)rant*   *sev(e)ral*

2 three syllables, not four:

    comf(or)table   *secret(a)ry*   *temp(e)rature*
    veg(e)table   *us(u)ally*

3 silent letters:

    shou(l)d   *cou(l)d*   *wou(l)d*   *ca(l)m*   *wa(l)k*   *ta(l)k*
    ha(l)f   *whis(t)le*   *cas(t)le*   *lis(t)en*   *fas(t)en*   *Chris(t)mas*
    of(t)en   *(w)rite*   *(w)rong*
    (k)now   *(k)nife*   *(k)nee*   *(k)nock*   *(k)nob*
    si(g)n   *forei(g)n*   *champa(g)ne*
    clim(b)   *com(b)*   *dum(b)*   *hym(n)*   *autum(n)*
    w(h)ere   *w(h)y*   *w(h)at*   *w(h)en*   *w(h)ich*   *w(h)ether*
    (h)onest   *(h)onour*   *(h)our*
    cu(p)board   *i(s)land*   *i(r)on*   *mus(c)le*   *(p)sychology*
    han(d)kerchief   *san(d)wich*   *We(d)nesday*
    (w)ho   *(w)hose*   *(w)hole*
    g(u)ess   *g(u)ide*   *g(u)itar*
    dau(gh)ter   *hi(gh)*   *hei(gh)t*   *li(gh)t*   *mi(gh)t*   *ri(gh)t*
    strai(gh)t   *throu(gh)*   *ti(gh)t*   *wei(gh)*   *nei(gh)bour*
    bou(gh)t   *brou(gh)t*   *cau(gh)t*   *ou(gh)t*   *thou(gh)t*

4 gh = /f/

    *cou**gh**   enou**gh**   lau**gh***

5 ch = /k/

    *ar**ch**itect   **ch**aracter   **ch**emist   **Ch**ristmas   heada**ch**e*
    *tootha**ch**e   stoma**ch***

6 a = /e/

    ***a**ny   m**a**ny   Th**a**mes*

7 ea = /e/

    *br**ea**kfast   d**ea**d   d**ea**th   h**ea**d   h**ea**lth   h**ea**vy*
    *l**ea**ther   pl**ea**sure   r**ea**d (past)   r**ea**dy   br**ea**d   sw**ea**ter*
    *inst**ea**d*

8 ea = /eɪ/

    *st**ea**k   br**ea**k   gr**ea**t*

9 o = /ʌ/

    *br**o**ther   m**o**ther   l**o**ve   c**o**mpany   c**o**me*
    *c**o**ver   m**o**nth   m**o**ney   **o**ne   n**o**thing   **o**nion*
    *o**th**er   s**o**me   s**o**n   st**o**mach   g**o**vernment   w**o**nder*
    *w**o**rry   L**o**ndon   h**o**ney   gl**o**ve   t**o**n*

10 ou = /ʌ/

    *c**ou**ntry   c**ou**ple   c**ou**sin   d**ou**ble   en**ou**gh   tr**ou**ble*

11 u = /ʊ/

    *b**u**tcher   c**u**shion   p**u**ll   p**u**sh   p**u**t*

12 words pronounced with /aɪ/

    dial   either   neither   buy   height   idea   iron
    microphone   biology   science   society

13 strange spellings:

minute /ˈmɪnɪt/	*theatre* /ˈθɪətə(r)/
woman /ˈwʊmən/	*one* /wʌn/
women /ˈwɪmɪn/	*once* /wʌns/
friend /frend/	*two* /tuː/
Europe /ˈjʊərəp/	*area* /ˈeərɪə/
Asia /ˈeɪʃə/	*heard* /hɜːd/
Australia /ɒsˈtreɪlɪə/	*biscuit* /ˈbɪskɪt/
bicycle /ˈbaɪsɪkl/	*busy* /ˈbɪziː/
blood /blʌd/	*fruit* /fruːt/
foreign /ˈfɒrən/	*moustache* /məˈstɑːʃ/
juice /dʒuːs/	*heart* /hɑːt/

330 still, yet and already

1 Meanings

Still, *yet* and *already* are all used to talk about things which are going on, or expected, around the present. We use these words to say whether something is in the past, the present or the future.

a   *Still* says that something is in the present, not the past—it has not finished.

> *She's **still** asleep.*
> *It's **still** raining.*

b   *Not yet* says that something is in the future, not the present or past. We are waiting for it.

> *'Has Sally arrived?' '**Not yet**.'*
> *The postman hasn't come **yet**.*

In questions, *yet* asks whether something is in the future or not.

> *Has the postman come **yet**?*

c   *Already* says that something is in the present or past, not the future—perhaps it has happened sooner than we expected.

> *'When's Sally going to come?' 'She's **already** here.'*
> *'You must go to Scotland.' 'I've **already** been.'*

2 Position

Already and *still* go in 'mid-position' (see 13.2).

> *He's **already** gone.*
> *When I was fourteen I **already** knew that I wanted to be a doctor.*
> (NOT *~~Already when I was fourteen~~* ...)

> *She's **still** working.*
> *I **still** remember your first birthday.*

Yet usually goes at the end of a clause.

> *She hasn't gone **yet**.*
> *I haven't done the shopping **yet**.*

3 Tenses

We usually use *already* and *yet* with the present perfect tense in British English.

> *She **hasn't gone** yet.*
> *I've already **forgotten**.*

▷   For other meanings of *still* and *yet*, see a good dictionary.
   For the meaning of *ever*, see 116.

331 subject and object forms

1 Six English words have one form when they are used as subjects, and a different form when they are used as objects.

subject	object
I	me
he	him
she	her
we	us
they	them
who	whom

Compare:

> *I like dogs.*   *We went to see her.*
> *Dogs don't like me.*   *She came to see us.*
>
> *This is Mr Perkins, who works with me.*
> *This is Mr Perkins, with whom I am working at the moment.*

2 In informal English, we use object-forms (*me, him* etc) after *be* and in one-word answers.

> *'Who's that?' 'It's me.'*
> *'Who said that?' 'Him.'*

In a more formal style, we prefer to use a subject form with a verb.

> *'Who said that?' 'He did.'*

3 *Whom* is not often used in informal English. We prefer to use *who* as an object, especially in questions.

> *Who did you go with?*
> *Who have you invited?*

We use *whom* in a more formal style; and we must use *whom* after a preposition.

> *Whom did they arrest?* (formal)
> *With whom did you go?* (very formal)

4 After *as, than, but* and *except*, we use object forms in an informal style.

> *My sister's nearly as tall as me.*
> *I'm prettier than her.*
> *Everybody but me knew what was happening.*
> *Everybody except him can come.*

Subject forms are used in a more formal style (usually with auxiliary verbs) after *as* and *than*.

> *My sister's nearly as tall as I am.*
> *I'm prettier than she is.*

332 subjunctive

1 The subjunctive is a special verb form that looks the same as the
infinitive. It is sometimes used to say that something should be done.

> *It's important that everybody **write** to the President.*
> *The Director asked that he **be** allowed to advertise for more staff.*

In British English that subjunctive is unusual. We usually express this
kind of idea with *should*.

> *It's important that everybody **should write** to the President.*
> *The Director asked that he **should be** allowed to advertise for more
> staff.*

2 We often use *were* instead of *was* after *if* and *I wish*. (See 165 and 367.)
This is also a subjunctive.

> ***If I were** you, I would stop smoking.*   ***I wish I were** on holiday
> now.*

333 suggest

We do not use *suggest* with object + infinitive.

> *My uncle suggested that I should get a job in a bank.*
> *My uncle suggested getting a job in a bank.*
> (NOT *My uncle suggested me to get* ...)

334 such and so

1 We use *such* before a noun (with or without an adjective).

> | *such* (+ adjective) + noun |

> *She's **such a fool**.*
> *He's got **such patience**.*
> *I've never met **such a nice person**.*
> *It was **such a good film** that I saw it twice.*

We use *so* before an adjective alone (without a noun).

> | *so* + adjective |

> *She's **so stupid**.*
> *He's **so patient** with her.*
> *Your mother's **so nice**.*
> *The film was **so good** that I saw it twice.*

We cannot use either *such* or *so* with *the* or a possessive.

> *I am happy to visit your country—it's so beautiful.*
> (NOT ... *your so beautiful country*.)

2 *So* and *such* can be followed by *that*-clauses.

> *It was* **so** *cold* **that** *we stopped playing.*
> *It was* **such** *a cold afternoon* **that** *we stopped playing.*

335 surely

Surely does not mean the same as *certainly*. Compare:

> *That's* **certainly** *a mouse.* (= *I know that's a mouse.*)
> **Surely** *that's a mouse?* (= *That seems to be a mouse. How surprising!*)

Surely expresses surprise.
We can use *surely not* to show that we do not want to believe something, or find it difficult to believe.

> **Surely** *you're* **not** *going to wear that hat?*

336 sympathetic

Sympathetic is a 'false friend' for people who speak European languages. It does not mean the same as *sympathique, sympathisch, sympatisk, simpatico* etc.

> *The people in my class are all very* **nice/pleasant**.
> (NOT *...very* **sympathetic**.)

Sympathetic means 'sharing somebody's feelings' or 'sorry for somebody who is in trouble'.

> *I'm* **sympathetic** *towards the strikers.*
> *She's always very* **sympathetic** *when people feel ill.*

337 take

Take has three main meanings.

1 The opposite of *give*

> *She* **took** *my plate and gave me a clean one.*
> *Who's* **taken** *my bicycle?*
> *'Could I speak to Andrew?' 'I'm sorry, he's not here just now. Can I* **take** *a message?'*

We take something *from / out of / off* a place, and *from* a person.

> *Could you* **take** *some money* **out of** *my wallet?*
> *They* **took** *everything away* **from** *me.* (NOT *They took me everything.*)

2 The opposite of *put*

> *I* **took** *off my coat and put on a dressing gown.*
> *He* **took** *a ring out of his pocket and put it on her finger.*

3 The opposite of *bring*

We can use *take* for movements away from the speaker, and in other directions (see 71).

*Can you **take** me to the station tomorrow morning?*
***Take** this form to Mr Collins, ask him to sign it, and then bring it back.*

▷ For *take* with expressions of time, see 338.

338 take (time)

We can use *take* to say how much time we need to do something. Three constructions are possible.

> person + *take* + time + infinitive

*I **took** three hours to get home last night.*
*She **takes** all day to wake up.*

> activity + *take* (+ person) + time

*The journey **took** me three hours.*
*Gardening **takes** a lot of time.*

> It + *take* (+ person) + time + infinitive

*It **took** me three hours to get home last night.*
*It **takes** ages to do the shopping.*

339 tall and high

1 We use *tall* for things which are this shape:

We can talk about tall people, trees, and sometimes buildings.

*How **tall** are you?* (NOT ~~How high are you?~~)
*There are some beautiful **tall** trees at the end of our garden.*

We do not use *tall* for things which are this shape:

   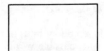

We use *high*.

*Mont Blanc is the **highest** mountain in Europe.*
(NOT ... ~~the tallest mountain.~~)
*It's a very **high** room.* (NOT ... ~~tall room.~~)

2 We use *high* to say how far something is above the ground. A child standing on a chair may be *higher* than his father, but not *taller*.

HIGH **TALL**

3 Parts of the body are *long*, not *tall*.

*She's got beautiful **long** legs.* (NOT ... ~~*tall legs.*~~)

340 taste

We can use *taste* in three ways.

1 *Taste* can be a 'copula verb' (see 91). We can describe the taste of food etc by using $\boxed{taste + \text{adjective}}$ or $\boxed{taste\ of + \text{noun}}$.

Progressive tenses are not used.

$\boxed{taste + \text{adjective}}$

*This **tastes nice**. What's in it?* (NOT *This **is tasting** ...*)
*The wine **tasted horrible**.* (NOT ... ~~*horribly*~~.)

$\boxed{taste\ of + \text{noun}}$

*The wine **tasted of old boots**.*

2 We can talk about our sensations by using *taste* with a personal subject. Progressive tenses are not possible; we often use *can taste*. (See 81.)

*I **can taste** garlic and mint in the sauce.* (NOT ~~*I am tasting* ...~~)

3 We can talk about using our sense of taste to find something out.

*'Stop eating the cake.' '**I'm** just **tasting** it to see if it's OK.'*

341 telephoning

1 We usually answer a private phone like this:

> *Hello. Abingdon three seven eight double two.* (= 37822)

Some people give their names.

> *Hello. Albert Packard.*

2 We ask for a person like this:

> *'Could I speak to Jane Horrabin?'*

3 We can identify ourselves with the word *speaking*.

> *'Could I speak to Jane Horrabin?' '**Speaking**.'* (= *That's me.*)

4 Note the difference between *this* (the speaker) and *that* (the hearer).

> ***This** is Corinne. Is **that** Susie?*

(Americans use *this* for both speaker and hearer.)

5 We ask for a number like this:

> *Could I have Bristol three seven eight seven eight?*
> *Could I have extension two oh four six?* (= *2046*)

6 The telephonist may say:

> *One moment, please.*
> *Hold on a moment, please.*
> *Trying to connect you. (The number's) ringing for you.*
> *Putting you through now.*
> *I'm afraid this number is engaged/busy.*
> *I'm afraid this number is not answering/there's no reply from this extension.*
> *Will you hold?* (= *Will you wait?*)

A possible answer to the last question:

> *No, I'll ring again later.* OR *I'll ring back later.*

7 If somebody is not there:

> *'I'm afraid she's not in at the moment. Can I take a message?'*
> *'Yes. Could you ask her to ring me back this evening?'*

8 Other expressions:

> *I'm afraid you've got the wrong number.*
> *I'm sorry. I've got the wrong number.*
> *Could you speak louder? It's a bad line.*
> *Could I possibly use your phone?*
> *What's the code for London?*
> *How do I call the operator?*

*I'd like to make a reversed charge call/transferred charge call to
Washington 348 6767.* (The person at the other end pays. Americans
call this a *collect call*.)

342 telling the time

1 There are two ways of saying what time it is.

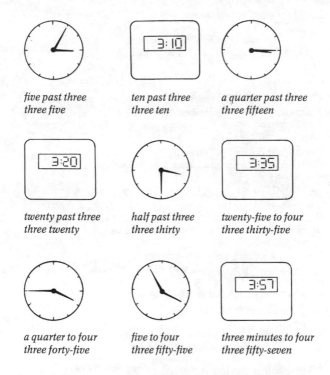

five past three
three five

ten past three
three ten

a quarter past three
three fifteen

twenty past three
three twenty

half past three
three thirty

twenty-five to four
three thirty-five

a quarter to four
three forty-five

five to four
three fifty-five

three minutes to four
three fifty-seven

2 In conversation, we do not usually use the 'twenty-four hour clock'. We
can make a time more precise by saying *in the morning, in the afternoon*
etc, or by saying *a m* (= 'before midday') and *p m* (= 'after midday').

3 We ask about the time like this:

What time is it?   What's the time?
What time does the match start?

343 tenses in subordinate clauses

1 In subordinate clauses (after conjunctions), we often use tenses in a special way. In particular, we use present tenses with a future meaning, and past tenses with a conditional meaning.
This happens after *if*; after conjunctions of time like *when, until, after, before, as soon as*; after *as, than, whether, where*; after relative pronouns; and in reported speech.

> present for future

> *She'll be happy if you **telephone** her.*
> *I'll write to her when I **have** time.* (NOT *... when I will have time.*)
> *I'll stay here until the plane **takes off**.*
> *She'll be on the same train as I **am** tomorrow.*
> *We'll get there sooner than you **do**.*
> *I'll ask him whether he **wants** to go.*   *I'll go where you **go**.*
> *I'll give a pound to anybody who **finds** my pen.*
> *One day the government will really ask people what they **want**.*

> past for conditional

> *If I had lots of money, I'd give some to anybody who **asked** for it.*
> (NOT *... who would ask for it.*)
> *Would you follow me wherever I **went**?*
> *In a perfect world, you could say exactly what you **thought**.*

2 Sometimes we use a future tense in a subordinate clause. This happens if the main clause is not about the future. Compare:

> *I'll tell you when **I arrive**.*   *I wonder when **I'll arrive**.*
> *I don't know if **I'll be** here tomorrow.*

344 that: omission

We can often leave out the conjunction *that*, especially in an informal style.

1 Relative pronoun

We can leave out the relative pronoun *that* when it is the object of the relative clause.

> *Look! There are the people (**that**) we met in Brighton.*

2 Reported speech

We can leave out *that* after more common verbs. Compare:

> *James said (**that**) he was feeling better.*
> *James replied **that** he was feeling better.*
> (NOT *James replied he was feeling better.*)

3 After adjectives

We can use *that*-clauses after some adjectives. We can leave out *that* in more common expressions.

> *I'm glad (**that**) you're all right.*
> *It's funny (**that**) he hasn't written.*

4 After *so* and *such*

We sometimes leave out *that* after *so* and *such*.

> *I came to see you so (**that**) you would know the truth.*
> *I was having such a nice time (**that**) I didn't want to leave.*

345 there is

1 When we tell people that something exists (or does not exist), we usually begin the sentence with *there is, there are* etc, and put the subject after the verb.

> **There's** *a hole in my sock.* (NOT *A hole is in my sock.*)

We use this structure with 'indefinite subjects'—for example, nouns with *a/an*, nouns with *some, any,* or *no*, nouns with no article, *somebody, anything, nothing.*

> **There's some beer** *in the fridge.*
> **Are there tigers** *in South America?*
> **There's somebody** *at the door.*

2 We can use this structure with all simple tenses of *be*.

> **There has been** *nothing in the newspaper about the accident.*
> **There will be** *snow on high ground.*

There may be, there might be, there can be etc also possible.

> **There might be** *rain later.*   **There must be** *some mistake.*

3 The infinitive of *there is* (*there to be*) is used after certain verbs and adjectives.

> *I don't want* **there to be** *any trouble.*
> *It's important for* **there to be** *a meeting soon.*

4 We can use *there* to introduce indefinite subjects of present and past progressive verbs.

> **There's a man standing** *in the garden.*
> **There was somebody looking** *at her.*

5 Note the expression *there's no need to*.

> **There's no need to** *worry—everything will be all right.*

346 think

1 *Think* can mean 'have an opinion'. In this meaning, it is not used in
progressive tenses.

>   *I **don't think** much of his latest book.*
>   (NOT ~~I'm not thinking much~~ ...)
>   *Who **do you think** will win the election?*
>   (NOT ~~Who are you thinking~~ ... ?)

2 When *think* has other meanings (for example *plan*, or *consider*)
progressive tenses are possible.

>   *I**'m thinking** of changing my job.*
>   *What **are you thinking** about?*

3 When *think* is used to introduce a negative idea, we usually construct the
sentence *I do not think ...*, not *I think ... not ...* (See 215.7.)

>   *I **don't think** it will rain.*
>   *Mary **doesn't think** she can come.*

▷   Note also the structures *I think so, I don't think so.* (See 311.)

347 this and that

1 We use *this* to talk about people and things which are close to the
speaker, and for situations that we are in at the moment of speaking.

>   *I don't know what I'm doing in **this** country.*
>   (NOT ... ~~in that country.~~)
>   ***This** is very nice—how do you cook it?*
>   *Get **this** cat off my shoulder.*

We use *that* to talk about people and things which are more distant, not
so close.

>   *I don't like **that** boy you're going out with.* (NOT ... ~~this boy~~ ...)
>   ***That** smells nice—is it for lunch?*
>   *Get **that** cat off the piano.*

2 We use *this* to talk about things which are happening or just going to happen (present or future).

> *I like **this** music. What is it?*   *Listen to **this**. You'll like it.*

We use *that* to talk about things which have finished.

> ***That** was nice. What was it?*   *Who said **that**?*

3 On the telephone, British people use *this* to talk about themselves, and *that* to talk about the hearer.

> *Hello. **This** is Elizabeth. Is **that** Ruth?*

Americans often use *this* in both cases.

▷ The difference between *this* and *that* is like the difference between *here* and *there* (see 159). See also *come* and *go* (83) and *bring* and *take* (71).

348 too

1 We can use an infinitive structure after *too*.

> | *too* + adjective/adverb + infinitive |

> *He's **too old to work**.*
> *It's **too cold to play** tennis.*
> *We arrived **too late to have** dinner.*

We can also use a structure with *for* + object + infinitive.

> | *too* + adjective/adverb + *for* + object + infinitive |

> *It's **too late for the pubs to be** open.*
> *The runway's **too short for planes to land**.*

2 We can modify *too* with *much, a lot, far, a little, a bit* or *rather*.

> ***much too** old* (NOT ~~*very too old*~~)   ***a little too** confident*
> ***a lot too** big*   ***a bit too** soon*
> ***far too** young*   ***rather too** often*

3 Don't confuse *too* and *too much*. We do not use *too much* before an adjective without a noun, or an adverb.

> *You are **too kind** to me.* (NOT ... ~~*too much kind to me.*~~)
> *I arrived **too early**.* (NOT ... ~~*too much early.*~~)

4 Don't confuse *too* and *very*. *Too* means 'more than enough', 'more than necessary'. Compare:

> *He's a **very** intelligent child.*
> *He's **too** intelligent for his class—he's not learning anything.*

> *It was **very** cold, but we went out.*
> *It was **too** cold to go out, so we stayed at home.*

349 travel, journey and trip

Travel means 'travelling in general'. It is uncountable (see 92).

>*My interests are music and **travel***.

A *journey* is one 'piece' of travelling.

>*Did you have a good **journey***? (NOT ~~Did you have a good travel?~~)

A *trip* is a journey together with the activity which is the reason for the journey.

>*I'm going on a **business trip** next week.*
>(= *I'm going on a journey and I'm going to do some business.*)

We do not usually use *trip* for journeys which take a very long time.

350 unless and if not

Very often, we can use *unless* to mean *if ... not*.

>*Come tomorrow **if** I **don't** phone / **unless** I phone.*
>*I'll take the job **if** the pay's **not** too low / **unless** the pay's too low.*

We cannot always use *unless* instead of *if not*. It depends on the sense.

a. The sentence says 'A will happen if B does not stop it.' We can use *if not* or *unless*.

>*I'll come back tomorrow **if** there's **not** a plane strike.*
>(OR ... ***unless** there's a plane strike.*)
>*Let's have dinner out—**if** you're **not** too tired.*
>(OR ... ***unless** you're too tired.*)

b. The sentence says 'A will happen because B does not happen'. We can use *if not*, but not *unless*.

>*I'll be glad **if** she **doesn't** come this evening.*
>(NOT ~~I'll be glad unless she comes this evening.~~)
>*She'd be pretty **if** she **didn't** wear so much make-up.*
>(NOT ... ~~unless she wore so much make-up.~~)

351 until and by

We use *until* to talk about a situation or state that will continue up to a certain moment.

>*Can I stay **until** the weekend?*

We use *by* to talk about an action that will happen on or before a future moment.

>*You'll have to leave **by** Monday midday at the latest.*
>(= *at twelve on Monday or before.*)

Compare:

> '*Can you repair my watch by Tuesday?*
> (NOT ... ~~until Tuesday.~~)
> '*No, I'll have to keep it until Saturday.*'

until twelve o'clock   *by twelve o'clock*

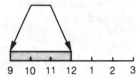   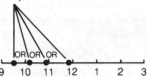

352 **until** and **to**

1   We usually use *until* (or *till*) to talk about 'time up to'.

> *I waited for her until six o'clock, but she didn't come.*
> (NOT ~~I waited for her to six o'clock ...~~)

2   We can use *to* after *from*.

> *I usually work from nine to five.* (OR ... *from nine till five.*)

We can also use *to* when we are counting the time until a future event.

> *It's another three weeks to the holidays.* (OR ... *until the holidays.*)

3   We do not use *until* for space—only for time.

> *We walked to the edge of the forest.* (OR ... *as far as ...*)
> (NOT ~~We walked till the edge of the forest.~~)

4   *Until* and *till* mean the same. They are used in the same way, except that
we prefer *until* in more formal situations.

▷   For the difference between *until* and *by*, see 351.

353 **used to** + infinitive

1   *Used to* + infinitive is only used in the past: it has no present form. We use
it to talk about past habits and states which are now finished.

> *I used to smoke, but I've stopped.*
> *She used to be very shy.*

To talk about present habits and states, we usually just use the simple
present tense (see 261).

> *He smokes.* (NOT ~~He uses to smoke.~~)
> *Her sister is still very shy.*

2   In a formal style, *used to* can have the forms of a modal auxiliary verb
(questions and negatives without *do*).

>   ***Did you use to** play football at school?* (informal)
>   ***Used you** to play football at school?* (formal)
>
>   *I **didn't use to** like opera, but now I do.* (informal)
>   *I **used not** to like opera, but now I do.* (formal)

A contracted negative is possible. (*I **usedn't** to like ...*)

3   We do not use *used to* to say how long something took, or how often it
happened.

>   *I **lived** in Chester for three years.*
>   (NOT ~~I used to live in Chester for three years.~~)
>   *I **went** to France seven times.*
>   (NOT ~~I used to go to France seven times.~~)

4   Note the pronunciation of *used* /juːst/ and *use* /juːs/ in this structure.

5   Don't confuse | *used to* + infinitive | and | *be used to ... -ing* |

(see 354). The two structures have quite different meanings.

354 (be) used to + noun or -ing

After *be used to*, we use a noun or an *-ing* form.

The meaning is quite different from | *used to* + infinitive | (see 353).

If you say that you are used to something, you mean that you know it
well. You have experienced it so much that it is no longer strange to you.

| *be used to* + noun |

>   *I'm **used to** London traffic—I've lived here for six years.*
>   *At the beginning, I couldn't understand the Londoners, because
>   I **wasn't used to** their accent.*

We can use an *-ing* form after *be used to*, but not an infinitive.

| *be used to* + ... *-ing* |

>   *I'm **used to driving** in London now, but it was hard at the beginning.*
>   (NOT ~~I'm used to drive ...~~)
>   *It was a long time before **she was** completely **used to working** with
>   old people.*

Get used to means 'become used to'.

>   *You'll soon **get used to** living in the country.*

▷   For more information about structures with | *to* + ... *-ing* | , see 181.

355 verbs with object complements

1 Some verbs are used with | object + adjective |.
They usually show how something is changed.

> | verb + object + adjective |

> *The rain **made** the grass wet.*
> *Let's **paint** the door red.*
> *Try to **get** it clean.*
> ***Cut** the bread thin.*

Keep and *leave* show how things are not changed.

> ***Keep** him warm.*
> *You **left** the house dirty.*

2 Other verbs are used with | object + noun |.

> | verb + object + noun |

> *They **elected** him President.*
> *You have **made** me a very happy man.*
> *Why do you **call** your brother 'Piggy'?*

356 verbs with two objects

1 We use many verbs with two objects—a direct object and an indirect object. Usually the indirect object refers to a person, and comes first.

> | verb + indirect object + direct object |

> *He gave **his wife a camera** for Christmas.*
> *Can you send **me the bill**?*
> *I'll lend **you some**.*

Some common verbs which are used like this:

bring	pay
buy	promise
cost	read
give	refuse
leave	send
lend	show
make	take
offer	tell
owe	write
pass	

2   We can also put the indirect object *after* the direct object, with a preposition (usually *to* or *for*).
We do this when the direct object is much shorter than the indirect object, or when we want to give special importance to the indirect object.

> verb + direct object + preposition + indirect object

*I took **it to the policeman**.*
*She sent **some flowers to the nurse** who was looking after her daughter.*
*Mother bought **the ice cream for you**, not for me.*

3   When both objects are personal pronouns, we more often put the direct object first.

*Give **it to me**. (Give **me it** is also possible.)*
*Send **them to her**. (Send **her them** is also possible.)*

4   In passive sentences, the subject is usually the person (not the thing which is sent, given etc).

I've just been given a lovely picture.
You were paid three hundred pounds last month.

But we can make the thing given etc the subject if necessary.

'What happened to the picture?' 'It was sent to Mr Dunn.'

5   We do not use *explain*, *suggest* or *describe* with the structure

> indirect object + direct object   .

*Can you explain **your decision to us**?*
(NOT ~~Can you explain us your decision?~~)
*Can you suggest **a good dentist to me**?*
(NOT ~~Can you suggest me ...?~~)
*Please describe **your wife to us**.*
(NOT ~~Please describe us your wife.~~)

6   When *write* has no direct object, we put *to* before the indirect object. Compare:

Write me a letter.
Write to me. (Write me is not common in British English.)

▷   For structures like *They made him captain*, see 355.2.

357 way

1 We often use *way* (= *method*) in expressions without a preposition.

> *You're doing it (in) **the wrong way**.*
> *You put in the cassette **this way**.*
> *Do it **any way** you like.*

In relative structures, we often use *the way that...*

> *I don't like **the way (that)** you're doing it.*

2 After *way*, we can use an infinitive structure or *of... -ing*. There is no important difference between the two structures.

> *There's no **way to prove / of proving** that he was stealing.*

3 Don't confuse *in the way* and *on the way*.
If something is *in the way*, it stops you getting where you want to go.

> *Please don't stand in the kitchen door—you're **in the way**.*

On the way means 'during the journey' or 'coming'.

> *We'll have lunch **on the way**.*
> *Spring is **on the way**.*

▷ For *by the way*, see 97.1.

358 weak and strong forms

1 Some words in English have two pronunciations: one when they are stressed and one when they are not. Compare:

> *I got up **at** /ət/ six o'clock.*
> *What are you looking **at**? /'æt/*

Most of these words are prepositions, pronouns, conjunctions, articles and auxiliary verbs. They are not usually stressed, so the unstressed ('weak') pronunciation is the usual one. This usually has the vowel /ə/ or no vowel. The 'strong' pronunciation has the 'written' vowel. Compare:

> *I **was** late. /w(ə)z/*
> *It **was** raining /w(ə)z/*
> *Yes, I '**was**. /wɒz/*

> *I **must** go now. /m(ə)s/*
> *I really '**must** stop smoking. /mʌst/*

> *Where **have** you been? /(ə)v/*
> *You might **have** told me. /(ə)v/*
> *What did you '**have** for breakfast? /hæv/*
> *(Have is not an auxiliary verb in this sentence.)*

Contracted negatives always have a strong pronunciation.

> *can't /kɑːnt/   mustn't /mʌsnt/   wasn't /'wɒznt/*

2 The most important words which have weak and strong forms are:

	Weak form	Strong form		Weak form	Strong form
a	/ə/	/eɪ/*	some	/s(ə)m/	/sʌm/
am	/(ə)m/	/æm/	than	/ð(ə)n/	/ðæn/
an	/ən/	/æn/*	that†	/ð(ə)t/	/ðæt/
and	/(ə)n(d)/	/ænd/	the	/ðə; ðɪ/	/ðiː/
are	/ə(r)/	/ɑː(r)/	them	/ð(ə)m/	/ðem/
as	/əz/	/æz/	there	/ðə(r)/	/ðeə(r)/
at	/ət/	/æt/	to	/tə/	/tuː/
be	/bɪ/	/biː/	us	/əs/	/ʌs/
been	/bɪn/	/biːn/	was	/w(ə)z/	/wɒz/
but	/bət/	/bʌt/	we	/wɪ/	/wiː/
can	/k(ə)n/	/kæn/	were	/wə(r)/	/wɜː(r)/
could	/kəd/	/kʊd/	who	/hʊ/	/huː/
do	/də/	/duː/	would	/wəd; əd/	/wʊd/
does	/dəz/	/dʌz/	will	/(ə)l/	/wɪl/
for	/fə(r)/	/fɔː(r)/	you	/jʊ/	/juː/
from	/frəm/	/frɒm/	your	/jə(r)/	/jɔː(r)/
had	/(h)əd/	/hæd/			
has	/(h)əz, z, s/	/hæz/	† conjunction		
have	/(h)əv/	/hæv/			
he	/(h)ɪ/	/hiː/			
her	/(h)ə(r)/	/hɜː/			
him	/ɪm/	/hɪm/			
his	/ɪz/	/hɪz/			
is	/z,s/	/ɪz/			
must	/m(ə)s/	/mʌst/			
not	/nt/	/nɒt/			
of	/əv/	/ɒv/			
our	/ɑː(r)/	/aʊə(r)/			
Saint	/s(ə)nt/	/seɪnt/			
shall	/ʃ(ə)l/	/ʃæl/			
she	/ʃɪ/	/ʃiː/			
should	/ʃ(ə)d/	/ʃʊd/			
sir	/sə(r)/	/sɜː(r)/			

*unusual

359 well

1 *Well* is an adverb, with the same kind of meaning as the adjective *good*.
Compare:

> It's *a **good** car.* (adjective)
> It runs ***well***. (adverb)

> She speaks ***good*** English.
> She speaks English ***well***. (NOT ~~She speaks English **good**.~~)

Note that we cannot say *She speaks **well** English.*
(Adverbs cannot go between the verb and the object—see 13.1).

2 *Well* is also an adjective, meaning 'in good health'.

> 'How are you?' 'Quite ***well***, thanks.'
> I don't feel very ***well***.

Well is not usually used before a noun.
We can say *She's **well***, but not *~~a **well** girl.~~*

▷ For *ill* and *sick*, see 169.

360 when and if

We use *if* to say that we are not sure whether something will happen.

> I'll see you in August, ***if*** I come to New York.
> (Perhaps I'll come to New York; perhaps I won't.)

We use *when* to say that we are sure that something will happen.

> I'll see you in August, ***when*** I come to New York.
> (I'm sure I'll come to New York.)

We can use both *if* and *when* to talk about things that always happen.
There is not much difference of meaning.

> ***If/When*** you heat ice, it turns into water.

361 whether and if

1 In reported questions (see 284), we can use both *whether* and *if*.

> I'm not sure ***whether/if*** I'll have time.
> I asked ***whether/if*** she had any letters for me.

We prefer *whether* before *or*, especially in a formal style.

> Let me know ***whether*** you can come ***or*** not.
> (... *if* ... is possible in an informal style.)

2 After *discuss*, only *whether* is possible.

> We ***discussed whether*** we should close the shop.
> (NOT *~~We **discussed if** ...~~*)

362 whether ... or ...

We can use *whether ... or ...* as a conjunction, with a similar meaning to *it doesn't matter whether ... or ...* The clause with *whether ... or ...* can come at the beginning of the sentence or after the other clause.

Whether you like it or not, you'll have to pay.
You'll have to pay, whether you like it or not.

363 which, what and who: question words

1 Determiners

We can use *which* and *what* before nouns to ask questions about people or things.

Which teacher do you like best?
Which colour do you want—green, red, yellow or brown?

What writers do you like?
What colour are your girl-friend's eyes?

We usually prefer *which* when we are choosing between a small number, and *what* when we are choosing between a large number. Before another determiner (for example *the, my, these*) or a pronoun, we use *which of*.

Which of your teachers do you like best?
Which of them do you want?

2 Pronouns

We can use *which, what* and *who* as pronouns, without nouns. We use *who*, not *which*, for people.

Who won—Smith or Fitzgibbon?
Which would you prefer—wine or beer?
What would you like to eat?

We usually use *who*, not *whom*, as an object.

Who do you like best—your father or your mother?
(*Whom do you like best ...?* is very formal.)

▷ For *who* and *which* as relative pronouns, see 277. For relative *what*, see 278.

364 who ever, what ever, how ever etc

These express surprise, or difficulty in believing something.

Who ever is that girl with the green hair?
What ever are you doing?
How ever did you manage to start the car? I couldn't.
When ever will I have time to write some letters?

Where ever have you been?
Why ever didn't you tell me you were coming?

▷ For *whoever, whatever* etc, see 365.

365 whoever, whatever, whichever, however, whenever and whether

These words mean 'it doesn't matter who', 'it doesn't matter what' etc.
They are conjunctions: they join clauses together.
Whoever, whatever and *whichever* are also relative pronouns: they can
be the subjects or objects of clauses.

> *whoever* etc + clause + clause
> clause + *whoever* etc + clause

Whoever telephones, tell them I'm out.
I'm not opening the door, whoever you are.

Whatever you do, I'll always love you.
Keep calm, whatever happens.

'Which is my bed?' 'You can have whichever you like.'

However much he eats, he never gets fat.
People always want more, however rich they are.

Whenever I go to London I visit the National Gallery.
You can come whenever you like.

Wherever you go, you'll find Coca-Cola.
The people were friendly wherever we went.

366 will

1 Forms

Will is a 'modal auxiliary verb' (See 202). It has no *-s* in the third person
singular; questions and negatives are made without *do*; after *will*, we use
an infinitive without *to*.

> *Will the train be on time?*

Contractions are *'ll, won't.*

> *Do you think it'll rain?* *It won't rain.*

2 Future

We can use *will* as an auxiliary verb when we talk about the future. After
I and *we, will* and *shall* are both possible with the same meaning.

> *I will/shall be happy when this is finished.*
> *What will you do when you leave school?*

For the different ways of talking about the future, see 134–140.

3 Willingness and intentions

We can use *will* (but not *shall*) to say that we are willing to do something, or to offer to do something.

> *'Can somebody help me?' 'I will.'*   *'There's the doorbell.' 'I'll go.'*

Will can express a firm intention, a promise or a threat.

> *I really **will** stop smoking.*   *I'll kill her for this.*

We can use *won't* to talk about refusal.

> *She **won't** open the door.*
> *'Give me a kiss.' 'No, I **won't**.'*
> *The car **won't** start.*

We can use *wouldn't* for a past refusal.

> *The car **wouldn't** start.*   *She **wouldn't** open the door.*

4 Requests and orders

We use *will you* to tell people what to do.

> ***Will you** send me the bill, please?*   ***Will you** come this way?*

Would you is 'softer', more polite.

> ***Would you** send me the bill, please?*   ***Would you** come this way?*

Will you have . . . ? can be used for offers.

> ***Will you have** some more potatoes?*   *What **will you have** to drink?*

5 Habits and characteristics

We can use *will* to talk about habits and characteristic (typical) behaviour.

> *She'll sit talking to herself for hours.*

Would is used for the past.

> *On Saturdays, when I was a child, we **would** all get up early and go fishing.*

6 *will* and *want*

Don't confuse *will* and *want*. *Will* is 'interpersonal'—we use it when our wishes affect other people: when we promise, offer, request etc. *Want* simply describes our wishes. Compare:

> ***Will** you open the window?* (an order)
> *Do you **want** to open the window?* (a question about somebody's wishes).

> *She **won't** tell anybody.* (= She refuses to . . .)
> *She doesn't **want** to tell anybody.* (= She prefers not to . . .)

▷ For more information about *would*, see 369.
For information about *shall*, see 292.

367 wish

1 We can use *wish* + infinitive to mean *want*. *Wish* is more formal.

> I **wish to see** the manager, please.

For the differences between *wish*, *want*, *expect*, *hope* and *look forward to*, see 122.

2 We can also use *wish* to express regrets—to say that we would like things to be different. We use a past tense with a present meaning in this case.

> | *I wish* + subject + past tense |

> **I wish I was** better-looking.
> **I wish I spoke** French.
> **I wish I had** a yacht.
> **I wish it wasn't** raining.

In a formal style, we can use *were* instead of *was* after *I wish*.

> **I wish I were** better-looking. (formal)

We can say *I wish ... would* (but not *I wish ... will*).

> **I wish** she **would** be quiet.
> **I wish** something interesting **would** happen.

To talk about the past, we use a past perfect tense (*had* + past participle).

> | *I wish* + subject + past perfect |

> I wish **I had gone** to university.
> I wish **I hadn't said** that.

If only is used in the same way. (See 167.) For other structures where we use a past tense with a present or future meaning, see 239.

3 We do not use *wish* in progressive tenses.

> **I wish** I knew why. (NOT ~~I am wishing~~ ...)

368 worth ... -ing

We can use *worth ... -ing* in two structures.

> | *it is (not) worth ... -ing (+ object)* |

> It isn't **worth** repairing the car.
> Is it **worth** visiting Leicester?
> It's not **worth** getting angry with her.

> | subject + *is (not) worth ... -ing* |

> *The car isn't* **worth** *repairing.*
> *Is Leicester* **worth** *visiting?*
> *She's not* **worth** *getting angry with.*

369 would

1 Forms

Would is a 'modal auxiliary verb' (see 202). There is no *-s* in the third person singular; questions and negatives are made without *do*; after *would*, we use the infinitive without *to*.

2 Meaning

We use *would* as a past form of *will*, or as a less definite, 'softer' form of *will*. Compare:

> *I'll be here at ten tomorrow.*
> *I said I **would** be there at ten the next day.*

> *She **will** talk to herself for hours.* (present habit)
> *She **would** talk to herself for hours.* (past habit)

> *He **won't** do his homework.* (present refusal)
> *He **wouldn't** do his homework.* (past refusal)

> ***Will** you open the window, please?* (firm request)
> ***Would** you open the window, please?* ('softer' request)

Would is the auxiliary verb for the 'conditional' of other verbs (see 88).

> *I **would** tell you if I knew.*

▷ For the difference between *would* and *should*, see 296.
For more information about *will*, see 366.

370 would rather

1 *Would rather* means 'would prefer to'. It is followed by the infinitive without *to*. We often use the contraction *'d rather*: this means 'would rather, not 'had rather'.

> | *would rather* + infinitive without *to* |
> | --- |

> ***Would you rather** stay here or go home?*
> *'How about a drink?' **'I'd rather** have something to eat.'*

2 We can use *would rather* to say that one person would prefer another person to do something. We use a special structure with a past tense.

> | *would rather* + subject + past tense |
> | --- |

> ***I'd rather** you **went** home now.*
> *Tomorrow's difficult. **I'd rather** you **came** next weekend.*
> *My wife **would rather** we **didn't** see each other any more.*
> *'Shall I open a window?' **'I'd rather** you **didn't.'***

▷ For other structures where a past tense has a present or future meaning, see 239.
For another way of using *rather*, see 124.

Index